1964

Dante and his Comedy

Dante AND HIS
Comedy

ALLAN H. GILBERT
Professor Emeritus of English Literature
Duke University

1 8 1 8

". . . they might scout at Moby Dick as a
monstrous fable or, still worse and more de-
testable, a hideous and intolerable allegory."
Melville, *Moby Dick*, Chap. 45.

NEW YORK UNIVERSITY PRESS 1963

CONTENTS

To attempt writing on Dante is to pronounce judgment—expressed or implied—on Dante scholarship. Yet at present the most industrious specialist can hardly master Dante literature, if he also spends part of his time in writing. My bibliography of Dante studies from 1930 to 1960 shows about six hundred volumes and an enormous number of articles. Further, many books and articles written earlier than 1930 are cited in the philological magazines; indeed, they extend back to the fourteenth century. Francesco da Buti's commentary alone runs to some 2,700 printed pages. Dante, moreover, is not to be abandoned to specialists, however helpful they may be or however well they fit the spirit of the present age. The great poet must be dealt with by those who have steeped themselves in an abundance of poetry in various languages. Attentive reading of poets before and after Dante who form an indispensable background for enjoyment, understanding, and criticism is enough to occupy the lives of most of us who, while devoted to study, strive also to be teachers.

Having in more than half a century of university teaching been able to devote but one year exclusively to Italian literature, I am far from being a specialist. I can only hope that from many years in the classroom with Spenser, Shakespeare, and Milton I have gained something not usual among writers on Dante. My volume on him in 1925 and several short studies since show me returning from time to time over many years to serious examination of his poetry. I have also given long periods to Italian followers of Dante, especially Ariosto and Machiavelli.

For reasons hinted above, I do not in this study proceed by

the bibliographical method, though from such books and articles as I have read I have taken, as Kipling says, "what I thought I might require." Scholars who recognize matter seemingly borrowed from their writings will, I hope, forgive me for slighting their names as they recall that even the most original notions commonly have been at least adumbrated by still other workers, and that in half a century of sallies into a subject one easily comes to suppose his own what he has borrowed. And what is scholarship for except to be used in making the poets more accessible to men in general?

The bibliographical procedure of specialists can hardly be interesting or useful to laymen. Moreover, it is easily deflected from its justifying purpose, the spread of truth, to utterance of partisan views. The charity of any experts who condescend to this volume will, I trust, sometimes give me credit for having turned the pages of scholarly books and articles which, rightly or wrongly, I am unable to endorse. Wishing entirely to avoid personal controversy, I intend to offer only such explications as the material itself makes probable; I am ready to abandon any of my conclusions or surmises when I encounter destructive evidence. That I have not concealed my own preferences in explication, I well know. But whatever my views, I hold that poetical interpretation is free. Granting such freedom to all, for myself I apply to Dante the principle of minimum interpretation, even as an experiment to find out how much of the essential poetry of the *Commedia* will be touched by exegesis which most men can accept as a beginning if not as an end. Though artists may sometimes wield complex ideas, is not their accomplishment essentially simple, perhaps simple in proportion as they are great?

Few poets have suffered more than has Dante from the deeply rooted fear of art as a vain thing. It was rife in his day and affected the poet himself, especially when he turned critic. It is in our time powerful; to the advertising man a simple versifier on rural life is not merely a poet; he must be called "poet and philosopher." Current novelists are esteemed because of what are taken as their personal sociological views. Certainly poets and novelists often deal with great and serious matters, but themes do not make poets. Philosophers, historians, reformers, and others also deal with them. The supposition that poets are profound and difficult has in all ages fattened the scholar. In our day the literary researcher may try to make his material seem as remote from the layman as are the arcana of the physicist. If a poem can be read by any educated man, what sort of scholarship does it require? Dante's multitude of little-known historical characters inevitably excites the curiosity of readers, yet this natural curiosity is not always wise. For example, historical knowledge about Folco of Marseilles (*Paradiso* 9) must include his part in the extirpation of the Albigensian heresy. This activity, however, is unnoticed in the *Paradiso*, where he utters a poet's geographical passage, speaks with mythological adornment on love and on himself as a lover, explains the heaven in which he appears, and attacks the worldliness of the Church, with promise of coming purification. In none of this does Folco the stern judge of heretics appear. Did Dante know him in that character? The modern reader, whether he condemns or praises the militant bishop, risks diversion from the poetry by such irrelevant information. So sometimes one who enjoys poetry shows prudence in remaining ignorant, unless he so controls his mind that on taking up the *Commedia* he lays aside all erudition not in harmony with the poet's verses. No man needs to be so awed as to class himself with the bluestocking whom Ben Jonson satirized in her assertion: "Dante is hard and few can understand him." Medieval as the poet is, he is not for the learned only but for all who have an ear and an eye for poetry. Interpretation such as comes easily and naturally —reading that does not attempt too curiously to summon from fancy what is not set down—minimum interpretation, in short, is usually enough to secure enjoyment. In attempting such interpretation, though I welcome the severest examination of my volume by any specialist, I design my book first of all for the "gentle reader."

I express thanks to the Research Council of Duke University, to the libraries of that university and the University of Pennsylvania, and to Mr. Enzo Orvieto, who loaned his photographs of Guido da Pisa's commentary on Dante.

All translations are the work of the author.

1 · *Fact or Fancy?*

The *Commedia* presents two Dantes. One is the poet who wrote the work. The other is the traveler who, according to Dante's "beautiful lie" (*bella menzogna*—*Convivio* 2. 1), went on an imaginary journey through Hell, Purgatory, and Paradise. For clarity the poet might have given his hero some name other than his own, as Swift did his. Gulliver may at times express Swift's considered beliefs, yet no alert reader will so assume; at least we need not be author-conscious. But a wary reader of Dante may now and then find himself caught in the autobiographical assumption. Sometimes the traveler's fictitious reminiscences on returning to the land of the living become the historical Dante's poem, with its seventeen addresses to the reader (e.g., *Inf.* 8. 94; 22. 118; *Purg.* 10. 106; *Par.* 22. 106). Isn't the poet he who would bribe souls with hope of fame (e.g., *Inf.* 32. 94), and who is to expose papal wickedness, even though Saint Peter's speeches in Heaven are but poetical fancies (*Par.* 27. 40)? Without doubt the historical Dante wished to return from exile, but did he expect his poem, in which he attacks Florence, to be his means for restoration? Can even his hope for return be touched with the fiction of the traveler in the world of the dead? Manifold references to the Virgin in the *Comedy* and their support in the *Monarchia* and other works show Mary important in Dante's thought. Yet does the historical exile or the fictitious traveler declare that he invokes her morning and evening (*Par.* 23. 88)? The dramatic Dante says that in the Florentine Baptistery, in order to rescue a person who was suffocating, he broke the sides of one of the pits cut in the marble of the font as "a place for the baptizing priest" (*Inf.* 19. 18). Benvenuto da Imola embroiders the story, but Dante's sons Pietro and Jacopo and other early commentators do not. Such a font was reported found in excavations at the Baptistery not many years ago. Modern comment is sometimes incredulous, though the storyteller furnishes an apparent guarantee with the words: "Let this be a testimony that will keep every man from error" (*Inf.* 19. 21). The traveler also swears that he saw the monster Geryon swimming through the air (*Inf.* 16. 128). Further, the visitor's fear of the Malebranche, remembered in later security, is illustrated by comparison: "So once I saw the infantry afraid who came out of Caprona under safe-conduct, on seeing themselves in the midst of so many enemies" (*Inf.* 21. 94).

If this is factual statement, the historical Dante was with a Florentine army at Caprona. The simile, however, flows along in reminiscences of experience with the devils of the fifth *bolgia* —obvious fiction. Yet the storyteller several times relates how in that *bolgia* he saw, as with his own eyes (*e.g.*, 22. 31; 23. 35). Shall we assign the narrative of Caprona to Dante as a factual writer and the fiction of the Malebranche to the feigned traveler? Otherwise what was seen near Pisa and what was seen in the fifth *bolgia* are both either prosaic or invented. Dante's presence at the surrender is affirmed only in the verse quoted and by commentators taking it as fact. Boccaccio and Leonardo Aretino in their biographies of Dante do not mention Caprona, nor do Dante's sons. The prosaic verity of the statement is thus unproved, though not disproved. But whether or not Dante witnessed the surrender of Caprona, the comparison makes more poetically vivid the tourist's tale of his adventure with the Malebranche. For such a purpose fact and fiction are indiscriminately at the poet's service.

The Florentine exile, the Dante looking forward to poetic immortality, appears unmixed with the frequently comic traveler called Dante in invocations of the Muses and of Apollo, in personal statements such as that he worked years on the *Commedia*, in the passage *Ahi serva Italia*, "O enslaved Italy" (*Par.* 25. 3; *Purg.* 6. 76), not assigned to any dramatic speaker.

Yet such passages have their poetical quality; the last is the digression not of a mere politician or reformer but at the worst of a poet in politics, more influenced by artistic effect than historical accuracy. Or are we to allow that sometimes Dante is not poet at all? Surely autobiography was not the versifier's chief concern. He was writing a comedy, in which he could work his will on the fictitious Dante whom he made his leading character. The reader may beware that he does not dull the edge of imaginative effect by taking as mere knowledge what Dante wrote as poetry.

At times Dante confuses or identifies himself as poet and exile with the fictitious Dante often frightened and dependent like a child on Virgil and Beatrice. The traveler who is examined on theology as a student seeking a further degree is also the poet who asserts himself a worthy opponent of a triple-crowned pope or a Florentine government (*Par.* 24. 34; 26. 66). Thus the poet forwards the tendency of his readers to make his achievement an autobiography rather than a comedy. Comedy suffers in the reader's confusion of the sometimes distinct and sometimes united aspects of poet and protagonist, with over-emphasis on the exile's woes. Similarly, Ben Jonson intended his V*olpone* as comic, yet deliberately showed the punishment of evil. As a result, the unwary have called the play a tragedy. So the Dante who is frightened by Saint Paul's sword, or rebuked by Virgil for listening to the billingsgate of Sinon and Adam—unless Dantists beware—acquires too much of the dignity belonging to Dante the author (*Purg.* 29. 141; *Inf.* 30. 131). Yet to wary readers, and subconsciously to all, the poem gains by the apparent confusion. What work surpasses it in vivid realism or—for the sympathetic—in comic improbability cloaked by outward gravity?

VISION OR REALITY?

From early times the *Commedia* has been thought of as a fictitious vision. Such Guido da Pisa considered it about the time of Dante's death (British Museum ms., pp. 32ff., 153, etc.). Benvenuto da Imola accepted the idea, writing:

First I must say that our author feigns that he had this wonderful beneficial vision in the year 1300. . . . He writes of this vision of his as spread over a length of time, though he had it all at one time, as Moses writes Genesis and John the Apocalypse. I wished to tell this so that many points would be clear which if it were not realized would seem obscure. For our author writes of many things which happened after 1300 and were spread over many years. Thus as a prophet he seems to predict the future, though really he knew of those events as having already happened when he wrote. Yet he feigned that he foresaw them in that vision of his in that year, whereas actually he wrote them later at various times (On Canto 1).

Landino in his commentary writes that some say the poem "is nothing other than a vision which appeared to the author in his sleep" (ed. 1507, p. 2). Illustrations of the first canto in the Venetian editions of 1491 and 1512 show Dante asleep, dreaming his journey. The Padova edition of 1613 is entitled *La Visione*, and Cary called his translation *The Vision*. That the work was thought a dream is not strange. Medieval visits to the other world, as though following the *Somnium Scipionis*, commonly are presented as visions, such as *The Revelation to the Monk of Evesham* and *The Vision of Tugdale*. A reader of such literature would assume that Dante presented a visit in a dream, as perhaps Chaucer did when he imitated Dante in his *House of Fame*. Virgil, though representing Aeneas' excursion to the world of the dead as factual, nevertheless has his hero return to the upper world through one of the gates of sleep (*Aeneid* 6. 893). Improbabilities not acceptable in a feigned experience can be excused to a dreamer.

A few passages in the *Commedia* may darkly hint that Dante once did intend to relate his journey as a dream. At the beginning he says that he does not know how he got into the dark forest: "So very sleepy I was when I entered it" (*Inf.* 1. 11). Cacciaguida, with a view to the tourist's return to earth, commands him to make his "vision" evident (*Par.* 17. 128). Saint Bernard speaks to him of "the time that makes you slumber" (*Par.* 32. 139). We read among the last verses of the poem: "To the lofty phantasy here strength failed" (33. 142). On *Paradiso* 32. 139, the fourteenth-century commentator Buti writes: "The author here feigns this to continue the fiction he adopted at the beginning of his *Comedy*, that is, that in 1300 in the night of Good Friday and Holy Saturday he had this vision, and that in vision were shown to him the matters contained in this poem." Against all the passages mentioned can be brought objections precluding proof that Dante presents his poem as a vision. Yet may some of them be survivals from a time when the *Commedia* was planned as a dream?

Possibly the dreams narrated in the poem are other survivals. On the brink of the abyss of Hell, the traveler sinks down as asleep, to awake in a different place (*Inf.* 3. 136; 4. 1). On hearing Francesca's story he swoons; on recovery, he is in the next circle of Hell. In Purgatory he has three symbolical dreams (*Purg.* 9. 19; 19. 7; 27. 97). In the Earthly Paradise, lulled by a Biblical song, he sleeps in the midst of action and awakens to find that a scriptural allegory has ended. Though his slumber is described with elaboration, its significance is hidden and the sleeper relates no dream (32. 68). Buti in his commentary says that the traveler "experienced the greatest sweetness and consolation in this vision," but he infers from the situation rather than from a statement in the poem. Though in Paradise the traveler does not dream, he approaches a dreamer's state: "As is a man who sees when he is dreaming, and after his dream the emotion impressed on him remains, but the rest does not come back to his memory, such am I, for what I saw almost wholly disappears, and still the sweetness it caused suffuses my heart" (*Par.* 33. 58).

When presenting a fictitious vision, an author normally writes an introduction announcing that he slept and dreamed. For example, John Bunyan at the beginning of *Pilgrim's Progress* does so; and now and then in the course of his book writes: "I saw in my dream." At the end: "So I awoke and behold it was a dream." Dante's poem begins abruptly, without notice whether it is a vision or not. How different Chaucer in his somewhat Dantesque poems, *The House of Fame, The Parliament of Fowls,* and *The Book of the Duchess!* All have explanatory prologues. Dante also ends his poem abruptly, without suggestion of means by which his hero returns to earth to relate his experiences. May one or two of the passages I have mentioned be survivals from a time when the *Commedia* was an avowed dream, with prologue and conclusion? Another possible remnant is the frequent use of the words "I saw." Were some of these once "I saw in my dream," as Bunyan has it? In his dream poems Chaucer frequently declares: "I saw."

If Dante ever planned his poem as a dream, he abandoned it for his present fiction in which the traveler, to whom he gives the name of Dante and some of the qualities befitting it, is supposed an actual visitor to the three kingdoms of the other world. The feigned quality of this visit should ever be in the reader's mind. Buti gives constant warning by the formula with which he begins sections expounding passages: "In these tercets our author feigns," etc. In other words, we are dealing with a work of fiction. Dante the traveler is never exactly the historical Dante who lived in Florence, though fact and fiction may interpenetrate each other. But fiction is master. If in the passage on enslaved Italy in *Purgatorio* 6 the factual Dante is uttering sentiments similar to those in his letter to the Florentines, the verses nevertheless emerge from the fictitious meeting of Virgil and Sordello, the poet's language is figurative and his ideas are less specific than those of the letter. If these are political verses, they are not untouched by the universalizing power of poetry.

THE FEIGNED TRAVELER'S EXPERIENCE

Whether or not he ever contemplated writing *Dante's Dream*, when Dante decided to tell of his visit to the other world as though he made it in the flesh, his artist's instinct assured him that he needed to make the events he imagined appear real. In this he so well succeeded that too easily we assume that the historical Dante pulled hair from the helpless Bocca degli Abati's head (*Inf.* 32. 104). The incident may be true or untrue to the author's feelings, but it is adapted not to Dante the poet but to the feigned visitor to the shades, who could deceive Frate Alberigo, justifying himself with the proverbial: "It was courtesy to act like a brute to him" (*Inf.* 33. 150). Dante the Florentine may or may not have approved such deception; Dante the visitor enjoys the deceptive joke. He swears to the Frate: "If I do not disencumber you, may I have to go to the bottom of the ice" (*Inf.* 33. 116). The swearer knows, though the other man does not, that he is going to the bottom. The trick is not unlike that in one of the stories about Dante. When the exile was at Porciano, a Florentine officer was sent to demand that the town authorities surrender the poet. Being warned, he left the place. On the road he met the officer who, not recognizing him, asked if Dante were at Porciano. The answer was: "When I was there, he was there." Did this come from one of Dante's favorite authors, Ovid? Part of the story of Erysichthon, mentioned in *Purgatorio* 23. 25, is that, falling into poverty, he sold his daughter. Having power to change her shape at will, and being on the seashore, she metamorphosed herself into a fisherman. Her buyer, amazed at her disappearance, asked the fisher if he had seen a woman but now on the shore, to be answered: "I have not looked up from the water and have been attending to my business. That you may have less doubt, I swear—as I hope the god of the sea will assist me in my work—that for a long time there has been nobody on the shore but me, certainly no woman" (*Metamorphoses* 8. 864). May there be some truth in the story about Porciano, and did Dante write the traveler's false oath with Ovid's story of the deceived buyer in mind?

THE EYEWITNESS IN THE INFERNO

Toward accepting the journey through the realms of the shades as a reality, we are moved by the feigned observer's frequent use of the words "I saw." Virgil early told his charge: "You will see in pain spirits from remote ages. . . . You will see those who are satisfied in the fire" (*Inf.* 1. 115). The pupil wishes to be led "to see Saint Peter's gate" (1. 134). He invokes "Memory, you who write what I saw" (2. 8), as a reporter back from a journey for the sake of seeing. He often tells how he carried out that purpose. In the passage on Limbo, "I saw" occurs a dozen times. (In some texts Virgil says "see," pointing at various shades [*Inf.* 5. 65; cf. 7. 115].) The traveler's heart was pierced as he saw the avaricious and prodigal at their useless toil of rolling weights (7. 25, 36). After otherwise reporting what he saw (*e.g.*, 12. 52; 14. 19), the witness becomes more emphatic, asserting of Geryon's approach: "By the notes of this *Comedy* (as I hope they will not fail to be accepted in the future), I swear to you, reader, that through that thick and murky air I saw a figure come swimming up" (16. 128).

Similar in its amusing mock-seriousness is another reinforcement of veracity. Coming to the *bolgia* of the simonists, the traveler reports:

Along the sides and the bottom I saw the dark rock full of holes all of the same size; each was round. I took them to be not smaller or larger than those which in my beautiful San Giovanni are provided as standing-places for the baptizers. One of those, not many years ago, I broke for the sake of a person being smothered there. And let this be a testimony that will keep every man from being led into error. Out of the mouth of each hole were thrust the feet of a sinner and the legs to the thick part, and the rest was inside. The soles of both feet were entirely on fire (*Inf.* 19. 13).

The narrator will convince the incredulous that he saw such holes by asserting experimental knowledge of similar ones. Doubtless the poet enjoyed assigning such specious logic to the wayfarer striving to win belief in his supernatural adventures.[1] In the *bolgia* of the fortune-tellers, the traveler is moved by what he sees: "Now reader, . . . imagine from the effect on yourself whether I could keep my face dry when I saw close to me our image so twisted that the tears from the eyes bathed the buttocks through the divide" (20. 19).

Remembering how he gazed into the *bolgia* of the dividers, the pilgrim gives more strength to his device for gaining credence as an eyewitness:

I stood still to look at the crowd, and I saw a thing that I would be afraid merely to relate without more proof, if it were not that I gain safety from conscience—that good companion who sets a man free under the armor of knowing he is blameless. Absolutely I saw—and I think I see it still—a body walking along without a head, just as the others in that wretched flock were walking along (28. 112).

To give a sense of reality, or mock-reality, to this travesty of the miracle of San Miniato, asseveration is needed. And the

---

[1] This use of asserted experience as proof commonly receives an autobiographical rather than an artistic explanation.

protestation is the more comic the more zealously conscience is invoked.

Sometimes the wording is varied, as "My eyes hit upon" (18. 40). Or "There struck my eye one who was crucified on the earth" (23. 110). Or more elaborately: "I was bending down, but sharp eyes couldn't reach the bottom because of the darkness. So I said: 'Teacher, go over to the next bank and we can climb down the wall of the bridge, because just as I hear something from the bottom but do not understand, so I am trying to see what is down there but am making out nothing' " (*Inf.* 24. 70).

Descending until the *bolgia* was plainly visible (*fu manifesta*), the traveler "saw" there such terrible serpents that the "recollection of it still curdles my blood." One of the sinners is more pained "that you have caught me in the misery where you see me than I was when I died. But so that you may not take pleasure in what you see, open your ears to my declaration and hear" (24. 133). On this the traveler, reviewing his experience in Hell, comments: "Through all the dark circles of the Inferno, I saw no other spirit so haughty before God" (25. 13).

Still eager to observe, the narrator tells that on the next bridge "I stood bending over so far to see what was below that if I had not taken hold of a rock, I should have fallen without being pushed" (26. 43). He tells how intensely he used his eyes in the *bolgia* of the schismatics: "The many people and the different wounds had made my eyes so drunk that they wished pause for weeping" (29. 1).

Carefully he observes the giant Nimrod:

His face as I looked at it was as long and broad as the pine cone of Saint Peter's at Rome, and his other bones were in proportion. Hence the bank, which was a girdle of decency from his middle down, let me behold so much of him above it that three Frisians could not have boasted of reaching his hair. Thus I was looking at thirty great handbreadths of him between the place where a man fastens his mantle and the bank below (31. 58).

Having observed this giant so exactly, he seems to wish to compare him with another. At any rate he says to his guide: "If it is possible, I should like my eyes to have experience

of the measureless Briareus," but he must content his "gluttonous eyes" with what his guide can furnish. In telling of the
Ninth Circle, the returned traveler continues to insist that
he was an eyewitness; for example: "I saw a thousand faces
made purple by the cold. As a result, frozen streams make me
shudder, and always will" (32. 70). Moving on, he feels a
breeze. On enquiry, he learns from Virgil that his "eye will
give the answer, when he sees the cause" (33. 107). Ere long
his guide bids him look into the distance, and as they advance
exclaims: "Behold Dis" (34. 2, 20). By the sight the visitor
was so frightened that, recalling it, he says: "I did not die;
I did not keep alive" (34. 23). In the sixty-nine lines given to
viewing Satan are more than a dozen words related to sight.

The Observer in Purgatory. In Purgatory the visitor continues
an eyewitness. Virgil explains to Cato that he is guiding his
charge "to see and to hear" (*Purg.* 1. 69). Cato instructs him
not to allow his pupil to go before the guardian angel of Purgatory's gate "with clouded eyes" (1. 97). As the angel who conducts the souls from Tiber mouth appears speeding over the
water, the visitor glances at Virgil to ask a question and on
looking back "sees the angel more shining and larger" (2. 21).
Moving on, the traveler sees various persons (2. 76, 130; 3. 58,
85). When he fails to recognize Manfred, that king says, "Now
look," showing the wound in his breast (3. 110), and instructs
the beholder to tell Constance that he has seen her father (3.
143). After other references to the sight, the narrator tells how
Virgil instructed him to look at Sordello (6. 58). The Mantuan
then leads the newcomers to a position from which they get a
good view of the valley of the kings, and instructs him to look
especially at some of them (7. 89, 106, 107), influencing the
reader to feel that he too sees them. As the visitor approaches
Nino Visconti, darkness is coming on, but not so much but
that "between his eyes and mine what was at first concealed
became plain. He moved toward me and I moved toward
him. Gentle Judge Nino, how glad I was when I saw that you
were not among the wicked" (8. 49).

Seeing is believing. Not souls alone does he see; about to
look at the stars, he exclaims: "My gluttonous eyes were turn-

ing to the sky" (8. 85). In the *Comedy* the noun "eye" occurs more frequently than any other, and never are the observer's eyes other than greedy. In due time Virgil demonstrates that they have come near to Purgatory itself: "Look at the wall of rock that encircles it; look at the entrance where there seems to be a break" (9. 50). Then the visitor saw the gate and its guardian, but as he strained his eyes to see, the bright angel and his sword were too much for human vision (9. 79). To the topography of the terrace of pride, reality is imparted by the remark: "From the side of the terrace terminated by the abyss to the foot of the high rock, which ever rises up, was three times the measure of a human body. As far as my eye could throw its gaze, on either left or right, such the [width of the] cornice appeared to me" (10. 22).

Looking at a carving on the cliff, the visitor says, "I moved in front of Virgil and went nearer, so that it would have the right position for my eyes" (10. 53). On this terrace he well may speak of "my eyes, which were glad to look to see strange things, of which they are fond" (10. 103). Beholding the proud under heavy loads, he expresses pity through a visual figure: "As to hold up a ceiling or a roof, sometimes you see as bracket a figure pressing his knees against his breast, so that what is not true makes a true pang rise in him who sees it, so I saw them" (10. 130). On the terrace of envy he gets close enough to be sure of what he sees:

I do not believe there is today on earth a man so hard that he would not be pierced with compassion for what I then saw, for when I had come so near them that I was sure of their state, my eyes with tears relieved my hard pain. In wretched haircloth I saw that they were clad, and one supported the other with his shoulder, and all were supported by the bank (13. 52).

Properly the sightseer remarks that Virgil is "he who guides my eyes upward" (21. 124). Encountering the shade of his old friend Forese Donati, he weeps at seeing him so thin (23. 55).

Though eyes hardly could be greedier than those of the tourist, Beatrice yet unnecessarily exhorts him: "In behalf of the world that lives wickedly, keep your eyes on the chariot, and what you see, when you get back there, be sure to write" (32.

103). Then apparently satisfied with him as an observer, she exhorts him to courage as writer: "Keep in mind, when you write, not to hide what you have seen as to this tree that now is robbed here for the second time" (33. 55).

Eyesight in Paradise. In Paradise also Beatrice's lover uses his eyes, often on her beauty, which thus he makes vivid. Passing over Beatrice, I give instances in which he makes himself eye-witness of heavenly splendor.

From the first, preparing his readers for the belief demanded by his fiction, he writes, "I saw things which he who descends from there does not know how to repeat, and he has no power to do so" (*Par.* 1. 5). Yet what he recalls he will tell (1. 12, 24). Moreover, in Heaven the shades are not plainly seen, as they are in Purgatory. In the Moon, souls that appear like torches are willing to converse with him. Perceiving them like images reflected in mirrors, then "to see whose images they were I turned my eyes. But I saw nothing and turned back my eyes to my sweet guide" (3. 21). She explains that he is seeing the actual shades of the blessed. Later he beholds the lights in which they are enclosed, as when he sees the movement, in harmony with song, of the "glorious wheel" of which Saint Thomas' shade makes part (10. 145). He will further impress upon his reader what he saw in that heaven of the learned: "Let him imagine who strives to realize well what I saw (and let him as I write keep hold of the image as a firm rock)—let him imagine fifteen stars that in different quarters enliven the sky with such brightness as to surpass every airy mixture" (13. 1).

The marvelous eagle in the Heaven of Jupiter might be held incredible, so the narrator repeats that he saw it:

I beheld before me with wings spread the beauteous effigy which, happy in sweet mutual enjoyment, the united souls produced. Each one seemed a ruby in which a ray of the sun burned with such fire that in my eyes it was reflected. And what now comes to me to write, voice never spoke nor ink wrote nor was it by imagination ever grasped, for I saw and also heard the beak speaking and forming with its voice *I* and *mine*, though the concept was *we* and *our* (19. 1).

He repeats that he saw the lights of this heaven like "precious and shining jewels" (20. 16), and that he "saw the two blessed lights" moving in harmony with the eagle's words (20, 146). Less extraordinary and needing less asseveration is a sight in Saturn, yet he affirms that he beheld it: "I saw a stairway reaching so high that my eye could not follow it. I saw descending on the steps so many splendors that I believed every light appearing in the sky to be poured out there" (21. 29). Yet Pier Damiano explains that the beholder has only mortal vision (21. 61).

In his reporter's zeal to see what will interest future readers, and emboldened by the kindness which, he says, "I see and note in all the heavenly fires," he asks if he may see Saint Benedict's form without its mask of light (22. 60). The saint replies that such a view is possible only in the Empyrean. To that heaven reaches the wonderful stairway, so high that it is "stolen from the traveler's sight" (22. 69). Below him the enquirer sees the universe already traversed.

With my eyes I moved back through all seven of the spheres, and I saw this globe of the earth. . . . I saw the daughter of Latona. . . . There, Hyperion, I sustained the sight of your son and, Maia and Dione, I saw your motions around and near him. From my position the tempering of Jove between his father and his son, and their variation in place were evident. All seven were revealed to me in their size and their speed. The bit of ground that makes us so proud . . . appeared before me (22. 133).

Thus his knowledge of the heavenly bodies and of the Earth's insignificance is ocular. As he continues to see and to ask, Beatrice approves: "The great desire which now kindles and urges you to have knowledge of what you look at, pleases me the more, the more it swells" (30. 70). Yet, though his "eyes are not lofty enough" to attain all that is offered (30. 81), he can say: "O splendor of God, through which I saw the high triumph of the true kingdom, give me strength to write how I saw it" (30. 97). Looking up to Beatrice as she sits in the celestial rose, he thanks her for enabling him to see: "O lady in whom my hope lives . . . for seeing all the many things I have seen, I thank the grace and strength of your power and

goodness. . . . You have brought me from slavery to freedom. . . . You have made my spirit healthy" (31. 82). What
he saw affected himself, as well as gave him something to put
on paper when returning to earth as poetical recorder. Saint
Bernard in the highest heaven still encourages the alert eye:

"Son of grace, this rejoicing existence will not be known to you
if always you hold your eyes downcast. But look at the remotest
circles until you see seated the Queen to whom this realm is subject
and bound." I raised my eyes, and as in the morning the eastern
horizon surpasses that where the sun sets, so, raising my eyes from
the bottom to the top, I saw part at the very top outdoing in light
all the rest of the rim. . . . I saw more than a thousand angels in
festival. . . . (31. 112).

The visitor follows the saint's advice to the end. The last ninety-
six lines of the poem contain many words indicating that he
saw; my count is twenty-eight. As theologian he wishes "to see
how the image of the Son fits with the circle" (33. 137), but
also to the end he is the poet eager to see for the sake of the
"high imagination," which only at the final instant fails.

If we wish, we may suppose that some of the many assurances
that the observer saw with his own eyes once stood in the
form: *I saw in my dream*. But when Dante abandoned the
dream-poem (if ever he accomplished part of one) he made
what had been the visions of the dreamer into personal experiences contributing to the feigned reality of the fiction. What
the traveler saw with his own eyes we accept as convincing;
hearsay we reject. The narrator's constant seeing keeps before
us the movement of the journey. We accept a series of new
things beheld in their reality as the narrator moves from group
to group of shades in their settings.

Other Vivid Impressions. While the visitor to the world of
the dead often insists that he saw, he also tells of powerful
effects upon him without specifying the sense through which
the impression was made. After sight, hearing is most important. Virgil tells Cato that he is guiding his charge "to see
and to hear" (*Purg.* 1. 69). Yet smell, touch, and taste are not
unused. Often the emotional state of the visitor rather than
the sense by which it was excited is the poet's concern.

Hardly within Hell Gate, he weeps on hearing the lamentations of the souls neither wicked nor good (*Inf.* 3. 24). Listening to Francesca and seeing her lover weep, he is overcome with pity (5. 142). In his loathing for Filippo Argenti, he wishes for him a more severe punishment (8. 38). He feels compunction when ignorantly he misleads Cavalcante into believing that his son—still living—is dead (10. 109). In the circle of the suicides he cannot ask the questions that will satisfy his curiosity because pity sways him, so he requests Virgil to act for him (13. 84). In the presence of Ser Brunetto Latini—the only one of the damned honored with that courteous prefix—he shows respect (15. 30, 45, 101). Reverence alone restrains him from expressing to Pope Nicholas his indignation at the injury done the Church by papal avarice (19. 101). When he weeps over the fortune-tellers, Virgil rebukes him (20. 19). Though we can be glad of the visitor's human sympathy, we can commend the guardian for warning his charge against pitying criminal rather than victim. Nor was Virgil's exhortation effective, for on leaving the *bolgia* of the schismatics the observer declares: "The many people and the different wounds had made my eyes so drunk that they wished pause for weeping" (29. 1). Virgil does not understand his pause or—if we may guess—pretends that he does not, while the other finds an excuse in his desire to see one of his relatives among the damned. And further, in the *bolgia* of the falsifiers, "Varied lamentations pierced me like arrows headed with pity, so that I covered my ears with my hands" (29. 43).

In Purgatory, since the sufferers voluntarily take upon themselves their pains, the observer expresses less compassion, though he is sympathetic. Fascinated by Manfred's narrative of his death and the insults to his corpse, the traveler is oblivious of the passage of time (*Purg.* 4. 16). On the first terrace he looks with such engrossed attention at a relief of the Annunciation that Virgil is forced to remind him that he must look at others and hasten on (10. 46). Yet on seeing further reliefs, he must again be roused from his absorbed delight (10. 100). Omberto Aldobrandesco, one of the penitents, has no need to strive to make the observer "feel pity for my burden" (11. 57). Again

when the visitor forgets practical matters while gazing at and
meditating on the mosaics representing pride, Virgil recalls him
to the needs of the moment (12. 78). In pity and respect he is
about to kneel to Adrian V, but the Pope in humility restrains
him (19. 127). With evident, though expressed eagerness, he
follows Virgil and Statius listening to their conversation, which
"gave him mental power for poetry-writing," and made him
follow them without effort (22. 129; 23. 9). On the last terrace,
the poet-traveler is so moved when Guido Guinizelli announces
himself that for a long time he can only gaze in silence at the
father of love poets.

In the Earthly Paradise he delights in the fresh branches
and in the appearance and song of Matilda, who comes before
him like "something which displaces every other thought" (28.
36). The traveler experiences "the early flowers of everlasting
pleasure" (29. 31). On seeing Beatrice, he feels in himself "all
the signs of the old flame" which in the days of the *Vita
Nuova* struck him with awe and trembling (30. 36, 48). Turning to the Latin poet, he sees no one. Even the delights of the
Earthly Paradise do not keep the mortal from shedding his
first tears since Virgil wiped his face with dew (30. 54). By
Beatrice's rebukes the traveler is further affected to tears (31.
34).

In Paradise the visitor is little moved by the happiness of the
blessed. Indeed his own happiness is rather implied than expressed. He says, for example, that Beatrice uncovered to him
the "sweet form of beautiful truth" (*Par.* 3. 2), without telling
more of his own pleasure. Pleasure in truth is dealt with in
Convivio 2. 11, where Dante says that goodness of thought in
poetry is especially delightful. Heavenly truth is "sweet medi-
cine" (*Par.* 20. 141). Again and again the observer in Heaven
tells of Beatrice's beauty, though sometimes with the implica-
tion rather than the assertion of delight in it. Yet he does say
that "she turned upon me the rays of a smile that would make
any man happy in the fire" (7. 17), and "The eternal purpose,
which was directly sending its rays on Beatrice, pleased me with
its reflection from her beautiful face" (18. 16). In a passage on

Beatrice's eyes, he speaks of "holy pleasure" (14. 138); the word "holy" is usually—perhaps hastily—supposed to apply to them. He is delighted with heavenly music (*e.g.*, 14. 122; 21. 59; 23. 129; 26. 67). He is struck with amazement and joy (31. 40), and once with amazement and possibly apprehension at a shout of the blessed after Pier Damiano's denunciation of the clergy (21. 142). At the very end of the poem a lightning flash pierces the beholder's mind to give him understanding of the Trinity (33. 141).

In thus showing the various effects produced on his protagonist, Dante has gone beyond any purpose of presenting the dead either literally (but always in accord with his fiction) or as allegorically they figure life on earth, however vaguely. In an exhibition of divine justice, little attention need be given the beholder; what he sees is enough. Yet our author remembered how Virgil presented his hero in the lower world. Aeneas shed tears on meeting Dido and on greeting his father Anchises. By the clangor heard from within the walls of Tartarus he was terrified. Yet Virgil was writing an *Aeneid*, in which his title character is for his own sake important. But was the Italian poet writing a *Danteid*, with himself as the comic hero? So far as he was, the adventures of his traveler are to be vivid. To sights and sounds he gave reality when the narrator told what an impression they made on him, so that his terror or his pity or rapt interest—not always ruled by theological notions of the divine will—continued to live in his memory.

WHAT DOES THE VISITOR SHARE WITH THE DEAD?

Virgil tells Mohammed that no sin is driving his pupil "to be tormented" (*Inf.* 28. 47). The spectator is not a fit subject for Hell. On the contrary, he is a "good Christian" (*Par.* 24. 52) who after death will appear in Purgatory (*Inf.* 3. 93; *Purg.* 2. 91; 13. 133). But though not subject to punishment for mortal sin, the traveler is exposed to the climate of the regions he visits, as though journeying on earth.

On entering the Inferno, he is oppressed by the horrible noise and the darkness (*Inf.* 3. 22, 29). The "dark plain" is shaken

by earthquakes, so frightful that the visitor after his return to
earth sweats with terror on recollecting them (3. 130). He
cannot cross in Charon's boat because it is forbidden to "good
souls" (3. 127). From darkness the wayfarers enter the light of
a place inhabited by "honorable people" (4. 72); on leaving,
they reenter murky air. At the edge of the Sixth Circle, Virgil
suggests that they wait until they become accustomed to the
stench rising from below (11. 11); a similar stench rises from
the *bolgia* of the falsifiers (*Inf.* 29. 50). In the steep and path-
less descent to the Seventh Circle, loose stones move under the
unwonted weight of mortal feet (12. 9, 30). In that circle,
avoiding fiery sand, the companions walk along the levee of a
stream. The Florentine would like to descend to a level with
Brunetto Latini, but dare not risk the burning desert (14. 74;
15. 43; 16. 16, 49). Forced to climb out of the *bolgia* of the
hypocrites, he loses his breath on its steep slope (24. 43). In
the icy depths of Hell he trembles in the cold (32. 75). The
freezing wind so benumbs the mortal visitor's face that he
shelters himself behind Virgil, here treated as substantial rather
than as a shade (33. 101; 34. 8). Thus like an earthly explorer,
the visitor to Hell is subject to topography and climate.

In Purgatory, since Virgil does not know the country, he
often asks for directions (e.g., *Purg.* 3. 76; 19. 78). Topographical difficulties are the ascents from one level to another through
steep ravines, becoming easier as the mountain rises. In steep-
ness the first equals San Leo, where on a mountain sits a castle
supposed impregnable by situation; indeed it is more difficult,
for San Leo can, on some sides, be ascended on foot, but for
the hill of Purgatory wings are needed: "The summit was so
high that it was out of sight, and the slope more than that of
a line from the middle of a circle's quadrant to its center.
I was so tired that I said: 'O good father, turn and see how I
shall be left alone if you don't pause.' 'My son,' he answered,
'drag yourself up to there,' and he pointed to a shelf a little
above, which on that side circles all the hill. His words so
stimulated me that I made an effort, crawling on all fours up to
him, until the ledge was under my feet" (*Purg.* 4. 40). The

climb from the terrace of pride to that of envy is so much easier as to be like that from Florence to San Miniato (12. 100).

The other topographical difficulty in Purgatory is that the terraces are not secured with railings, though on the outer side there is a sheer and perilous cliff (13. 80; 25. 117). Two of the ledges offer the ascender difficulty. That of wrath is shrouded in dense smoke, through which the way leads, as through the murky air of Hell, less obscure than this (16. 1). Virgil, never subject to physical restriction, offers his shoulder and cautions his pupil not to separate from him. The terrace of lust is occupied by flames, except for a narrow path on the verge of the precipice (25. 112). Yet the mountain cannot be ascended without crossing through the flames to the inner side of the terrace. The living man hesitates, but when Virgil reminds him that Beatrice is on the other side, he plunges in. Though finding the flames intensely hot, he suffers no injury. In their search for moral significance, annotators assert that here the observer shares the torment of the dead. If so, his distress is a mere token, for sinners normally spend years in Purgatory. Can any traveler avoid the topography and escape the climate of any region he passes through?

The visitor to Heaven, raised by miracle from sphere to sphere, escapes the difficulties of mortal travel; he does not need the chariot of Elijah or of Astolfo (*Orlando Furioso* 34. 69). The climate of Heaven cannot cause distress. Yet his mortal eyes are blinded by celestial lights (*Par.* 14. 78; 23. 87; 25. 27, 138; 30. 51). In Saturn he also becomes unable to hear: "Tell me why in this round the sweet symphony of Paradise is silent, which in the others lower down makes such devout music." "Your hearing like your sight is mortal," answered Pier Damiano, "therefore no singing is heard here for the same reason that Beatrice does not smile" (*Par.* 21. 58). Beatrice's failure to smile has been explained:

My eyes were fixed upon my lady's face, and my mind with them, and from every other object it was taken away. She did not smile but said: "If I should smile, you would be in Semele's state, when she was burned to ashes, because my beauty, which burns brighter as I climb higher up the stairs of the eternal palace, as you have seen, would if not softened, so shine that at its glory your mortal power would be like a branch which lightning breaks" (21. 1).

Such reference to the visitor's mortal powers, made slightly comic by the comparison with Semele, does much for the realism of the visit to the celestial regions.

2 · Poetry

However much Dante learned from Virgil, he did not imitate the Latin master's plot, the story of a warrior's adventures. Aeneas travels to act, while Dante as protagonist makes his expedition to see and learn. The outline of the *Commedia* is simple movement: the traveler passes through Hell, Purgatory, and Heaven. But however interesting his personal experiences, they are secondary; we do not say: "Dante the visitor did something," so much as "Dante saw something." The inscription over Hell Gate makes clear that he enters to assure himself of divine justice, power, love, and wisdom. Or the few days of the journey are to give "full experience" (*Inf.* 28. 48; cf. *Purg.* 26. 75); or the traveler seeks liberty (*Purg.* 1. 71). Spiritual liberty he does thus achieve (*Par.* 31. 85), declaring at last that love—the love exalted on the portal of Hell—was impelling his will to move like a wheel turned steadily (*Par.* 33. 143–45). Yet little is shown of the mental processes working the chief character's change from the fear and "wearied vigor" (*Inf.* 1. 20; 2. 130) preceding his journey. The poet assumes that to present the evidence is enough; a man of sense cannot but draw the right conclusions. So in his journey the traveler is to see (*Inf.* 1. 116, 118; 3. 17; 10. 8; 12. 21; 22. 17; *Purg.* 1. 64, 69;[1] *Par.* 5. 5, etc.).

---

1 Virgil says to Cato, *a vederti e a udirti* (to see you and to hear you). The "you" is sometimes explained as flattering to Cato. I suspect (as by a sort of ethical accusative) a reference to all of Purgatory or even to all three realms of the dead. Perhaps necessary rhyme and meaning go together here. The author of the *Ottimo Commento* reports that Dante said he could give new meaning to rhyme words (On *Inf.* 10. 85).

Virgil "guides his eyes on high" (*Purg.* 21. 124). Especially in the *Paradiso* he also hears, as from Piccarda (*Par.* 4. 97). The pilgrim may be said to visit a museum arranged to display fundamental truths of human life. In the other world there are no deceptive appearances; all things can be seen as they are, as is suggested by the usual nakedness of the spirits. Such opportunity for seeing is all that is required to establish in the observer's mind confidence in divine justice and love.

As appears in *Inferno* 11 and later passages of exposition, Dante thought out the series of persons to be seen and heard. But sequence from one group of sinners or saints to another is slight. One interview does not lead to another. Thus the construction of the poem is that of beads on a string, each bead distinct. In the *Inferno* the chief division is into nine circles and divisions of circles, amounting in all to twenty-three. In each of these is used the same formula, skillfully varied. Dante enters or views the circle, sees the sinners and their punishment, learns who they are. Here then are twenty-three similar but far from identical beads. In Malebolge, repetition of material arrangement is at its utmost. The ten *bolge* are similar except that each succeeding one is on a lower level and, being included within the circle above it, of smaller diameter, but the connection by bridges is the same throughout, except for the variety of one broken bridge. Further precaution against monotony is the descent into some of the *bolge*, with the presence or absence of torturing demons. Thus the *Inferno's* general characteristic of exhibiting variety in similarity is at its most evident.

The central part of the *Purgatorio*—the description of the seven terraces—also illustrates Dante's love for variation within symmetry. An angel always presides over the ascent. On each terrace are the sufferers. Examples of those practicing contrary virtues are given as a "scourge"; one of these is always the Virgin. Those who have been guilty of the vice are given as the "bridle" (*Purg.* 13. 40). One of the beatitudes is sung, and one of the letters on the tourist's forehead is removed, though the removal is not always specified or even implied. Within this pattern variation is great. The scourge, for example, is sometimes graphically represented, sometimes spoken of by the sufferers, sometimes mysteriously heard. The order of the components is varied. On only some of the terraces does the sightseer hear a song or a prayer. Ante-Purgatory, though divided into four sections, the excommunicated (Canto 3), the lazy, those who died a violent death, those too lazy to repent (Canto 6), does not have obviously repetitive structure. In the cantos following *Purgatorio* 27 repetition disappears.

The *Paradiso* is also constructed according to formula, based on the heavens of medieval astronomy. In each of the first eight heavens the visitor encounters and talks with some of the souls adapted to the sphere visited. Each heaven is more brilliant than its predecessor, though this the reader is left to infer, if he wishes, from the descriptions. Likewise Beatrice is made more glorious with each ascent; she says: "My beauty along the steps of the eternal palace burns brighter . . . as it rises higher" (*Par.* 21. 7). (Note also 8. 15; 10. 38; 18. 57.) Yet one movement to a higher heaven is made without reference to her loveliness, whether in forgetfulness of symmetry or deliberately for variety (22. 100).

The long series of circles and terraces and spheres beginning at Hell Gate is made up of resembling units little connected with one another. These units, easiest reckoned as forty-four besides introductions, are primary in Dante's outline, yet they are far from covering the entire poem. Among them are to be placed many other harmonious units in the chain, having their own individuality. Obvious declarations of poetical quality are the similes and metaphors involving description, as of the River Montone (*Inf.* 16. 94), the Venetian arsenal (21. 9), the shepherd dismayed by the frost (24. 1), the messenger with the olive branch (*Purg.* 2. 70), the man in the street unconscious of some strange mark on his head (*Purg.* 12. 127), the cavalier riding out to defy an enemy (24. 94), the Argonauts on their voyage (*Par.* 2. 16), the lady coughing at the time of Guinevere's slip (16. 13), and the tailor who cuts out a gown as the cloth permits (32. 140). The number of similitudes in the *Commedia* has been reckoned as nearly 600. Many melt into the context as ornament on beads forming the necklace, but some of them are to be reckoned as independent beads—small ones, perhaps.

Another sort of independent passage treats political subjects. Among these are invectives against Florence, such as that of

Ciacco (*Inf.* 6. 49), of Brunetto Latini (15. 61), Rusticucci (16. 67), Dante (*Purg.* 12. 102), Guido del Duca (14. 25), Forese Donati (23. 94), Folco (*Par.* 9. 127), and Cacciaguida (15. 97). Such anti-Florentine passages, or those against the corruption of the Church, are often at least semi-independent of their context, as not dealing immediately with the punishments and rewards of the spirits in the world of the dead. Clearly they are among the themes Dante as poet thought his function required him to deal with, if we are to judge from the way they come into the poem throughout. Indeed the two passages labeled by the author as digressions are of this type. One is the lament beginning *Ahi serva Italia,* not assigned to any dramatic speaker (*Purg.* 6. 76). The other is Beatrice's denunciation of buffoonish preachers (*Par.* 29. 88).

Another topic to which Dante gives more independence than is required by his attempt to show the condition of the dead or to present divine justice in any limited sense, is poetry, whether that of the *dolce stil nuovo* (*Purg.* 24. 57) or of the classical authors. This is well illustrated by his treatment of Statius (*Purg.* 22). No firm foundation has been discovered for the belief that Statius became a Christian. Thus if Dante did not invent the conversion of that poet, he chose to follow a tradition obscure enough to elude modern students. He had before him the possibility of putting Statius in whichever he wished of his three realms. Having chosen Purgatory, he still retained the choice of any part of that kingdom. Here too he seems to have had no guiding authority. The ledge of avarice Dante perhaps selected as enabling him to use a quotation from Virgil: *Quid non mortalia pectora cogis,/ auri sacra fames* (*Aeneid* 3. 56)? Yet Statius is acquitted of avarice, though guilty of the less repulsive sin of lavishness. Dante's chief motive in devoting nearly two cantos to Statius is to write on classical poetry, with glorification of Virgil. He seizes also the opportunity to add another function for Statius, that of explaining the nature and laws of Purgatory.

Our poet's freedom to assign shades to any of the three kingdoms of the other world is often apparent. After Farinata degli Uberti's death, political opponents brought legal charges of heresy. Perhaps his reputation for freethinking required Dante to put him in Hell. Yet there is in the *Comedy* no discussion of the sin of this "magnanimous" man (*Inf.* 10. 73). Moreover, the traveler early declared Farinata one of the worthy, who set their intelligence to doing good (6. 79, 81). Had Dante wished Farinata in Purgatory he needed only to imagine tardy repentance, as for Manfred and Buonconte da Montefeltro. No one but the omniscient poet could know that Manfred repented as, deserted, he succumbed to two wounds, or that Buonconte, alone by the river, called on Mary with his dying breath (*Purg.* 3. 119; 5. 101).

If Dante so evidently wished to include in his poem much in addition to its basis in the punishment or reward of the dead, was this other material less interesting to him than that of his central theme? Did he not plan his poem with some of it in view? For its inclusion his method gave him opportunity. Each circle or terrace or heaven is a unit in itself, subject not to preceding action by the characters encountered but only to the requirements of the entire plan. Dante the traveler himself must usually be the eager enquirer, yet though he is sometimes so depressed as to be made a child, he also passes over into the role of Dante author of the inspired poem, worthy to be classed with the greatest, and anticipating centuries of fame. Beatrice may be the beautiful lady with sparkling eyes, glad to assist the visitor, or she may castigate a forgetful lover or act as a learned expounder of Plato. Virgil is more stable, though sometimes the Christian knowledge of this pagan astonishes moderns unaccustomed to thinking his Fourth Eclogue a prophecy of the Messiah (*Purg.* 3. 36). There is no plot whose interrelated actions must be kept harmonious. The many unrelated characters, but once encountered, make possible the most diverse interviews, limited only by the approximately uniform length of the cantos and by their total number of one hundred. The world is before the poet. This rejection of restraint fitted the author's habits as shown in the *Vita Nuova*, where the topic of the proper language for poetry is inserted with little regard for the story of adoration for Beatrice.

Though many beads are provided by the different places visited and the many interviews with souls, the poet still was unsatisfied. Can he be imagined as content to produce a string so uniform as adherence to the reward and punishment of the shades would provide? To secure length and variety, he needed many other beads. Variety required also that not too much of one sort of matter be put in one part of the poem. The political passages, for example, are distributed.

But above all, Dante chose to subject himself to the control of arbitrary numbers, in no way derived from his matter. Not only must his three *cantiche* be nearly of the same length (the utmost disparity being but thirty-eight lines), but there must be 100 cantos evenly assigned to the three, except for the extra one given to the *Inferno*, and these cantos are not to differ greatly in length. Their maximum variation, caused by two very short cantos and one exceptionally long, is forty-five lines; this disparity is not representative. Thus not infrequently Dante might find the material written for three cantos, for example, extending to five hundred lines. He then was obliged to remove some eighty lines, discarding them entirely or placing them elsewhere. Often some of these lines may have formed an independent group or bead. Sometimes the poet may have been fortunate to find in a remote part of his poem a gap of the right length, where such a section could be placed without conspicuous incongruity, perhaps with abridgement or extension. Passages must also have been composed in order to add a few lines, such as a long simile could supply, for example, the device of the Romans for managing crowds on the Ponte Sant' Angelo (*Inf.* 18. 28–33). The difficulty of adjusting rhymes might have led the poet to prefer the addition of afterthoughts at the beginnings of cantos; the first six lines of a canto present but one rhyming word to be adjusted to those following. Conceivably added to increase length are the initial lines of *Inferno* Cantos 12, 15, 21, 22, 23, 24, 28, *Purgatorio* Cantos 6, 16, 17, 19, 21, 24,[2] *Paradiso* Cantos 2, 10, 11, 16, 23, 25. Surely these initial lines are not to be explained only as late additions, though they are to be contrasted with initial lines which continue the narrative of the preceding canto. The extreme example of continuous movement appears when Beatrice speaks to the end of one canto and continues in the first line of the next, with the statement soon

2 The word of transition comes in line 7, though expected in line 1. Cf. *Inferno* 8. 1.

inserted: "She said further, continuing without pause" (*Purg.* 31. 4). Similarly we are told that Matilda "went on to end her words" (29. 2). The last half-dozen cantos of the *Purgatorio* give such slight indications of beginning or end that one imagines them written as a unit and divided into cantos having the required number of lines. But so simple a process is given complexity by the junction in these cantos of two kinds of matter: the allegorical or symbolical procession and Beatrice's dealings with her lover. Presumably the procession, unnecessary to the narrative of the journey, is the part of latest date.

Near the end of the *Purgatorio*, Dante combines with a reference to fixed length a variation of his device of declaring a description of his experience—here with the sweet waters of Eunoë—beyond his powers. He remarks that since the pages designed for the second *cantica* are full, he has no room for praising Eunoë. The amusement with which Dante wrote this did not escape Ariosto; developing Boiardo's habit, he writes: "But before I take my hero further, so that I will not abandon my custom, since I have filled my sheets on both sides, I am going to put an end to this canto" (*Orlando Furioso* 33). Yet joined to Dante's amusement at his own love for regularity is the actual excess of this canto above average length; indeed he would also have been watching the total length of the *Purgatorio*, which now stands as but three lines shorter than the *Paradiso*.

Dante planned, then, to use a large number of beads, none of which must be too large to harmonize with the remainder of his string. These beads he strung according to their fitness of whatever sort, whether contrast, immediate or ultimate harmony, amusement, or conviction—his reasons are manifold. With his iron limitation of 100 cantos and somewhat freer restriction to 133–154 lines per canto (with some unemphatic exceptions), he was deterred from addition to cantos nearing maximum length, unless he was ready to compress or to shift passages. With the wealth of matter at his command, including the information in which he took pleasure, he seldom was under any necessity for writing lines that any reader can call superfluous. On the contrary, his fertility normally enabled him to improve his work, even to modern eyes, when under pressure to

protract a canto to the required length. Perhaps he is overlong
on moon spots, but he more than atones by the richness of
simile sometimes required to bring cantos up to the limit fixed

TO PLEASE, TO TEACH, THE POET'S AIM

In Limbo the fictitious visitor encounters Homer, Horace
Ovid, and Lucan, who receive him, with Virgil, into their
"troop," so that he is "the sixth in the midst of such great poetic
power" (*Inf.* 4. 102). Whether under the traveler's delight in
meeting these masters of song there is any prophecy of his own
greatness by the historical Dante, who can say? With no other
group does the traveler connect himself because of his interest
in their achievement, though he looks with admiration on
Aristotle and many others. Do Dante the poet and Dante the
reporter of the other world unite here? In the Latin poets
mentioned, the Florentine was well read. Virgil asserts that his
pupil knew the *Aeneid* throughout (*Inf.* 20. 114), and the
wanderer in the dark forest, instead of hastening to explain his
pressing dangers, is so interested in the artistic achievement of
his rescuer as to exclaim first of all: "O glory and light of all
poets, may I profit from the continued study and great love that
has made me attentive to your volume! You are my teacher and
my maker; you are he only from whom I took the admirable
style that has brought me renown" (*Inf.* 1. 82). Under this
drama lies fact; long is the list of Dante's borrowings from
Virgil. Thus the *Commedia* presents itself as a poem quite as
the *Aeneid*, the *Metamorphoses*, and the *Pharsalia* are poems.
We may read it as we read them. Ben Jonson said that the poet
who sends out one of his products thereby parts with his right
to it; he must endure such interpretation as readers give, whether
or not to his pleasure. A fable represents Dante as taking an
opposite view. As he passed a potter's shop he heard the owner
barbarously repeating some of his verses. Entering, he threw
pieces of earthenware on the floor. Remonstrated with, he replied that he was treating the potter's vases as the potter was
treating the poet's verses.

Yet though we have liberty to interpret, a view of Dante's
concept of poetry may aid us in catching his intention. Actually,
however, we are to deduce any poet's intentions from the poems

exhibiting them rather than meekly to accept his statements; practice and theory may not harmonize. In explaining one of his *canzoni* Dante says that the "goodness and the beauty of any poem are separate and different; its goodness is in its idea, and its beauty is in the ornamentation of the words. Both give pleasure, though the goodness is especially pleasurable" (*Conv.* 2. 11). Since the idea of the *canzone* is difficult, he concedes that any who cannot understand it (ordinary readers, presumably) may pardonably pay more attention to beauty than to goodness. With similar dualism, he follows Virgil in declaring that Helicon must flow abundantly if he is "to put difficult things in verses" (*Aeneid* 7. 641; *Purg.* 29. 40). In his treatise *De vulgari eloquentia* (*On the Vulgar Tongue*) 2. 4, he makes a different specification for subject. Rightly considered, poetry "is nothing other than a fiction put in verses with verbal and musical skill." The allegorical meaning of poetry is hidden beneath the poet's fables; the truth is concealed under a "beautiful lie, just as when Ovid says that Orpheus with his lyre made the wild beasts mild, made the trees and the rocks walk like animals. The poet really is saying that a prudent man by using speech can make cruel hearts grow mild and meek" (*Convivio* 2. 1). A letter to Can Grande della Scala, attributed to Dante as *Epistle* 10, says, in partial harmony with the quotations just given, that in the *Comedy* the mode of treatment is "poetic, fictive, descriptive, digressive, transumptive, and also definitive, divisive, probative, improbative, and provided with examples." However the latter terms suggest logic, the list is headed by *poetic* and *fictitious*. The "fiction" or "beautiful lie" of the *Commedia* is evidently the journey itself in all its details. For the generality of readers the plain story of the imagined excursion, with its poetical embellishments, is enough, just as the story of Aeneas or an elementary narrative from Ovid's *Metamorphoses* is enough.

Yet to Dante as medieval theorist the literal meaning of a poem was not enough. He adds allegorical meaning to the literal sense (*Convivio* 2. 12). In the letter to Can Grande is analyzed the verse from the Psalms: "When Israel went out of Egypt." To refer this to the historical Exodus is but a beginning; the deliverance from Egyptian bondage is made to signify escape of three kinds: (1) allegorically, man's redemption by Christ; (2) morally, man's escape from the wretchedness of sin to a state of grace; (3) anagogically, the holy soul's deliverance from the servitude of worldly corruption and its attainment of liberty in eternal glory. Evidently further effort by interpreters can bring other allegorical meanings from the Psalmist's historical reference. The metaphor of release from Egyptian bondage fits various escapes, personal, economic, political. In the letter to Can Grande, the literal or factual subject of the *Comedy* is affirmed as "the state of the souls after death, taken simply, for from that comes and on that depends the whole course of the work." Allegorically and truly, however, the poem's subject, the writer of the letter reiterates, is "man insofar as, by showing merit or its opposite, in the freedom of his will, he is subject to [divine] justice, which is to reward or punish him." A modern reader cannot too often remind himself that even the letter to Can Grande does not apply to the *Commedia* moral and anagogical interpretations. Yet that letter is the only exposition of the *Commedia* assigned to its author.

With an allegorical and true meaning a seeker for delight who reads poetry as poetry is not primarily concerned. In Dante's poem he appreciates the effect of vivid words and harmonious verse, of lively exhibition of character in brief glimpses of many persons, the activity of the sightseer himself, and all the qualities that make the poem perennially fascinating. But to the allegorical meaning the poetically minded reader, as distinguished from the professional expositor or the seeker for some such matter as the spirit of the Middle Ages, seldom goes. Such profit as the lover of poetry gets—and it may be very great, for of all readers he profits most—is chiefly incidental. At the least he rejoices in the verse carrying the instruction as well as in the ideas, and any knowledge comes to him as something moving rather than static. Realizing the universal rather than the merely particular quality of the poem, he thinks of Francesca as revealing the human heart torn between conventional duty and mastering passion, of Ulysses the unquenchable adventurer, rather than of the meaning of their punishments.

For some of the penalties, the reader who asks about the allegory cannot but be puzzled. Attempting to retrace what he imagines the steps of Dante's ingenuity in inventing them, he may decide that burning pits into which sinners are thrust headlong are suitable for the simonists who perverted the activities of their ecclesiastical offices, changing charity to avarice. Such an interpretation requires ratiocination. Why is smoke the punishment of the angry in Purgatory? Is it irritating like anger or, on the contrary, does it oppose the swift violence of wrath? Did Dante not make the allegory clear enough to gain for it immediate recognition? Must the reader who penetrates it turn from rapid impression to delaying logic? Even then can he be sure his solution is correct?

Some of the punishments of Hell are more effective as aids to the reader's memory than as expressions of the sinner's life. Those who caused schism and civil war are themselves divided asunder by a devil, though in life they were not themselves divided; they caused division in states and families; as it were, they acted the part of the devil who slashes them. Allegorical explanation has been attempted for the panders and seducers in the first *bolgia* of Circle Eight, who are scourged by horned devils. One commentator has suggested that since every word of Dante's was written with thought, the horns are the figurative horns of the husbands whose wives have been seduced. Certainly Dante wrote with thought, but with what thought? How much meditation do the cuckold's horns require, and how frequently do devils have horns? Buti explains the opposite directions in which panders and seducers are driven (*Inf.* 18. 31–33, 65, 80, 97): "We can understand that he feigns, allegorically, that the two groups move in opposite directions . . . because the pander is avaricious and does what he does through avarice, but the seducer is prodigal and to indulge his lust would throw away everything." Buti then attempts explanation of the nakedness of the sinners and of their punishment by scourging. Could his words not be applied to many other sufferers in Hell? They are equally "naked of God's grace," as they are physically naked.

On the other hand, by an easy metaphor, tyrants who lived in the midst of bloodshed suffer their hellish punishment in a river of blood. Or in Purgatory the slothful can naturally be thought of as correcting their fault by rapid action, as in life they would have roused themselves to activity. Allegory and the universalizing quality of poetry, or even of slightly poetical narrative, come close together only when an easily grasped metaphor unites them, as when the flatterers are immersed in the filth of privies, since flattery is a filthy sin. Yet when the gluttons in Purgatory are exposed to continual desire for food that they refrain from, the punishment is literal rather than allegorical.

The *Paradiso* is less specific in its allegory of the individual than the other *cantiche*. In contrast to the damned who stole or caused dissension, the saints are not limited to appear as peacemakers or givers of charity. Since they have attained perfection, they cannot display the specifically directed efforts of Purgatory. Yet actually dwelling in the highest heaven, though displayed for the traveler's instruction in the lower ones, they become an allegory of the divine ordering of the world, in which each man has his function, equally sacred with that of others, whether more or less inclusive or elevated. Connection with the earth appears in the concern of various saints, such as Bonaventura and Peter, with human wickedness. Yet for any individual, allegory appears generally rather than specifically in harmony with the eternal love and participation in its light—light which is itself an allegory of the divine.

So Dante's attempts to adapt in detail the punishment or the reward to the sin or the virtuous action sometimes are successfully obvious and sometimes so hard to penetrate as to yield no assured interpretation. If the poet reflected long over the propriety of some of the punishments, does he require us to pause in reading to exercise ingenuity as on a puzzle? Did he expect the readers to whom he looked forward to arrive at solutions as a matter of course? The illustrations he takes for the explanation of allegory are usually metaphorical. His view of the "dark conceit" of Ovid's Orpheus has been observed. In *Convivio* 2. 1 the verse "When Israel came out of Egypt," explained as the issue of the soul from sin, is assigned not to the moral sense, as in the letter to Can Grande, but to the anagogical sense, perhaps with some overlapping of classes. Likewise, *Convivio* 2. 1 interprets Christ's visit to the Mount of Transfiguration with but three followers as meaning that "in very secret matters we should have little company." But is this more than an example worth following?

Dante wrote allegories less evident than that of stones as stony-hearted men. One such perhaps is his confinement to graves of those rejecting the immortality of the soul (*Inf.* 10. 15) as though to say: They hold that the soul ends with the grave. More debatable, as appears from the history of interpretation, is the lesson to be drawn from the wrathful in the Stygian swamp. Did Dante know that some of his symbols were not very evident? Could he have expected his readers to reach the right conclusion? Had he at times no allegorical intention? Here, as elsewhere, we may remember:

I intend to show the true meaning of these *canzoni*, for it cannot be understood by anybody if I do not explain it, because it is concealed under an allegorical image; and this explanation will not merely be heard with much delight but will give shrewd instruction both in writing allegorically and in understanding the allegorical meaning of other men's writings (*Convivio* 1. 2).

There is reason in applying to the *Commedia* the method Dante uses in the prose work, with allowance for the difference between *canzoni* and long narrative poem. Interpreters have attempted to do so, for example, by equating Beatrice with Theology, as the lady of the *Convivio* is Philosophy. We must, however, be cautious, for the liberty in which the poet left us, when he failed to provide the *Commedia* with such comment as he presents in the *Convivio*, has many dangers.

The first general allegory to be deduced from the *Commedia* is that of man as he deserves punishment or reward. On this Benvenuto da Imola writes:

The matter or subject of Dante's poem is the condition of the human soul both when joined with the body and when separate from the body. This condition is universally threefold; hence the author divides his work into three parts. Certain souls are in their sins, and these souls while they live in their bodies are morally dead; thus they are in a moral Hell. When they are divided from their bodies, they are in a material Hell, if in their obstinacy they died without cure. There are other souls that draw back from the vices; these while in their bodies are in a moral Purgatory, that is, they are subjecting themselves to penitence, by which they purge

their sins. When they are divided from their bodies, they are in a
material Purgatory. Thirdly, there are other souls perfect in their
practice of virtue. These while living in the body are in a sense
in Paradise, since they are in such felicity as is possible to man
in this life of misery. When divided from the body after death,
they are in the heavenly Paradise enjoying the vision of God,
in whom is true and perfect happiness. . . . Some describe Hell
morally only, as do the ancient poets Virgil and Homer, for all
the punishments these poets feign in Hell are found in this vicious
world, which is the Hell of living men. Others describe Hell as it
materially is, such as the sacred theologians and holy doctors. As a
thoroughly Christian poet, our author describes both Hells. Following both paths, he sometimes speaks of the moral Hell, sometimes
of the material Hell (Introduction, p. 16, ed. 1887).

Thus Benvenuto confirms in detail the assertion in the letter to
Can Grande that literally Dante's subject is the state of the
dead, but that allegorically it is man (in this world) as subject
to divine justice.

Within the poem, Dante calls attention only to allegory not
applying to the souls of the dead as symbols of the living. At
the gate of Dis, the fictitious traveler in terror hears the devils
on the wall above him planning to bring the Gorgon Medusa,
potent to turn him to stone. Thereupon " 'Turn around and
keep your face covered, because if the Gorgon does come and
you see her, you never can return to the world above.' So said
my teacher, and he himself turned me around and did not think
my hands enough but covered my eyes with his own as well"
(*Inf.* 9. 55). Abandoning his fiction for the moment, the poet
addresses his readers: "O you who have sound minds, look
closely at the teaching hidden under the covering of my strange
verses" (9. 61). Though Dante does not uncover the hidden
teaching, commentators have been zealous. Yet they differ
among themselves. Does the poet's adjuration apply to the
Gorgon alone or to the whole episode? Vernon, in his *Readings
on the Inferno*, attempts to demonstrate that the Furies are evil
conscience, Medusa is doubt, etc. Yet Benvenuto da Imola
(whom Vernon usually follows)—rejecting elaborate allegories
as superfluous—thinks that "the best and truest exposition is to
make Medusa represent Dante's terror." Guido da Pisa interprets
the scene as an exhortation to let no impediment turn us back
from good work begun. According to Jacopo della Lana's early

commentary, the three furies indicate incontinence, malice, and bestiality; in allegorical truth, a man who lets these vices conquer him becomes an insensible stone. Such an allegory of Medusa as Despair of Winning God's Mercy is more recent. The deliverer "sent by Heaven" (*Inf.* 9. 85) to secure Dante's entrance into the city of Dis has in modern times become an allegory of divine revelation. Benvenuto da Imola thought him Mercury, chiefly on the ground that Dante does not put angels in Hell.

Again Dante calls attention to his allegory when in Ante-Purgatory he hears the spirits pray for divine guardianship and sees descending two angels armed with fiery swords shortened by breaking their points. On this he addresses the reader: "Here, reader, sharpen your eyes to the truth, for the veil is now very thin, so that, certainly, to pierce it is easy" (*Purg.* 8. 19). Even these words have troubled some annotators, who ask: Why should the sight need sharpening when the veil of literal words drawn over the allegory hardly conceals its truth? Presumably Dante is here thinking of such readers as those of *Convivio* 2. 11, more attracted by beauty than by truth. Yet here even they can be sharp-sighted enough to get the easy allegory of the angels who come in answer to prayer to defend the souls by putting the serpent to flight. The angelic garments are green, for that, says Benvenuto da Imola, is the color of hope.

In an allegorical dream an ugly woman appears to the traveler (*Purg.* 19. 7). As he gazes, she becomes a beautiful siren, whose foulness is then revealed by a "holy lady." Strangely, the siren first appears repulsive, then beautiful. We expect beauty first, then the revelation of foulness, as Spenser presented his Duessa, the false witch. With this the commentators do little, though Vernon aptly quotes from Pope:

> Vice is a monster of so frightful mien
> As to be hated needs but to be seen;
> Yet seen too oft, familiar with her face,
> We first endure, then pity, then embrace.

Dante makes no attempt to explain this allegory of the Siren, with its unmistakable picture of the false attractiveness of evil. Benvenuto attempts to apply in detail her various deformities to the three terraces of Purgatory above, devoted to avarice, gluttony, and lust. The lady who exposes her is said to be

Wisdom, Lucia or Truth, the Church, Reason, Philosophy, etc. The number of choices—any one of them in some way acceptable—indicates that Dante is here indefinite. Another long allegorical passage, tenuously connected with the narrative of travel to observe the souls of the dead, is the procession in the Earthly Paradise. [See Chap. 4, Part 2.]

In one exhortation—whimsical, even comic, Dante calls on his reader to provide understanding. Having presented an aspect of the universe as depending on "the first and ineffable Power," he continues: "Now reader, keep sitting on your bench, thinking about what I have touched on, if you hope to be pleased rather than bored. I have put food before you; now eat for yourself. For my part, the matter on which I am required to write claims all my effort" (*Par.* 10. 22). Is Dante, like Ben Jonson, here saying that he has "parted with his right," and is little concerned with the reader's interpretation? That valuable medieval document, the letter to Can Grande, gives the *Commedia* a practical purpose, namely, to take those "who live in this life out of a state of misery and bring them into a state of happiness." The wish to instruct underlies Dante's interest in truth under a veil of narrative. He expected his more intellectual readers to look for the allegory, to eat the food he put before them. In the verses on the "ineffable Power" just referred to, he expected his audience to go beyond his scientific exposition to such a moral as God's care for man as revealed in his divine support of the universe. That is, he expected some of his readers to find the hidden meaning. So in all of Dante's avowedly allegorical passages the moral is not remote. As we have seen, enough of the punishments of Hell and Purgatory so evidently represent human wickedness, accepted or struggled against, as to produce a strong effect. Even when Dante's ingenuity fails to produce a fully representational punishment, he at least asserts that the wicked man lives unhappily and that the righteous live in the divine light of happiness.

So Dante fails to make all his punishments and rewards as clearly representative of man's earthly life as the early commentators held them to be or as the letter to Can Grande—if made rigid—demands. While some punishments may be so taken, generally the poet seems content with those merely harmonious with the criminal life of the sufferer. Ulysses and Guido da Montefeltro, who sinned through keenness of intellect, are shining in Hell. Such a punishment is too noble for the counterfeiters, more sordid in their vice. Yet why should those falsifiers be covered with scabs, instead of suffering some other disgusting affliction? The answer strains the ingenuity of Benvenuto da Imola. In Purgatory, though some of the terraces have puzzled commentators, some of the punishments—such as those of sloth and gluttony—are so obviously opposed to the vice as to justify ingenuity in seeking similar counteraction in all seven. In Paradise, as interpreters have now and then said, allegory of earthly life is not general among the blessed. From such carelessness of limited allegorical instruction and yet the highly wrought character of the poem, one may conclude that to narrative and poetical effectiveness the poet gave more effort than he did to ethical meaning. For the artist, practically if not theoretically, the claims of art outweigh those of morality.

In the Middle Ages, with its esteem for ethics, theory demanded moral precepts from the poet. The popular demand for instruction was then—we may guess—not very different in amount from modern eagerness for meaning—such as sociological meaning—in art, often to the neglect of beauty or even of elementary fascination with story. Other medieval likings are suggested by some of the secular literature and, for example, by comic and bawdy carvings in ecclesiastical buildings.

But however we estimate the medieval scene, the *Convivio* presents a Dante who enjoyed teaching. Moreover, he seems to have been familiar with Horace's *Ars Poetica*.[3] At least his thought is in the Horatian tradition, which tends to overestimate Horace's didacticism at the expense of his remarks on pleasure. Even in the year 1963 many scholars are still making Dante, Shakespeare, and Sophocles first of all moral and religious teachers. Yet Horace, recognizing that poetry may be instructive, says that he gets every vote who mingles the useful with the delightful, both pleasing and advising his readers. The poet should be brief in his teaching and make use of the delightfully fabulous.

---

3 *Vita Nuova* 25; *Convivio* 2. 14; *Vulg. Eloq.* 2. 4; *Epist.* 10. 10. Yet possibly he knew not the complete work but only quotations from it. In the Middle Ages books were harder to get than now.

Medieval lovers of poetry sought deep meaning—moral and allegorical—in fiction in order to defend poetry from condemna-
tion as vain and frivolous and even immediately injurious. In his
commentary on his father's poem, Dante's son Pietro accepts
such a view, though he was well read in the Latin poets, especially Ovid, the most suspect of the great ones. Against what
may be called puritan rejection of poetry, Boccaccio directed
the moral and religious interpretations in his *Genealogy of the
Gods*.

Yet such a moralist as Saint Thomas is philosopher rather
than artist. As moral teacher merely, Dante would not have
taken his place as one of the world's great writers of verse. His
perfection in *terza rima*, credited as his invention, was not the
achievement of a few months. The examination of meters in his
De vulgari eloquentia is not a piece of pedantic research, but the
result of consideration on the language most suitable for adorn-
ing thought, or for securing that *convenientia* or harmony between matter, tone, and language essential, as Dante thought, to
poetic art (*On the Vulgar Tongue* 2. 1). Whatever the importance of goodness (that is, value or power to benefit) in subject
matter, however pleasurable it may be, poetic qualities or beauty
reside in the adornment of the language (*Convivio* 2. 11). He
explains why he did not wish to write in Latin the commentary
on his Italian poems, so that it could be read outside Italy:

It would be contrary to the desire of the poems for their matter
to be explained in regions where they could not carry also their
beauty. For everybody ought to realize that nothing gaining harmony from musical unification can be translated from one language
to another without destroying its sweetness and harmony. For this
reason Homer has not been rendered from Greek into Latin like
other Greek authors. For this reason the verses of the Psalter have
no sweetness of music and harmony, because they were translated
from Hebrew to Greek and from Greek to Latin, and in the first
translation all their sweetness vanished (*Convivio* 1. 7).

Without beauty there is no poetry, though subject matter is
important. On this Dante says:

I say that the goodness (*i.e.*, value or profitable character) and the
beauty of each piece of writing are separate and different, because
the value is in the idea and the beauty is in the adornment of the
words; and both of these yield delight, though the goodness (profit-

able component) may be exceedingly delightful. Hence though the profitable part of this canzone may be hard to understand because of the different persons brought in to speak, since many things must be kept distinct, but the beauty is easy to see, I believe it essential to the canzone that most men [those who find the idea difficult] should give more attention to beauty than to profit (*Convivio* 2. 11).

Dante continues with a direct address to his poem:

If you happen to come where you think people doubt your subject matter, do not worry, but say to them: "Since you do not see my valuable content, at least give attention to my beauty." [Dante then speaks himself.] By this I do not intend to say anything other, according to what is said above, than this: "O men, who are unable to see the idea of this poem, do not therefore refuse it, but give your attention to its beauty, which is great both in its construction, which is the concern of grammarians, by the arrangement of its language, which is the concern of rhetoricians, and through the number of its parts, which pertains to the musicians. These things anybody who looks can see are excellent in this poem" (2. 11).

We may recall that earlier in the *Convivio*, Dante had spoken of the advantages of giving poetry wide circulation among those who did not know the Latin language (1. 7, 8), and that he had said that allegory could be understood only if the author explained it (1. 2).

The idea of "fit audience . . . though few" appears in Dante's address to his readers near the beginning of the *Paradiso*. Those attempting to follow his ship in a "little boat" had best turn back, but "You few others who have betimes furnished yourselves with angels' bread, on which we live here and are not sated, are able to go on a voyage over the salt sea, following my wake before the water gets smooth again" (2. 10). This is a journey to Heaven, it is true, but one under the conduct of Minerva, Apollo, and the nine Muses. Minerva is the goddess of wisdom, but Apollo and the Muses are for poetic beauty.

From the number of fit readers, how many whose eyes were opened to poetical beauty but who were little concerned with an allegorical and true meaning would Dante have excluded? How much indeed of the understanding signified by Minerva would he have required? He does not tell us much of allegorical meaning throughout his *Commedia*, save as we adhere to the letter to

Can Grande, though such passages as that of the serpent vanquished by the angels and of the Siren are evidently symbolical. If we may apply the *Convivio* to the *Commedia*, is it possible that Dante was far from demanding readers so eager for profit that they would spin their own allegorical interpretations? In his reference to readers who abandoned improvement for poetical beauty, was he showing respect for professed students, and yet covertly, with some amusement at his own didactic tendencies, indicating that since he was a poet, readers who accepted poetical beauty without further demands were enough for him?

Surely part of the pleasure he contemplated for his readers, as he (or some other critic) wrote at the end of the letter to Can Grande, was to come from the delightful truth presented. He has the poet's proper and necessary regard for the content of his verse. Thus he thinks of the pleasure derived from religion and moral observation as part of that to be found in poetry—as widely inclusive. As a practical poet (who might serve as an example to students of aesthetics) he felt no need to analyse the reader's pleasure and reject part of it. For example, to devout Catholics, Saint Bernard's prayer to the Virgin will give more or at least different pleasure than to those not practicing hyperdulia. At the beginning of the *Paradiso*, Dante makes his fitness for a poetical crown dependent on two things: his matter and his poetical skill (1. 27). For success as an author he calls for Apollo's aid, with his eye fixed on the beauty of poetry. Indeed when any poet or wise critic talks of instruction in verse, he assumes, if he does not mention, all that the Delphic god indicates. If poetry is teaching, it is delightful teaching. The delight makes the poet. Had Dante wished merely to teach, he would have been content to return to Florence as philosopher or scholar or preacher, but he aspires to the poet's crown.

From the beginning, most writers on Dante have shown less concern with him as poet than as teacher. On the early annotators generally, we must echo Professor Grandgent's observation that they "were deficient in poetic insight." Even Boccaccio is disappointing, often using a Dantesque reference as an excuse for mythological or historical disquisitions suitable for an encyclopedia, and giving pages to farfetched allegory. Guido da Pisa recognizes the poetical quality of the *Comedy* by listing with comment the comparisons with which cantos are adorned. We cannot know the estimate through the centuries of the non-professional reader, who has written nothing. The incidental remarks of Machiavelli and Milton hint that they read the *Comedy* as they read other poetry, without undue emphasis on instruction. In later years Dante's audience doubtless has contained independents, though many going through the *Comedy* as a duty—even when of a higher order than those Italians who read a prose version—have taken seriously the medieval comments printed in their books. In part as a heritage from the Middle Ages, emphasis still rests on ecclesiastical allegory.

The poem is also offered as a medieval encyclopedia, presenting varied knowledge. Something of medieval theology, philosophy, and science surely can be learned from the poem. Indeed, to an acute reader perusing the poem for pleasure, the work furnishes so much information as to be in great part its own commentary. Dante carried to excess the application of his theory that much of the delight offered by poetry comes from its good ideas (*Convivio* 2. 11). Professor Grandgent, insisting that the didactic is an integral part of Dante's conception, yet remarks on the discussion of angels in *Paradiso* 29 that "to the modern reader such speculations seem otiose; and we are perhaps justified in believing that they did not appear very important to Dante." [4] Yet even in such passages Dante does not cease to be the poet, for whom it is not enough to teach; he will teach beautifully. Only secondarily is he an encyclopedist. Our modern judgment, however humdrum in justifying poetry, would hardly send a student of medieval philosophy to Dante rather than to Aquinas. More than incidental insistence on the *Comedy* as encyclopedia is homage to the perennial desire to justify poetry as prosaically improving. Yet a poet's science or theology suffers because subordinate to fiction and used for poetical rather than informative purposes. His didactic passages—unless reduced to mere versified information—are to be regarded with scepticism. Dante had read widely, but would the professional learned men of his age have thought him an adequate expositor rather than an apt pupil? To a literary merchant like Giovanni Villani, Dante appeared a philosopher, but would schoolmen have taken

4 In his edition of the *Comedy*, 1933, pp. 648, 924.

this party agitator and vernacular versifier as their equal? What of some early growlings about Dantesque heresy?

When a modern reads the poem as poem he can feel secure. Not only can he lay aside anxiety about medieval thought, but he can neglect the allegory as produced by the annotators. If it occurs to him that the avaricious as they push heavy weights typify the useless toil of men intent on riches only, he is gaining Horatian profit. To more farfetched allegories, such as the seven walls of the noble town in Limbo meaning the seven liberal arts, he need not attend. If as free reader he wishes to pause and ask for meaning, let him do so, even though he pass out of the realm of poetry into that of the puzzle. Allegories demanding attention, such as that of the siren, are apparent. When speculating beyond what is set down, the interpreter is in peril when he identifies his own development of the poet's suggestion with the author's wish. The *Comedy* offers enough of the reasonably plain to satisfy legitimate desires. If Dante is a great poet, why attempt to raise his stature with our own inventions?

A POEM ON POETRY

Inferno. Beginning his fictitious narrative as a returned traveler, Dante writes of the forest in which he was lost: "To deal with the good that I found there, I shall write of the other things I saw there" (*Inf.* 1. 8). The word translated "write" is *dire*, in the *Vita Nuova* often standing in the clause: "I wrote a sonnet." In the midst of his fears, as he rushes downward to escape beasts impeding his ascent of a mountain, the wanderer sees a human figure to whom he calls for aid. The shade addressed hoarsely replies that he lived under Augustus Caesar, adding: "I was a poet and I sang of that just son of Anchises who came from Troy after proud Ilium was burned" (1. 73). Then he inquires about the petitioner, who delays his answer, saying first:

"Are you that Virgil and that spring which pours out such a broad river of poetry?" I answered bashfully. "O honor and light of all the poets, I am relying on the years of devotion and the great love that has made me pore over your book. You are my teacher and my original; you alone are he from whom I learned the beautiful style that has given me fame" (1. 79).

Only after this expression of poetical love does the suppliant turn to his pressing physical danger; poetry comes first. Virgil's answer, though beginning with the wanderer's peril, then goes to the material of the *Aeneid*, for the Veltro "will rescue that lowly Italy for which the virgin Camilla died, and Euryalus, Turnus, and Nisus of their wounds" (1. 106). Even the expression "lowly Italy" is quoted from *Aeneid* 3. 522. Virgil then lays out his pupil's journey. The latter begins his answer by addressing the poet, though dealing with him only as guide.

In the second canto, Dante calls upon the Muse for aid— something the abrupt beginning of Canto 1 prohibited: "O Muse, O lofty genius, now aid me! O Memory, you who write what I saw, here your excellence will be seen" (2. 7). Then in the fiction he again addresses Virgil as "Poet," and gives some lines to the theme of the *Aeneid*. As the Latin author further explains, Beatrice requested him to use his "well-wrought" language (2. 67) in aiding the bewildered traveler; she came to him "trusting in your patrician language, which elevates you and those who have heard it" (2. 113). At last the Dante who has lost his way decides to go on the journey with his admired "original" as "leader, lord, and teacher." As they move on, Virgil, usually the guide, is still sometimes the "Poet" (e.g., 4. 14). They find the clear air of Limbo resembling that of the Elysian fields, of which Virgil wrote that they were clothed with purple light (*lumine purpureo*—*Aeneid* 6. 640), as Dante speaks of bright light (*lumera*—*Inf.* 4. 103). Here Virgil is greeted as "the most eminent poet" (4. 80), though Homer is "sovereign." With Homer come Horace, Lucan, and Ovid. They receive the living visitor as "the sixth in the midst of such great poetic power" (4. 102). Of antiquity's other famous men the narrator sees many but cannot list them all, "because my extensive theme so pushes me on that often my writing falls short of the fact" (4. 145). Whatever Dante's feeling for other celebrated names, his eye is first and last on the poets.

On entering the circle of the lustful, the observer again addresses Virgil as "Poet" (5. 73, 111), as though not wishing to submerge the Latin's right to immortality in his service as guide. (Note also 9. 51; 10. 122; 12. 113; 13. 80; 18. 20; 27. 3; 29. 121.)

Did Francesca interest Dante partly because the reading of a romance entered her story (5. 127)?

In the circle of the gluttons, Ciacco asks that the traveler on return recall him to the recollection of men (6. 88). This, without actual mention of poetry, is one of many suggestions that the poet can bring his subjects fame.

When about to enter the city of Dis, the traveler gives up his disguise for a moment, to let Dante the poet speak: "You who have healthy intellects, look upon the teaching concealed under the veil of the unusual verses" (9. 61). In the circle of the heretics, as both feigned visitor and real Florentine, he is seen by Guido Cavalcanti's father, who addresses him:

"If through this dark prison you go because of your excellent talent [for poetry], where is my son, why is he not with you?" And I replied: "I do not come alone, that man waiting there is guiding me here; him perhaps your Guido objected to" (10. 58).

We are to recall that Guido was the "first of Dante's friends" to whom the *Vita Nuova* was dedicated (Chap. 30, end), and was considered by him the chief of the poets of his day (*Purg.* 11. 97). What Guido had against Virgil we can only guess. He wrote short poems and wished Dante to write to him only in Italian (*Vita Nuova* 30). Did he represent a modern opposition to the classics?

In the circle of the suicides, Virgil refers to the incident in the *Aeneid* of the bleeding tree, which Dante adapts here:

"If my pupil here had earlier been able to believe, O injured soul, what he has experienced only in my verses, he would not have stretched out his hand upon you. . . . But tell him who you were, so that as some sort of amends he may renew your reputation in the world where he is permitted to return" (*Inf.* 13. 46).

Here we have both Virgil the author and Dante the author-to-be. Virgil is properly again referred to as "Poet" (13. 80).

As they come to a new region, Dante, again the author back from his journey, says: "To make clear these strange things, I write that we came to a plain where the soil rejects every tree. . . . O vengeance of God, how much you should be feared by every one who reads of what was brought before my eyes" (14. 7)! Here he speaks with Brunetto Latini, who addresses to him words which we now apply to Dante's poetic ambition: "If you follow your star, you cannot fall short of a glorious harbor, if I estimated you well in the happy life; and if I had not died so early, seeing the heavens so favorable to you, I would have encouraged you in your work" (15. 55). In his hasty departing words, Brunetto mentions his *Tesoro*, "in which I still live" (15. 120). Brunetto exemplifies the author whose greatest concern is his book. Another inhabitant of this circle asks the visitor to speak of him on his return to living men (16. 85), as though knowing him as poet. On leaving the circle, our author, addressing his reader, swears "by the notes of this *Comedy*" (16. 128).

In the circle of the simonists, Dante the visitor pronounces over Pope Nicholas a speech which he calls "singing such notes" (19. 118), as though contemplating including his words in his poem.

On beginning the twentieth canto Dante makes one of his infrequent references to the structure of his poem: "I need to write verses on a new penalty and to furnish matter to the twentieth canto of the first *canzone* [*cantica*], which is on those plunged beneath [the earth's surface]" (20. 3; cf. *Purg.* 33. 140; *Par.* 5. 139). These lines evidently were written when the first twenty cantos were at least approximately as now. They even hint that the whole poem existed in its hundred cantos. Yet they say less than any other of Dante's groups of initial lines or tercets, being what Robert Herrick called "farcing buckram in our books," as though intended chiefly to bolster length. The fourth line of the canto continues the last of the preceding canto, as though the initial lines were an insertion, and still the canto is of only 130 lines, below the average for the *Inferno*.

Having seen the soothsayers, Dante expresses the hope that his readers will get profit, seemingly moral, from their reading (20. 19). In spite of the poet's didactic interest, such allusions to the benefit to be derived from his poem are infrequent.

Before long Virgil refers to the *Aeneid* for his line on Eurypylus, adding: "So in a certain passage my high tragedy sings it. You well know that, because you know my poem from beginning to end" (20. 112). This autobiographical truth is supported by 200 quotations or references to the *Aeneid* listed by Dr. Moore in his *Scriptural and Classical Authors in Dante*.

As teacher and pupil move on, they discuss matters "which my *Comedy* does not care to sing" (21. 1). The clause appears another space-filler. A little later Dante the poet calls the attention of readers to the "sport" he writes of (22. 118). The serpents in the *bolgia* of the thieves remind him of what he has read in Lucan and Ovid (25. 94, 97). Further he says of the entire *bolgia*: "Let its strangeness excuse me, if my pen writes confusedly" (25. 143).

In the circle of the tricksters, Virgil knows that the spirits of Ulysses and Diomede are approaching, though concealed in the flames. Restraining his charge, who cannot speak Greek, Virgil addresses them: "Oh you . . . if I deserved anything from you when I lived, if I deserved from you little or much when in the world I wrote my noble verses, do not pass on, but one of you tell where, unknown, he died" (26. 79). Here Virgil reminds us that he is guide because he is poet, and emphasizes again that poets confer renown.

To tell of the *bolgia* of the dividers requires great power of language:

Who could ever write fully even in prose of the blood and of the wounds I now saw, even though telling it many times? Every tongue of a surety would fail, because human speech and memory have little capacity for taking in so much. If an author even should bring together all the men in the storm-beaten land of Apulia whose blood was shed by the Trojans, and in the long war which made such noble spoils of finger rings, as Livy writes, who errs not, and if he added those who felt the pain of wounds in resisting Robert Guiscard, and those others whose bone heap still remains at Ceperan, where every Apulian was a traitor, and at Tagliacozzo, where without weapons the old Alardo won, and if one man should show his pierced limb and another his limb cut off, nothing would they be to compare with the loathsome order of the ninth *bolgia* (*Inf.* 28. 1).

Here the earliest commentators pay no attention to the reference to prose; Pietro di Dante quotes from Virgil: "If I had a hundred tongues and a hundred mouths and a voice of iron, I could not gather together all the forms of wickedness, all the names of sufferings" (*Aeneid* 6. 625). Guido da Pisa quotes from Ovid: "If the god would give me a hundred mouths ring-ing with tongues and great ability and all of Helicon, I could not set forth . . ." (*Metamorphoses* 8. 532). Dante's *parole sciolte*, from the Latin *verba soluta*, is most simply rendered "prose," to be thought of as simple and easy in contrast with verse. If so, Dante is saying something like this: Livy, though he wrote in prose of the battle of Cannae, could not have written adequately of the ninth *bolgia*; if it is difficult in prose, much more so in verse. Was Dante endeavoring to imitate Virgil and Ovid and yet vary their idea and advance beyond it, as modern poets when they imitate the ancients often attempt to do? While beholding these sinners, the visitor thinks of returning to the world. To one shade he speaks of carrying news (28. 92).

In the *bolgia* of the falsifiers, the traveler turns to "the poets" (29. 63) for illustration. In saying that they "hold as solidly based" the legend of the origin of the inhabitants of Aegina from ants, he ironically implies that poetry is fictitious. The only poet whom Dante's son Pietro cites here is Ovid, *Metamorphoses* 7. 625; later annotators add no other. In this *bolgia*, as a variant to his frequent suggestion that as poet to return to the world of the living he can give immortality, the visitor merely wishes that a soul to whom he speaks may attain continued fame; yet the soul is unnamed and scholars disagree on his identity. Did Dante omit the name by accident, or is he playing with his readers? Still further in this *bolgia* he illustrates from Ovid, with no suggestion that the stories are fictitious (30. 1).

Before undertaking to sing of the lowest part of Hell, Dante calls upon the pagan muses:

If I had verses harsh and hoarse such as would fit the mournful pit above which all the cliffs overhang, I would press out the juice of my conception more fully, but because I do not have such verses, not without fear I go on to write. For to describe the depth of the whole universe is not an enterprise to be taken as a joke, nor for a tongue that says "mamma" and "papa." But I call on those ladies to help my poem who helped Amphion build the walls of Thebes, so that from the deed my word may not be different (32. 1).

Here is Dante's frequent theme of poetical powers inadequate to relate experience. He insists, too, on the poetical reality of his fiction, seemingly with amusement in calling his "beautiful lie" a fact, a "deed."

In the Antenora he reverts to the theme of immortality conferred by poets. For variety, Bocca refuses such patronage (32. 91), but the visitor is not discouraged, making a similar offer to Ugolino, "if that with which I speak does not wither" (32. 139), that is: "If I retain my poetic power."

Remembering how he beheld Satan, the returned traveler as poet exclaims: "Do not ask, reader, that I write as I felt, because every account would be too slight. I did not die, I did not keep alive. You can imagine for yourself, if you have the least native wit, what I was, deprived of both states" (34. 23). Dante varies his method of stating the poet's difficulty and strengthens his effect of actuality in the sights beheld by pretending that even a stupid reader can imagine more than a poet can express.

Purgatorio. Beginning the *Purgatorio,* Dante invokes the Muses and especially Calliope, whom he asks to "rise somewhat," as though to be more dignified than in the *Inferno,* though less so than in the *Paradiso.* Dante's early commentators, however, did not know Calliope as the muse of epic poetry. Pietro di Dante, for example, speaks of her as indicating "the best language and sonority," and the others are not much different.

In Ante-Purgatory, the sightseer encounters his friend Casella, to whom he says:

"If new law does not take from you the memory and the practice of love song, which once could quiet all my desires, be so kind as to comfort my spirit a little with such a song, since by coming here my body is greatly wearied." "*Amor che nella mente mi ragiona,*" he then sang, so sweetly that its sweetness still rings within me. My teacher and I and those people who were with him seemed so pleased that nothing else touched the mind of anybody (*Purg.* 2. 106).

Cato breaks into their absence of mind to send them hurrying on to prepare themselves for Heaven. Dante valued Casella's performance, but he took care to give him what he thought good material to work with, namely one of his own poems, from *Convivio* 3.

Having been begged by some of the shades to pray for them, the traveler asks Virgil about a passage in the *Aeneid* representing heavenly decrees as immutable. The conversation shows both author and enquirer believing a poet's words valuable as evidence. This seems Dante's belief in his *Monarchia* 2. 3, whether he actually held it or whether he thought lines from the *Aeneid* would influence readers. Soon the travelers meet Sordello, who becomes their guide. On learning that one of them is Virgil, Sordello shows great respect: "O glory of the Latins, through whom our language showed what it could do, O eternal credit to the place where I lived" (*Purg.* 7. 16). In *On the Vulgar Tongue*, Dante shows knowledge of Sordello as a writer, but in the *Comedy* does not mention his poetry, though we may suppose he chose the Mantuan for the part he plays because of his literary reputation. While in Sordello's company, the traveler heard a Latin hymn sung so sweetly that it absorbed his attention. From the effect of the singing, he passes to the easy allegory of either the hymn or what immediately follows: "Reader, sharpen your eyes to the truth, because the veil is now so very thin that passing through it is easy" (8. 19). Still the author thinks of his audience.

Soon he again asks to be thought of as poet: "My guide moved along the ledge and I behind him toward the height. Reader, you surely see how I am lifting up my matter, and therefore do not be astonished if I hold it steady with more art" (*Purg.* 9. 68). These lines have puzzled commentators, who often have taken them as a grave introduction to what is to come, though with little specific application. Such a serious estimate is summed up in Mrs. Sayers' destruction of Dante's simplicity: "I . . . [moved] onward toward the height. / Look, Reader, how my theme would scale the sky! / Marvel not, therefore, if with greater art / I seek to buttress what I build so high." The original speaks of a high place, not of climbing to the sky. To some readers, to be distinguished from scholars, the passage has seemed an amusing assertion of effort by the reporter-poet, with perhaps a pun on the "height" of the purgatorial mountain which is to be his "matter," and the poetic elevation proper for that "matter." At least the author here speaks in his own person rather than as fictitious visitor.

On the ledge of purification from pride or egotism, the visitor listens as Oderisi speaks on the primacy in Italian letters. It is now Guido Cavalcanti's but perhaps soon is to be another's. The three lines on poetry by Oderisi the illuminator cannot be called unfitting for him, though perhaps Dante had his own interests rather than dramatic fitness in mind as he wrote (11. 97).

From Marco Lombardo, on the terrace of wrath, Dante asks enlightenment on the wickedness of the world, "so that I may explain it to others" (16. 62). Here the writer gathering his material again speaks, though he also wishes to "see" for himself. As the visitors leave the smoke that penalizes wrath, the poet compares the brightening light with the breaking of a mountain mist, directing to the figure the eyes of his future readers (17. 1).

On the terrace of avarice and prodigality, the hopeful author assures one of the souls that on returning to the world he can reward kindness (20. 37). Though this assertion may apply only to prayers for souls in Purgatory, it suggests earlier offers of such fame for the dead as poets can assure. Here is the most extensive treatment of poetry for its own sake to be found in the *Comedy*, as the poet Statius accompanies the two visitors. Why did Dante not mention him among the poets in Limbo? Dr. Moore's statistics (see Index) show that Dante quotes Statius more often than Horace, though less often than Lucan. Statius tells of his regard for the *Aeneid*, his poetic nurse, and thus brings on an amusing scene in which he comes to know that the shade of Virgil is before him. This discovery leads to further talk, partly devoted to Statius' conversion but even more to the poetry of ancient Rome (*Purg.* 21. 88–22. 114). Then "they went ahead, and I by myself behind, listening to their talk, which gave me understanding of poetry-writing" (22. 128).

While with Virgil and Statius, the neophyte encounters his old friend Forese Donati. The two do not speak of their exchange of sonnets. The omission does not imply that Dante was ashamed of the content of those productions, though per-

haps he was of their quality.[5] The chief indications that the
two men had been associated—other than the question about
Forese's sister Piccarda—is that the visitor speaks to the shade
as one to whom Beatrice and presumably the *Vita Nuova* are
well known (23. 128), and that Forese shows him—among
others—the poet Bonagiunta of Lucca, who eagerly speaks with
the visitor, quoting the lines of a *canzone* from the *Vita
Nuova*. Thereupon Dante the poet declares the principle of
the *dolce stil nuovo*: "I am one who, when Love breathes into
my heart, observe, and as he dictates, so I report" (24. 52).
The other answers, whether in character or whether as Dante
thought perception of the truth required:

O brother, now I see the knot that kept back the Notary and
Guittone and myself from attaining the sweet new style which
I hear. I see clearly how your pens follow straight after the dictator
—something that certainly was not the way with ours. And he
who tries to look beyond does not see further difference between
the two styles (24. 55).

Forese then turns to Dante's second great interest, Florentine
political strife, but soon leaves the visitor, who is going more
slowly behind the two "great marshals" or "doctors," the
Latin poets (24. 99, 143). Much of the following canto is
given to Statius' discourse on the union of soul and body.
Since he does not speak of his poetry, we may suppose him
taking Virgil's place as mentor for variety. Like the older poet,
he addresses his hearer as "son" (25. 35). Statius' action also
fits the guess that once he was more important in Dante's plan
than now.

On the topmost ledge of Purgatory, the visitor is still mind-
ful that he must learn in order to write; on making his demand,
"Tell me who you are and who are in that crowd which comes
behind you, so I may put it on paper" (26. 64), he soon is told
that he is speaking with Guido Guinicelli's shade. Then,

as at the time of Lycurgus' affliction the two sons felt on seeing
their mother once more, so I felt (but I didn't go as far) when I
heard my father—and the father of all my betters who ever wrote
sweet and graceful love poems—give his name. Without hearing
and speaking, I for a long time walked on thoughtfully gazing at

5 For Forese, see Chapter 3, p. 88, below.

him, but on account of the fire I didn't get close. When I had my
fill of staring, I put myself wholly at his service with the sort of
assertion that makes people believe. And he replied: "You make
on me so deep and plain an impression, because of what I am
hearing, that Lethe cannot take it away or make it dim. But if in
your last speech you swore truly, tell me the cause for which in
word and look you seem to be fond of me." So I answered: "Your
sweet poems which, as long as the modern style lasts, will make
your ink marks precious." "O brother," he said, "that man at whom
I point my finger"—and he indicated a shade ahead of us—"was
a better workman in the mother tongue. All love poems and prose
romances he outdid, and let the foolish say that he of Limousin
was better. They turn their faces to rumor rather than to the
truth, and so settle their opinions before they listen to experience
or reason. So many earlier acted about Guittone, shouting his praise
over and over, until for the majority truth has now conquered"
(26. 94).

On taking leave of Guido Guinicelli, the visitor hurries on
to the man pointed out, politely expressing a desire to know
his name. He proves to be Arnaut Daniel, who answers in
eight lines in Provençal.

In the Earthly Paradise, the three poets listen to Matilda's
account of the place. She concludes by declaring: " 'Those who
in antiquity wrote poetry on the age of gold and its happy state,
perhaps in Parnassus dreamed of this place. Here human origin
was innocent; here it is always spring and every fruit grows;
this is nectar, of which everyone writes.' I then turned quite
around to my poets and saw that with a smile they had heard
the final clause" (28. 139). So Dante brings classical and
modern poetry together.

About to deal with the mysteries of the Garden, he follows
the custom of poets attempting a difficult theme:

O most holy Virgins, if ever for you I suffered hunger, cold, and
sleepless nights, a cause now drives me on to ask for my reward.
Now I need Helicon to pour out for me and Urania to aid me
with her chorus, that I may put in verse things hard to imagine
(29. 37).

Dante, like his son Pietro and like Benvenuto da Imola, thought
Helicon a fountain on Parnassus, of which poets were believed
to drink; Urania they knew as the heavenly Muse. The spirit
of the passage is classical, though the invocation of Urania is

not found in Virgil or even Lucan. Like Dante, Ovid makes her the representative of the sisterhood of Muses. Having seen part of the procession of the Church, Dante again appears as working poet, writing of the four animals symbolizing the Gospels:

In describing their forms I do not pour out more verses, reader, because other expense so presses me that I cannot be generous in this. But read Ezekiel, who represents them as he saw them coming from the cold country with wind and with clouds and with fire; and as you will find them in his pages such they were, except that as to the wings John is with me, and departs from Ezekiel (29. 97).

The poet abbreviates his description. This canto is already longer than the average; more than six additional lines on the four animals would have made it the longest in the poem. Presumably he liked also the colloquial touch by which he escaped describing the symbols of the Evangelists so familiar in sculpture and other arts.

In the course of Beatrice's arraignment, the lover does not actually appear as poet, yet her words "la sua vita nova," "his new life," go far toward representing the title of Dante's early book. Beatrice's whole speech and the culprit's reaction carry the reader back to the *Vita Nuova*, as maybe Dante intended they should. So even when the traveler is reduced to the state of a small boy found out in a fault, he still remains the author. When actually in the River Lethe up to his neck he hears the Fifty-first Psalm "so sweetly sung that I cannot remember it, much less write of it" (31. 98).

Next, seeing Beatrice with her eyes fixed on the griffin, he remarks: "Exactly as the sun in a mirror, the double beast was shining out in her eyes, now with the attitudes of one animal, now with those of the other. Imagine, reader, if I was astonished when I saw the thing in itself remain quiet, yet in its image it was shifting" (31. 121). The reflection shifts, though the object reflected does not. Dante is here making use of a passage in Ovid's *Metamorphoses* (4. 348) in which the sunlight reflected in the mirror is unlike that of the sun itself, perhaps because lively or flickering rather than steady. He is interested not merely as one who can experience but

also as one who can write verses on it. When Beatrice un-
veils, he tells not of the effect on himself as lover, but what
it would be on a poet:

O glory of the living eternal light, who has become so pale in the
shade of Parnassus—or who drinks from its fountain—whose
thought would not seem clumsy if he tried to tell of you as you
appeared—there where the heavens, moving in harmony, depict
you—when you were revealed in the open air (31. 139)?

Of a further experience, he cannot write, though a painter might
picture it:

If I could relate how the pitiless eyes went to sleep when they
heard about Syrinx—the eyes which much waking cost so dear—
like a painter who works from a model I would picture how I fell
asleep. But let him who wants to try make a good fiction of sleep!
So I omit everything until the time when I awoke (32. 64).

Beatrice warns him to observe carefully, not urging moral
profit but commanding him to write on his return to the world
(32. 105). To the same effect she speaks a second time (33.
55).

   After telling how Matilda led him and Statius to the fountain
of Eunoë, Dante the visitor unites with Dante the poet:
"Reader, if I had more room for handwriting, I would surely
sing in part the sweet drink that never would have satisfied
me; but because all the pages laid out for this second cantica
are full, the bridle of art does not let me go farther" (33. 136).
Here for three lines Dante abandons his fiction to speak as
author. Only here—and even here indirectly—does he refer to
the carefully regulated uniform structure of the *Commedia*.
The immediate concern is the length of the *Purgatorio*, which
—with its 4,755 lines—has 35 more than the *Inferno* and three
fewer than the *Paradiso*. Such uniformity came from unweary-
ing attention, from the labors that made the poet thin for
many years (*Par.* 25. 3). Does he imply when saying that he
has filled the pages designed for the *Purgatorio* that this *cantica*
did not easily reach the length required by the total plan? In
structure it is unlike the others. Its strictly purgatorial part,
devoted to the purification of souls on the seven mountain
terraces, consists of eighteen cantos (10–27). The approach to

these purging sufferings (*Purg.* 4. 128), or Ante-Purgatory, oc-
cupies nine cantos; at the end six (28–33) are given to the
Earthly Paradise. The other *cantiche* offer no space for such
prefaces and epilogues. Does their addition to the core of the
Purgatorio give some indication of the author's effort to ex-
pand that *cantica* until it filled the pages exacted by his design,
and hint that with a sense of achievement he reached a point
where the bridle of art checked him?

Paradiso. After the first tercet of the *Paradiso*, Dante turns
to the poet and the poet's subject:

In the heaven that gets most of God's light was I, and I saw
things that he who descends from up there neither knows how
to put in words nor can, because, drawing near to its desire, our
intellect goes so deep that memory cannot follow it. Yet all I saw
of the holy kingdom that I could store in my memory will now be
the matter of my song. O good Apollo, for my finishing task make
me such a partaker of your strength as you require for the giving
of your beloved laurel! Up to now one peak of Parnassus has been
enough for me, but now with both I need to undertake the race
still left to run. Enter my bosom and breathe as when you pulled
Marsyas from the sheath of his limbs. O divine power, if you allow
me to make known that shadow of the blessed realm which is
written in my brain, you will see me come to your cherished tree
and crown myself with the leaves of which the matter and you
make me worthy. So seldom, father, they are gathered for the
triumph of ruler or poet (for which human wishes should be
blamed and shamed) that the Peneian leaf should bring gladness
to the glad Delphic deity when it makes any one thirst for it.
A huge flame results from a little spark. Perhaps after me some
with better voices will so pray that Cyrrha will answer (*Par.* 1. 4).

With whatever modesty Dante speaks, whatever his concern
with his theme, he is frank in his desire for the laurel crown.
Soon he again alludes to the difficulty of his poetic task:
"Transhumanizing cannot be expressed in words" (1.70).

As poet he warns his readers that further reading will have
its difficulties, mingling with much pagan a little Christian
symbolism:

O you who in a tiny boat, eager to hear, have followed behind my
ship that moves on singing, turn back to see again your own lands;
do not go upon the sea, because perhaps, failing to follow me, you
will be lost. The water I go upon has never been sailed. Minerva

breathes upon me and Apollo guides me and the nine Muses show me the Bears. You other few who have betimes partaken of angels' bread—on which we live here and never are surfeited—are able to go on a voyage over the salt sea, following my wake before the water gets smooth again. Those famous ones who went to Colchis did not wonder, when they saw Jason made a plowman, as you are going to do (2. 1).

Pagan language Dante uses here and elsewhere as a poet taught by the great poets, the Romans. The reference to angels' bread, from Psalms 78. 25, suggests that the feeling is not altogether pagan. We do not need, like some Renaissance and later commentators, to avail ourselves of a doublet in Italian and make the "nine Muses" of Dante into "new Muses," those of Christian poetry. None of the medieval commentators feel any necessity to abandon *nine*, well understanding what classical reference meant in poetry.

To the structure of his poem Dante not often refers, yet he does so twice in this canto (5. 16, 139; cf. *Inf.* 20. 2). It is strange that in his concern with his hundred cantos Dante did not more often allude to them, since he so willingly and often appears as author. He assumes that his reader will be as eager to learn what went on in Heaven as the fictitious traveler is (5. 109). A little further he again refers to his method of beginning a canto (8. 10). Soon a soul is encountered who says: "Folco those called me to whom my name was known" (9. 94). One of these was Dante, who quotes a line of his verse in *De vulgari eloquentia* (2. 6). Yet here he makes no use of Folco as poet; indeed much of what he says seems to have little relation to what is known of Folco's character.

About to deal with the Heaven of the Sun, the poet writes a preface, in part to reinforce for the reader how difficult is the poem's subject: "Now sit, reader, upon your bench, thinking upon what I have given you in advance, if you want to be pleased rather than tired out. I have set food before you; now eat for yourself. [I can do no more] because the material of which I am made the penman wrenches all my effort to itself. . . . Though I call upon native endowment and skill and experience, still I cannot say what never would be imagined, but yet readers can believe and hope to see. And if our imaginings are too lowly to reach such a height, that is no wonder, because no eye has attained the sun" (10. 22). The last clause may refer to Saint Paul's rise to the third heaven, the highest reached by a mortal (2 Cor. 12. 2). Does the word "imaginings" hint that Dante's traveler does not relate a visit to the high heavens which—in the fiction—he actually made, but that the poet is telling what he imagined? (Cf. *Purg.* 29. 42; *Par.* 18. 86.) Can the line come from a time when Dante was writing of a dream rather than of a bodily visit? A little later the narrator informs readers that he has "returned" from Heaven (*Par.* 10. 70). Still further, he is the reporter asking attention from listeners: "If anyone wishes to understand well, let him imagine what I now saw, and let him while I speak hold the image like a solid rock" (13. 1). The author himself often says that he has difficulty; he must omit what his memory did not retain, and his genius is weaker than his memory (14. 81, 103). Yet he will excuse himself for his boldness, even to the imaginative reader (14. 130).

In his interview with Cacciaguida, the Florentine traveler becomes poet, hesitating between present refuge and future fame:

"I had better arm myself with foresight, so that if the city dearest to me is taken from me, I shall not lose other places through my poems. Down in the region endlessly bitter, and on the mountain from whose fair summit the eyes of my Lady raised me, and then through the heavens from light to light, I have learned things which, if I write them, to many will have a very sour flavor. Yet if I am a timid friend to the truth, I fear to lose my claim to live among those who will speak of this present year as long ago." Cacciaguida replied: "Discarding all lies, tell openly everything you have seen, and let men scratch where they itch. For even though your poem may be unpleasant when first tasted, later when digested it will leave its readers vital nutriment. This outcry of yours will be like the wind which hits hardest the highest peaks; and that is no slight indication of renown (17. 109).

Better to be famous, though exiled, than happy in Florence! Fame appears when the poet again invokes the Muse for aid in describing the marvelous letters in the Heaven of Jupiter: "O Pegasean goddess, you who give fame to poetical talents and make them live long—and they with your aid give fame to

cities and kingdoms—shed your light upon me that I may describe those letters as I have imagined them" (*concette*) (18.
82). Here the word translated *imagined*, if pressed, indicates
Dante as poetically devising things in the heavens rather than as
visitor beholding them. Thus he is immediate poet. Yet soon
he says the opposite as he deals with the eagle: "What now
I must write voice never uttered nor ink wrote nor did imagination ever grasp, for I saw the beak and even heard it speak"
(19. 7). As reporter-poet, he gladly utters "Things unattempted
yet in prose or rime" (*Paradise Lost* 1. 16).

Drawing toward the Heaven of the Fixed Stars, Dante as
traveler-poet, without naming any classical gods, calls on the
stars in the zodiacal sign of Gemini to aid him: "O glorious
stars, O light teeming with great power, which I thank for all
my [poetical] genius, whatever it be! . . . To you my soul now
devoutly breathes in order to gain strength for the difficult
experience coming upon it" (22. 112). As he goes on, he repeats
his need for aid, with emphasis on his weakness before his
difficult task:

If all the tongues that Polyhymnia and her sisters nourish with their
sweetest milk should now make music to give me help, to the
thousandth part of the truth they would not come, singing Beatrice's
holy smile and how shining it made her holy face. In the same
way, delineating Paradise, the inspired [*sacrato*] poem has to jump
like one who finds his road blocked. But any one who thinks on
the weighty theme and the human shoulder burdened with it,
will not blame that shoulder for trembling. Not for a little boat
is this voyage on which the ardent craft goes cutting the waves,
nor for a steersman who spares himself (23. 55).

Inevitably this is compared with a later passage:

If ever it happens that the inspired [*sacro*] poem—on which sky and
earth have labored, so that for many years it has made me thin—
is victor over the cruelty that shuts me out of the fair sheepfold
where I slept as a lamb hostile to the wolves that attack it, then
with another voice, with another fleece I shall come back as poet,
and at the font of my baptism receive the wreath (25. 1).

Much debated have been the words *sacrato* and *sacro* ("conse-
crated," "sacred"?), applied by Dante to his poem. They may
mean that the whole is religious and that the *Paradiso* especially
so; they go easily with the poet's insistence that his theme is

difficult; they suggest the devotion of his long labor, perhaps his hope to benefit readers. I have ventured the translation *inspired*, that is, inspired by the Muses and Apollo (*Inf.* 2. 7; *Purg.* 1.8; *Par.* 1. 13; 2. 8, 9), or by the "Highest Light" (*Par.* 33. 67). The Muses are for Dante *sacrosante*, "especially holy" (*Purg.* 29. 37). A poem inspired by them may properly be called *sacro*, "inspired by Heaven." At the same time Dante associates poetical achievement with personal advantage and honor, return from exile and the poet's crown suggesting ages of fame. Yet however lofty any part of his poem, that poem is still his comedy, not his tragedy. He wrote in an age when the human spirit more easily mingled a variety of things than it does in the present, when in our minds classification outdoes integration. Religion could wear its clothes more easily than now, and patriotism—not less sincere—could be more casual. So we can allow Dante to call his poem "sacred" without thinking that he ruined it as human poetry. Nor need we be disturbed because he was so open in his hope that it would do something practical for him. He merely expected the Florentines to act faster than they did in conferring on him the highest honors.

Saint Peter recognizes him as poet: "You son, who for your human burden will return to earth, open your mouth and do not conceal what I do not conceal" (27. 64). Saint Peter's poetry is that of indignation against wickedness in the world.

Not merely the beauty of Heaven but that of Beatrice affects our singer, somewhat as when he was writing in the *dolce stil nuovo*. As poet he speaks:

If all I have written about her up to now were fused into one speech of praise, it would be too little to supply this need. The beauty I saw is not merely far beyond our poetical strength, but I hold for certain that only its maker enjoys it in full. By this passage on her beauty I grant that I am beaten more completely than ever by part of his subject comic or tragic poet has been overcome (30. 16).

Tragic parts of the *Comedy* may be, but Dante does **not think** himself tragic only, in Virgil's sense of the word (*Inf.* 20. 113). He adds that he cannot continue to sing of Beatrice, but must give up the impossible attempt to celebrate her beauty in po-

etry (*poëtando*). When so high in Heaven, we expect something other than the *dolce stil nuovo*, concerned with an earthly
mistress, however raised among the angels.

Looking on the saints seated in the rose, Dante turns to his
poetical habits to express his feeling: "If I had in writing so
much wealth as in imagining, I would not be bold enough
to try to reach the least part of its delight. . . . What I saw
was greater than our power of speech" (31. 136; 33. 55). Yet
still he cannot be other than poet; almost at once he asks:
"O Highest Light, raised so far above mortal imaginings, lend
back to my memory a little of how you appeared [in the Empy-
rean] and make my tongue so mighty that I can leave to future
men just one spark of your glory! Because through returning
in part to my memory and giving a little music in these verses,
your victory will be better understood" (33. 67). And still of
heavenly love his experience is proved by poetic testing: "The
universal form of this knot I am sure I saw because as I write
this I feel my joy more ample" (33. 91). He now says, as he
moves toward the end, that he will write briefly, and soon
exclaims: "O how scant is my speech and how hoarse compared
with my concept! and that—put against what I saw—is such
that to call it meager is not enough" (33. 121). At the height
of his religious experience when moved by love, one impression
still is: "To the lofty imagination power now failed" (33. 142).
The poet's vigor, long striving against difficulties, here gives up
the struggle.

Did ever poet glancing "from heaven to earth, from earth
to heaven," show himself more preoccupied with his own craft?
In the *Vita Nuova*, Dante writes not only about Beatrice but
also about his own procedure as poet. When he makes an ex-
cursus, it is on the artist's language. Likewise, in the *Commedia*
he writes not only about the sights in the three realms—and
they interested the fictitious observer—but on the observation
of those sights by a man intending to write, and how they fit
into verses, and the author's power to handle them. In no small
measure the *Commedia* presents the practicing poet. Is that
one of the reasons—even though perhaps literary men have
often seemed not to realize it—why Dante has to such an
extent been a "poet's poet"?

3 · Comedy

COMEDY THROUGH DANTE'S EYES

Conventionally, Dante's poem is entitled *The Divine Comedy*, yet he called it "my comedy" (*Inf.* 16. 128; 21. 2). In 1568, a Venice edition is still the *Comedia*. The adjective "divine" may come from the poet's words *poema sacro* and *sacrato poema* (*Par.* 25. 1; 23. 62). In classical times the word "divine" traveled so far as to mean "extraordinary," "excellent," with the notion of "godlike" in the background, when applied to poets and orators by Horace and Quintilian (*Ars Poetica* 400; *Instit. Orat.* 2. 16. 7). In Dante's time, a poet wished to be crowned with Apollo's laurel, as inspired by that god (*Par.* 1. 26). Hence, to early writers calling Dante's poem "divine," the word denoted excellence. In our day, when the laurel-crowned poet is less familiar, the word has again taken on a more sacrosanct flavor, as though signifying the sacred book of a religion, to be opened with awe by true believers. To readers thus influenced by semantics, the nature of Dante's comedy can hardly appear. As a step toward their liberation, why not drop "divine," so that again, as to its author, the poem can be Dante's *Comedy*? It then can be read as he intended it.

Defending himself for writing in what Giovanni del Virgilio thought undignified language, Dante stands firm for his words befitting comedy, *comica verba* (*Eclogue* 1. 52). In *De vulgari eloquentia* he deals briefly with comedy, saying that comic language is of the middle or lowest type, while that of tragedy is of the highest and that of elegy of the lowest. He promises

61

further discussion in a later book never written. The letter to Can Grande, in dealing with comedy, says that the *Paradiso*, though elevated, is essential to the *Commedia* as furnishing the happy ending, "prosperous, desirable, and pleasant." Because the entire work is a comedy, its language is "careless and lowly, being the speech of the crowd, in which even ignorant women converse."

Such colloquial language fits the tone of the *Commedia*, although, as Horace permitted, at times a higher or tragic tone is heard. The poet seemingly wished to make plain at the beginning that his plan is to have his wanderer give the narrative of his journey on his safe return to the world of the living: "In order to deal with the good that I found there, I shall write of all the other things I saw there" (*Inf.* 1. 8). Near the end of his experience in Heaven, the traveler compares himself with a pilgrim who stares with pleasure at the church he has vowed to visit and with satisfaction foresees himself relating its wonders to stay-at-homes (*Par.* 31. 43). However intelligent the pilgrim, the scene of the traveler's tales told on return is one of informality, delighting the narrator even more than the hearer. Such rapport with his audience as that of the returned tourist is Dante's wish. He may even be thought of as contemplating speaking rather than writing (*Purg.* 13. 150).

Seventeen times putting himself in the position of the returned traveler, he addresses his reader. He tells his audience how afraid he was at the gate of the city of Dis (*Inf.* 8. 94). On beholding the twisted soothsayers, he exclaims: "If God allows you, reader, to get profit from your reading, now imagine for yourself how I could keep my face dry when I saw our form actually so twisted that the tears from the eyes were wetting the buttocks through the divide" (20. 19). With variation of his accost, he writes of the sinners on the burning sands: "O vengeance of God, how much you should be feared by every man who reads what was displayed to my eyes" (14. 16). And of the lights in the Sun: "Let him imagine who longs to understand well what I saw" (*Par.* 13. 1).

He promises his readers a juicy bit of comedy about the two devils caught in the pitch of their *bolgia* (*Inf.* 22. 18). Intro-

ducing the transmutations in the *bolgia* of the thieves, he allows
for slow belief in those conning his book because he himself,
after seeing, hardly believes (*Inf.* 25. 46). He assures his reader
that his fright on beholding Lucifer surpasses his power to
write (34. 23). At the Valley of Princes, he who reads should
sharpen his eyes for the truth (*Purg.* 8. 19). This has been
anticipated by a variation: "You who have healthy intellects,
look upon the teaching hidden under the veil of the strange
verses" (*Inf.* 9. 61). Soon the reader's eyes are directed to the
author's art (9. 70). The reader is not to be diverted from
penance by the terrors of purgatorial penalties, and can imagine
the thickness of the smoke on the terrace of anger from his own
experiences in mountain fogs (10. 106; 17. 1). Lacking time,
the poet apologizes for his brevity on the four allegorical animals of the Earthly Paradise, sending his reader to Ezekiel,
for except in number of wings, the author saw them as did
the prophet (*Purg.* 29. 100). Similarly, he explains that for lack
of space he cannot describe Eunoë (33. 136). Let the reader
imagine how the tourist was impressed by the griffin (31. 124).
He who cons the poem will realize how eager the visitor to
Heaven was to learn about the blessed, if he will think of
his own disappointment on the observer's failure to tell about
them (*Par.* 5. 109). Here is the amusing vacationist, familiar
to us, who becomes a bore in his assumption that his interests
are those of his polite hearers. The narrator directs the reader's
attention to the heavens to show where he has visited, and
then gives warning that he is not responsible for any benefit
derived from perusal (10. 7, 22). By his hope of salvation he
swears to his audience that his transit to the Fixed Stars was
swift beyond imagination (22. 106). Such an oath for the reader's benefit is that by which he seeks credence in the bulky
Geryon as a flying boat (*Inf.* 16. 128). Similar is the asseveration that Bertran de Born was dangling from his hand his severed head, where address to the reader is only implied (*Inf.* 28.
118). In other instances persons addressed are inferred. For example, may Polyhymnia aid him as he tells the truth about
Beatrice's smile (*Par.* 23. 55). If he were as rich in speech as
in imagination, he would not dare attempt, for the benefit

of others, the smallest part of the Virgin's splendor (*Par.* 31. 136).

To make his hearers believe that Caina is frozen hard, the reminiscent asserts: "I saw a thousand faces made doglike by the cold. Because of that sight, shuddering comes over me, and always will come, from frozen brooks" (*Inf.* 32. 70). If on remembering his early terror in Hell, he is soaked with sweat (*Inf.* 3. 132), a sweet song in Paradise so pleased him that "its delight never has left him" (*Par.* 23. 129; cf. 33. 62, 93; *Inf.* 26. 12, 19), as in recollection he assures his circle. He also joins himself with other men when in giving his recollections he speaks in various ways of "this life," or contrasts the world of the dead with that of the living in such a way as to show his pleasure in relating wonders to those who read or listen (*Par.* 1. 55; 2. 37; 10. 46, 70; 12. 16; 13. 8; 14. 25; 23. 93, 98; 24. 14; 30. 29; 31. 124). Thus many passages convey the spirit of his seventeen direct addresses to the reader.

Intimacy of tone, suggesting a returned traveler relating his adventures to a sympathetic circle at a social gathering or in a public square, is thus Dante's aim as author. Novelists have endeavored to achieve the same sort of informal relation with the "gentle reader," as did Sterne in *Tristram Shandy* (Bk. 2, Chap. 6). Did they learn from Dante? They could not have learned from the epics so pleasantly used by Fielding in his confidences to the reader on his methods of writing. So Dante did not draw his informal method from Virgil. Indeed, the habit of intimacy marks his departure from the *Aeneid* to adopt a comic method. Could he have learned to accost the reader from medieval preachers? Is his achievement of close relation with his reader one more mark of his original comic genius?

The letter to Can Grande does not distinguish the kinds of matter suited to tragedy and to comedy. The medieval tendency to think of style rather than of content in making the separation appears in Benvenuto da Imola, who says of Dante's poem as a comedy:

You are not to say, as some have done, that the matter of the book is comedy, for comedy is style, not matter. Hence just as some improperly say that Virgil's matter is tragedy, Horace's is satire, and Ovid's is comedy, so we should consider this case (Introduction).

Benvenuto modified this declaration, however:

There are three poetical styles, namely tragedy, satire, and comedy. Tragedy is a high and proud style, for it deals with memorable and terrible actions, such as overthrows of kingdoms, destructions of cities, conflicts in war, falls of princes, murders and deaths of men, and other terrible things. Those who describe such events are called tragedians or tragic writers, such as Homer, Virgil, Euripides, Statius, Simonides, Ennius, and many others. Satire is a medium and temperate style, for it deals with virtues and vices. Those describing such things are called satirists or satiric poets. There are also satiric poets who censure vices, such as Horace, Juvenal, and Persius. Comedy is a low and humble style, for it deals with the ordinary and trifling actions of farmers, citizens of low station, and humble men. Those describing such actions are called comedians or comic poets, such as Plautus, Terence, and Ovid. Yet here it must be carefully observed that just as in Dante's book every part of philosophy is present, so is every part of poetry. Hence if anybody wishes to investigate carefully, here is tragedy, satire, and comedy: tragedy because Dante describes the deeds of popes, princes, kings, barons, and other magnates and nobles, as appear in the whole book; satire, or censure, for he censures wonderfully and daringly all sorts of vices, nor does he spare any man's dignity, power, or nobility. So the poem can more properly be entitled a satire than a tragedy or a comedy. It can also be called a comedy, for according to Isidore, comedy begins with sorrowful material, namely Hell, and ends with gladness, namely with Paradise or the divine being. But perhaps, reader, you will say: "Why do you want to baptize the book for me with a new name, when the author himself called it his *Comedy?*" I answer that the author wished to call the work his *Comedy* because of its humble and lowly style, since truly it is lowly in respect to its writing, though in its kind it is distinguished and excellent (Introduction, p. 18).

Boccaccio carries his objections farther:

Dante deals with excellent persons and with noteworthy deeds; and even though his poem is written in Italian, in which we know that ignorant women converse, it is still ornate and graceful and lofty—qualities by which the current language of women is untouched. I do not say, however, that if it were in Latin verses, but yet with the meaning of the Italian sentences unchanged, it would not be much more artistic and more lofty, since there is much more art and weight in the Latin language than in our native language (Preface to Comment on the *Comedy*).

Boccaccio decides: "The name of *Comedy* is not suitable to this work." Yet he admits that, in *Inferno* 21. 2, Dante calls it his *Comedy*. As Dante himself observes, Giovanni del Virgilio also censures the language of comedy, used by the poet, as the ordinary language of women (*Eclogue* 1. 52).

Like Benvenuto and Boccaccio, Dante had read in Horace's *Ars Poetica* (the lines just precede those quoted in the letter to Can Grande della Scala):

Comic events are not to be presented in tragic verses; the banquet of Thyestes disdains to be narrated in verses suited to private matters and fit for a comic actor. Let individual things properly selected keep their place (*Ars poetica* 89).

The letter continues with the exceptions allowed in the style of both tragedy and comedy. In *On the Vulgar Tongue*, 2. 2, 3, 4, Dante deals with subject and style, though with application not to a long poem but to *canzoni*. Here he indicates certain great subjects (*magnalia*),[1] namely excellence in arms, fire of love, and control of the will, which are suitable for the *canzone*; thus they are suitable for the highest language. The first of these subjects could hardly have been out of Dante's mind when some pages later he quoted the beginning of the *Aeneid: Arma virumque cano*. To that poem he makes Virgil refer as his "tragedy" (*Inf.* 20. 113).

Is it possible to justify Dante's choice of title against the objections of Boccaccio? Or must we suppose that he applied the word "comedy" in a mood of humility when, knowing his tendency to egotism (*Purg.* 11. 118; 13. 136), he wished to remove his work from competition with the tragic *Aeneid* (*Inf.* 20. 113), or even with Lucan's *Pharsalia*? How seriously are we to take the traveler's reception by the poets in Limbo (*Inf.* 4. 100)? Does this mean that the historical Dante believed his own product equal with that of Virgil and the others,

---

1 Guido da Pisa says that Dante deserves to be called a tragic writer because of the great deeds (*magnalia gesta*) of lofty men which he narrates (Proem, p. 32a).

or is the fictitious sightseer a literary critic, as it were, delighted to enter the company of the great, just as later he was privileged, as an admiring listener, to catch something from the conversation of Statius and Virgil (*Purg.* 22. 128)?

As Boccaccio suggests, Dante's choice of the Italian language rather than the Latin for his *Comedy* meant that he chose to include in his audience the unlearned. Like Boccaccio, Dante thought the Latin tongue in some sense more noble than the Italian (*Convivio* 1. 5), and to him the great or "regular" or "regulated" poets were Virgil, Ovid, Statius, and Lucan (*De vulgari eloquentia* 2, 4, 6). By writing in the popular language, Dante condescended to popular taste. Boccaccio, though he too did so in both poetry and prose, was nevertheless distressed to think that the exalted Dante had spoken directly to the common herd. If we take literally some of Boccaccio's verses, he regretted having commented on the *Commedia* in Italian, laying bare to the populace some of its secrets, fit only for the learned (*Rime* 122, 123, 124, 125). By insisting on its esoteric character, Boccaccio removed Dante's *Comedy* from the class signified by its name. Yet Dante shows his own inclination by addressing the *Convivio* (1. 9) to the unschooled reader.

THE COMIC HERO

But whatever Boccaccio thought or Dante said, is the poem that within itself is twice called a comedy (*Inf.* 16. 128; 21. 2) really one or not? The *Aeneid*, which Virgil says the Italian poet knew by heart and which he called his "tragedy," is a proper standard (*Inf.* 20. 113).

The hero of the *Aeneid* is the leader of an army and the founder of Roman power. The medieval visitor to the other world is at times identified with Dante the poet who looks ahead to centuries of fame (*Par.* 17. 119). At other times that traveler does not act with dignity. At the beginning he is frightened into violent flight from the animals blocking his ascent of the mountain. He calls for aid from the first person he meets. He trembles and weeps. Anything Virgil suggests he will do, if only he can escape (*Inf.* 1). Yet having consented, he cannot hold to his determination, fearing that the journey will be foolish (*Inf.* 2. 35). Virgil accuses the vacillator of cowardice, explaining that his terror has been observed in Heaven and a messenger sent in his behalf, and asking "Why do you keep such great cowardice in your heart? Why do you not have vigor and courage" (*Inf.* 2. 122)? The wanderer then rouses his spirits to follow. When they have entered Hell, Virgil repeats his warning against cowardice, encourages his pupil by taking his hand, and addresses him as "Son." Yet the pupil is so dismayed that, after his return to earth, he is bathed with sweat on recalling his terror (3. 131). When they see Plutus, Virgil again cautions against fear (7. 5). Before the gates of the city of Dis, when the devils suggest that Virgil abandon his charge, the latter in the role of returned traveler addresses the reader, telling of his apprehension. He asks Virgil if they cannot at once retrace their steps. The master again tries to brace him against fear (8. 104). Yet, on returning unsuccessful from his attempt at entrance, he sees on Dante's face the color of cowardice, increasing as the guide speaks (9. 1, 13). With such apprehension the traveler is looking at the fiery summit of the tower that he does not attend to everything Virgil says. On the wall appear the Furies, shrieking so loud that the timid mortal clings to Virgil in terror. Looking down, the Furies shout: "Have Medusa come, so we can turn him to stone" (9. 52). Then, " 'Turn your back and keep your eyes covered, because if the Gorgon appears, and you see her, there never will be any going back up again.' So my teacher spoke, and he himself turned me around, and he did not rely on my hands enough not to cover my eyes with his own hands as well" (9. 55). As a responsible guide, Virgil is eager that his charge run no risks through failing, in his fear and nervousness, properly to cover his eyes. This is the first of the instances in which the tourist's guides—Virgil and Beatrice—treat him as a child. Perhaps there is something further here. Even as early as this in his other-worldly experience, the unheroic hero has exhibited the insatiable, though laudable, inquisitiveness that made his journey worth recording. Repeatedly, he has asked questions from Virgil and others (*e.g.*, 3. 32; 4. 49; 5. 50, 120; 6. 82), and has been eager to see. Of his view of the great spirits in Limbo, he says: "I was exalted by the sight" (4. 120).

In the *Aeneid* and Livy's *Histories* he had learned of the shades in Limbo; in the *Metamorphoses* and the *Pharsalia* he had read of Medusa, the Gorgon. Did Virgil, knowing he was not dealing with a firm-minded man, fear that his pupil, overcome by curiosity, would venture to peep at the Gorgon? So the Latin poet takes precautions against the ill effects of too great zeal to learn.

When told to seat himself on the back of the monstrous Geryon, the rider-to-be trembles like one about to be shaken by quartan fever, yet shame enables him to make a feint at appearing stouthearted (17. 85). Nevertheless, when they begin to move in the air, the aviator's panic is like that of Phaeton when the Sun's horses went astray, or that of Icarus when he felt his waxen wings melting (17. 104). Cautiously looking over the monster's side, he is still more disturbed, and hearing the screams of the damned, he trembles. On the bridge to the fifth *bolgia*, the sightseer is aghast when a devil appears carrying a sinner. Virgil, about to negotiate with the devilish guardians, tells him to squat behind a rock, yet to dread nothing (21. 59). Summoned from his hiding place, the squatter hastily seeks the security of his guardian's side, gazing at the devils in continued terror:

"O Teacher, what do I see?" I said, "Oh dear, let's go alone, without any escort, for I don't want any, if you know where to go. If you are as quick as usual, you see how they grind their teeth and threaten us with their scowls" (21. 127).

Notwithstanding Virgil's confidence, as they move off the visitor's hair stands on end and all the time he looks behind him (23. 19).

Seeing one of the giants around the pit of Hell, the observer's terror is enough to kill him (31. 109). When Antaeus stoops to take the wayfarers in his hand to set them down in the lowest pit, the Italian is so frightened that he wants to go in some other way (31. 141). Remembering his terror in the pit of Hell, he writes: "With fear I put it in verse" (34. 10). Though Virgil exhorts to fortitude when they behold Satan, the pupil is so affected that he is icy and his voice fails, so that he is neither living nor dead.

In Purgatory there is less reason for apprehension, though the nature of the mountain offers some danger, with its steep cliff on the outer side of each terrace, from which the unwary might fall, as the visitor is warned (*Purg.* 13. 80; 25. 117; 26. 3). When an earthquake shakes the mountain, the alarmed tourist is as cold as a man going to execution. Virgil tells him: "Never fear while I am guiding you" (20. 135). In the smoke of the Third Terrace, the escort tells his charge to keep close to him to avoid danger, seemingly that of the cliff. Otherwise, but one of the punishments threatens such personal injury as the burning sleet in the Seventh Circle of Hell. On the last terrace of Purgatory the fire that purifies lust so terrifies the adventurer "vividly imagining" human bodies he has seen burnt that he will not pass through. The Latin poet urges him on, recalling other dangers in which he has protected his pupil and exhorting him to courage. Still the traveler hesitates. Vexed, his director tells him that Beatrice is beyond the flames. Even this stimulus is not enough, but when Virgil smiles on him as on a boy bribed with an apple, he plunges in—to pass unharmed. How different the conduct of Tasso's Rinaldo when faced with a fiery wall restraining him from the duty before him! He considers that his leader is relying on him, wonders whether the fire will be less terrible than it appears, then exclaims: " 'Let come of it what can.' With these words he plunged in" (*Jerusalem Delivered* 13. 35). Like Spenser's knight in a similar experience, he is unharmed. It seems likely that Dante knew some such chivalrous story, which he adapted to the timid, unheroic character of his fictitious traveler.

In the Earthly Paradise, on the opposite bank of the River Lethe, moves the procession of the Church. One of the characters, identified as Saint Paul representing his Epistles, is armed, as is usual from the thirteenth century on, "with a sword shining and sharp, so that on my side of the river it frightened me" (*Purg.* 29. 140). The traveler exaggerates his fear by putting the swordbearer across the river. Perhaps he also indicates the reality of effect from the procession. But however genuine the characters for the purposes of their allegory, a symbolic figure will hardly abandon its place in a procession for an attack on the beholders. We have here a very timid hero.

In the *Inferno*, the tourist shows physical helplessness. When mounted on Geryon, he tries to ask Virgil to hold him tight. The traveler's voice fails because of his fear, but Virgil sees what is wanted. Down into the *bolgia* of the simoniacs, Virgil carries his pupil. Clasping his charge to his breast, he slides with him down the bank of the sixth *bolgia*; up the opposite slope he pushes him (*Inf.* 24. 32). The guide drags the traveler from the thieves' ditch (*Inf.* 26. 15). When Antaeus sets the two down in the lowest Hell, Virgil holds his living companion so tight that they are "one bundle" (*Inf.* 31. 105). On emerging from Hell, Virgil climbs down and then up the hairy sides of Lucifer with the narrator hanging around his neck. No wonder the shade of the Latin gasped "like a man tired out" (34. 83) when at last he deposited his burden on a rock. Only once is amusement expressed at the spectacle of "something solid" assisted by a shade in its emptiness (*Purg.* 21. 135). Virgil, because he is "light" (*Inf.* 24. 32) cannot merely get easily out of the ditch of the hypocrites but can push his charge upward. Is this situation intended to diminish still further the dignity of the traveler? In such a relation, comedy is always implicit. For the most part, references in the *Inferno* to Virgil as a shade come in the first twelve cantos (1. 67; 2. 44, 58; 3. 88; 4. 81; 8. 27; 12. 30, 81; cf. 28. 49; 29. 95); instances of physical assistance to the traveler come after Canto 12. Yet a hero who is carried like a child, even if not by a shade, is hardly heroic. Virgil's attitude is suited to his actions, for he addresses his charge as "Son" up to the last (*Purg.* 27. 128).

A touch of childish quality remains in a scene which nevertheless symbolizes the serious difference between Hell and Purgatory. Cato, warder of the second kingdom, directs Virgil to cleanse the new arrival from the blackness of Hell: "See to it that you wash his face so well that you get off all dirty discoloration, because it is unfitting that with a visage in any way soiled he should appear before the first ministering angel of Heaven" (*Purg.* 1. 94). Soon, therefore, "when we were in a place where the dew struggles with the sun and, being in a cool spot, evaporates little, my teacher gently put both his spreadout hands on the grass. So I, understanding his purpose, turned toward him my tear-soiled cheeks. Then he brought to light all my color that

Hell had concealed" (*Purg.* 1. 121). With Cato's strict injunction, the inadequacy of this cleansing is incongruous. Instead of a thorough washing, Virgil provides—to use modern language— a token purification. If Dante had seen a small boy's face after hasty washing, could he suppose that readers would not imagine the traveler's smeared face after such ablutions? (More probable is Ariosto's treatment of a body blackened by descending to Hell. His Astolfo found on emerging that the smoke of the infernal pit had penetrated beneath his garments; so he sought a fountain "in which he washed himself from his feet to his head" [*Orlando Furioso* 34. 47]). Yet if Dante were amused by his protagonist's dew-bedaubed cheeks, would he later have called them "cleansed" (*Purg.* 30. 54)? Certainly to call Dante, or Chaucer, naive is risky.

In Paradise, the miraculous ascent through the heavens precludes physical assistance, but there is much belittling of the protagonist. In Hell, Virgil does much of the talking with the shades, sometimes on request, though he also instructs his charge to speak, and sometimes does not interfere with unauthorized speech (e.g., *Inf.* 24. 127; 27. 33; 32. 43). In Purgatory the pupil avoids speaking without the teacher's approval (*e.g.*, 19. 85). In Heaven, the securing of permission from Beatrice before addressing any of the shades becomes a formula, sometimes not observed (e.g., *Par.* 9. 74). In her care she is like a mother (22.4).

Once Virgil carries his disciple as a mother does her baby (*Inf.* 23. 40) but most suggestions of the traveler as puerile come when he is with Beatrice. As she rebukes him, he is like disgraced children looking on the ground (*Purg.* 31. 64); she treats him as a mother would a child talking wildly (*Par.* 1. 102); his thought is boyish (3. 26); see also *Purg.* 27. 45; 30. 79; *Par.* 22. 5; 30. 82.

The purpose of Dante's imaginary journey is his *salute*, his well-being. To this end, the dead are shown (*Purg.* 30. 137); he needs to see and hear (*Purg.* 1. 69). Hence he does well to observe all he can. But his zeal also has another purpose. To Guido Guinicelli, met on the Seventh Ledge of Purgatory, he says: "Tell me, so that some time I may put it on paper, who you are and who are in that crowd that is coming behind you"

(*Purg.* 26. 64). The questioner is like the friend of whom Burns
wrote:

> Hear, Land o' Cakes, and brither Scots
> Frae Maidenkirk to Johnie Groat's,
> If there's a hole in a' your coats,
>   I rede you tent it;
> A chiel's amang you takin' notes,
>   And faith he'll prent it.

So the zealous reporter is always intent on what he shall write
on his return. This insatiable curiosity is the first characteristic
of the traveler. From most of the shades he meets, from the gate
of Hell to the symbol of the Trinity, he asks, "Tell me who you
are" (e.g., *Inf.* 6. 46; 29. 106; 32. 43; 33. 116; *Purg.* 13. 91; 20. 35;
21. 79; 23. 52; 24. 11; *Par.* 5. 127; 8. 44; 15. 87; 32. 103). Many
methods for obtaining this information are used, by means of
the guides and the souls themselves; especially in Heaven the
spirits are glad to furnish the facts that they know the traveler
is interested in. One of the most elaborate devices for getting a
name occurs in the lowest Hell. By destiny or fortune the visitor
struck his foot in the face of a spirit frozen in the ice:

Groaning he shrieked: "Why do you kick me? If you do not come
to magnify the vengeance of Montaperti, why do you injure me?"
So I said: "My teacher, now wait for me here, so that I may get
rid of my uncertainty about this man. Then I shall make all the
haste you can ask." My guide stood still, and I said to the man
who was still cursing violently: "Who are you, who are so abusing
me?" "And who are you," he replied, "who go through Antenora
whacking our cheeks so hard that if you were alive you couldn't
do it?" "I am alive, and I can be of use to you," was my answer,
"if you ask for fame, for I can put your name in my notebook."
He returned: "The opposite is what I want. Be off, and give me
no more trouble, for little do you know how to flatter in this
swamp." Then I seized him by the scalp and said, "You'll tell
me your name or I'll not leave you any hair." He returned: "If
you do scalp me, I shall not tell you who I am; I wouldn't reveal
it to you if you hit me on the head a thousand times." I already
had his hair gathered in my hand and had pulled out more than
one lock, while he barked with his eyes turned down, when another spirit shouted: "What is wrong with you, Bocca? Isn't it
enough for you to chatter with your jaws, without barking? What
the devil ails you?" "Now," I said, "I don't care about your talking,

wretched traitor, because to your disgrace I shall spread true news about you." "Go away," he answered, "and tell what you wish to; but don't keep quiet, if you get out of here, about this man who just now had such a ready tongue. He weeps here for the French money. You can say: 'I saw the man from Duera in the place where the sinners are kept cool.' If you are asked who else was here, nearby is that Beccheria man, whose throat Florence cut with a saw" (*Inf.* 32. 79).

In addition to giving variety to the naming of the sinner, Dante the poet is so interested in the identification that he is willing to make Dante the traveler take ignoble advantage of the helpless. So he exaggerates the reporter's zeal to collect information such as the world, in its love for scandal about individuals, will listen to. To what lengths will the writer's desire for matter carry him? Our sightseer is not—so far as this passage goes—interested in learning what will improve his character or influence men against treachery. He is intent on collecting facts as material for popular poetry. The passage satirizes—with comedy grim enough for the depths of Hell—the unquenchable desire of the writing man to get something to put on paper.

Even in Heaven comic curiosity breaks out. Beatrice presents her charge before Saint Benedict who, wishing to do all he can for the traveler's assistance, launches into an account of Monte Cassino marked by strong feeling. He concludes with the lines: "Here is Macarius, here is Romöaldo, here are my brothers who in the cloisters planted their feet firmly and kept their hearts sound" (*Par.* 22. 49). Clearly the saint is about to continue in the same vein, but the eager traveler, as though availing himself of a pause, says, though with a polite preface: "I beg, Father, tell me whether you will do me the great favor of letting me see you with your bodily form revealed" (*Par.* 22. 58). Instead of eagerness to learn of righteous lives, here is curiosity about external appearance. This is the mental state of the peasant from remote and uncultured Croatia who looks on the Veronica in Rome, saying: "My Lord Jesus Christ, true God, now was your appearance like that" (*Par.* 31. 107)? In the place of such a simple man, the traveler Dante, not the philosophic Dante of history, puts himself in his eagerness about Saint Benedict's outer aspect, not about his holy zeal. Addressing his questioner as "Brother," the saint answers with a polite but firm dismissal of the irrelevance, yet with doctrinal explanation, and then resumes where Dante interrupted him. There had been men strong in faith, but now no one desires Heaven; "My rule stands simply to blot paper. The buildings that once were abbeys are caves, and the cowls are sacks full of spoiled flour" (22. 75). He continues his jeremiad to the end and moves away with no further recognition of the questioner.

Thus the sightseer of Dante's imagination is commendably eager to see and to learn, but his desires are not the lofty aspirations of a saint or a philosopher. His eagerness—in itself often amusing—is that of a character deliberately kept mediocre to fit him for comedy as Horace describes it. Possibly Beatrice confirms this when she says: "The strong desire which now inflames and urges you to get knowledge of what you see, pleases me more the more it swells" (30. 70). The swelling eagerness of the visitor is both commendable and amusing. Nor is it enough. As Beatrice speaks, she stands by the river of light, saying to her infantlike charge: "You must drink of this water before such great thirst as you have can be sated" (30. 73). Only at the very end of the *Paradiso* does divine love possess the seeker's spirit. Otherwise, he is still on the comic level, quite unable to do more than lament weakness preventing expression; his narrative will be that of an infant (33. 107). He is a character fit for comedy, not for tragedy or epic.

This essentially comic quality of the protagonist, the poet puts dramatically before his readers at the beginning of the poem. The character to whom the author gave his own name must be argued into visiting the other world by Virgil's "splendid language." Trying to escape, he declares:

"I am not Aeneas; I am not Paul; neither I myself nor any other man thinks me fit for such an affair. If I am persuaded into going, I fear the journey will be a mad act" (*Inf.* 2. 32).

Quite different is the spirit of Aeneas, the hero of Virgil's "tragedy" (*Inf.* 20. 113). He asks to visit his father in the realm of the dead, supporting his request with the names of heroes who entered Pluto's realm in the flesh: Orpheus, Pollux, Theseus, Hercules. If they could go, why not he, also descended from

Jove? Though the sibyl calls the journey a madman's act
(*Aeneid* 6. 135), in the *Inferno* such words are those of the re-
luctant traveler. Far as is Virgil's timid protégé from the spectacular fortitude of Aeneas, he is equally far from Saint Paul's
declaration, which the wanderer assumes is known to the wise
Virgil:

In labors more abundant, in stripes above measure, in prisons more
frequent, in deaths oft. Of the Jews five times received I forty
stripes save one. Thrice was I beaten with rods, once was I stoned,
thrice I suffered shipwreck, a night and a day I have been in the
deep; in journeyings often, in perils of waters, in perils of robbers,
in perils by mine own countrymen, in perils by the heathen, in
perils in the city, in perils in the wilderness, in perils in the sea,
in perils among false brethren; in weariness and painfulness, in
watchings often, in hunger and thirst, in fastings often, in cold
and nakedness (2 Corinthians 11. 23).

Such resolution can give "heroic name to person or to poem" on
the "better fortitude of patience and heroic martyrdom," but the
hero of the *Commedia* lacks Pauline vigor.

As Dante knew, Horace licenses comic actors to speak tragi-
cally now and then and admits that tragic kings sometimes
adopt the style of the lowly. Like all great artists, Dante ignores
pedantic considerations of literary type. Shakespeare and Milton give their tragedies variety with a judicious mixture of comedy. *Comus* stands on the wreck of Ben Jonson's formulas for
the masque. Even more delightfully, Dante confuses tragedy
and comedy. Through the world of the dead his fiction takes
the timid and insatiably curious reporter to whom the poet has
given his own name. In his intention to relate on returning to
earth what he has seen and heard, that reporter is at times one
with the historical Dante, author of the poem, as in this passage:

O Highest Light, raised so far above mortal imaginings, lend back
to my memory a little of how you appeared [in the Empyrean] and
make my tongue so mighty that I can leave to future men just one
spark of your glory! Because through returning in part to my memory and giving a little music in these verses, your victory will be
better understood (*Par.* 33. 67).

Most of the invocations are by the poet alone, with no inter-mixture of the feigned traveler. One long passage of political indignation, *Ahi serva Italia* (Oh enslaved Italy) (*Purg.* 6. 76), is spoken directly by the poet. Generally such passages are assigned to a shade, who may thinly disguise the exile-poet. For much of the poem, however, the wary reader will not let the melancholy Dante of tradition or even the historical politician, exile, and poet drive off the stage the timid and comic Dante who is central in the *Commedia*.

EPIC FIGURES LOWERED

Exhorting his great-great-grandson—here uniting fictitious traveler and poet, partly ideal but partly literal—Cacciaguida says:

This outcry of yours will be like the wind which strikes hardest the highest peaks; and this is no slight indication of renown. Therefore in these spheres, on the mountain and in the valley of pain, are presented to you only the souls marked by fame, because the hearer's mind is not confirmed in faith by an example that has unknown and hidden roots or by any proof that is not well known (*Par.* 17. 133).

That the old crusader's assertion now seems exaggerated need not disturb us. Many of the characters are still known to history or fiction. Ulysses is an epic hero, and Capaneo comes from Statius' *Thebaid*. In various guises we see popes, emperors, conquerors, famous scholars, founders of religions: Boniface VIII, Justinian, Alexander the Great, Thomas Aquinas, Mahomet, Brutus, King David, Saint Peter, Hugh Capet. These and such less noted men as Guido da Montefeltro, Manfred, and Farinata are hardly suitable for Horatian comedy, though we can again recall the quotation from that poet in the letter to Can Grande: "The tragic king can lament in commonplace language." That is, the normal epic figure may be lowered in dignity to fit a comedy. Thus he loses his distinction from the citizens who normally play comic roles. Boccaccio and Guido da Pisa overlooked the flexibility of Horace's theory when they affirmed that by writing of men in high position Dante falsified his title of *Comedy*.

Some heroic figures Dante the traveler does see. Noble is the "magnanimous" Farinata degli Uberti (*Inf.* 10. 73); yet even he is the great man visited by the tourist, not the dauntless hero saving Florence at Empoli. Capaneo, however horrible an example, is in contrast still actively defying Jove (14. 51). Ulysses gives a vigorous account of his final voyage (26. 90); yet his words, like those of Farinata, are rather the reminiscences of an old man than like the narrative which Aeneas, still in the midst of his adventures, relates at Dido's court. In addition to sadness of spiritual failure, retrospect rather than immediate power flavors Guido da Montefeltro's story (27. 60).

In the *Purgatorio*, Hugh Capet speaks like a man who has been a king rather than like one who still rules (20. 40). The setting planned by Dante indeed forbids anything other than the pained observation of one who has retired from action.

In *Paradiso* 6, Justinian's noble oration has some of the qualities of heroic poetry, but it too—as its setting requires—has a tone of regret and sadness rather than the immediate vigor of the speeches in the eleventh book of the *Aeneid*, or even of orations by Dante's admired Lucan, such as Caesar's address to his troops in *Pharsalia* 1. 299–351. The powerful attacks on corruption in the Church, as by Aquinas, Saint Bonaventura, and Saint Peter, fall into the class of satire rather than of epic or tragedy.

Possibly there is sometimes a touch of the comic where moderns have been accustomed to look for something quite different. After Francesca has apparently finished her story, the inquisitive traveler presses on with his "Tell me." Francesca does continue her narrative, with some of the best-known verses in the *Comedy*, concluding: "That day we read no further there" (*Inf.* 5. 138). On this Benvenuto da Imola commented: "That day they did not return any more to the reading they had begun, since they gave their attention to other reading that made them forgetful of that first reading." In the sixteenth century, Bernardino Daniello commented: "[Francesca decently indicates] that they would give their attention to something else, carrying out what Ovid in his *Art of Love* says in the first book: He who has enjoyed kisses, if he does not also enjoy other things, deserves to lose even those that were given to him."

Even by some moderns the double quality of Francesca's words has been admitted, though generally they have been made altogether pathetic, or perhaps sentimental, without regard for any bawdy tone or undertone. Each reader is free to choose what interpretation he will, while allowing the same liberty to others. This famous passage, early in the *Comedy*, may suggest that many others are not simple but in various ways are of manifold and—at first glance—even mutually destructive significance.

Can some such ambiguity be found in the episode of Cacciaguida, in *Paradiso* 15, 16, 17, and 18? The seriousness of many lines can hardly be doubted, with their expression of various ideas elsewhere found in Dante's writings. For example, the notion of nobility (*Par.* 16. 1) is discussed in *Convivio* 4 and touched in *Purgatorio* 7. 121. There are also remarks on Dante's exile, Florentine politics, and Dante's fame as a poet. Such serious matters have properly attracted attention from commentators. But is there something else different in tone? At least the poem once represents Beatrice as laughing in the course of the episode (*Par.* 16. 14). So doing, she is like the woman who coughed when Guinevere first strayed. Modern comment has attached her amusement to Dante's sudden respect for his ancestor on learning his rank.

Among the commentators of Dante's century another explanation for Beatrice's laughter was given, which seems later to have been abandoned. I quote Lana's version, not essentially different from that of Buti, the *Anonimo Fiorentino*, and Benvenuto da Imola:

Dante attempts to show that Beatrice steadily encouraged him and indicates that she made a signal that he should present his desire to the blessed Cacciaguida, just as the lady in the romance gave a signal when she coughed at Guinevere's first slip. To understand the illustration, one needs to know that Queen Guinevere fell in love with Lancelot because of the many great deeds she saw him do and also because he was handsome and eloquent in speech. So the Queen decided to reveal her love to Prince Gallehaut, to whom, after he had promised secrecy, she revealed her purpose, adding: "So that you may be more zealous in my affair, keep in mind that I know you love Manoalt's wife and that I shall get her to do as you wish." So, if I may summarize the story, that prince worked so skilfully on his part, and Queen Guinivere on her part, that those four alone met at the proper hour in one room, so that on one side were Lancelot and the Queen, and on the other side were Gallehaut and Manoalt's wife. Now Lancelot under the power of love stood timidly near the Queen and did not speak or show any intention of doing anything. Manoalt's wife, understanding the place and what they were there for, coughed and gave a signal to Lancelot that it was time for him to get some satisfaction. He then, thus encouraged, threw his arms around the Queen's neck and kissed her. This is the kiss mentioned in the fifth canto of the *Inferno*. That which then followed between them and between the Prince and Manoalt's wife can be found by any one who wishes in the book dealing with it, compiled by the same Prince Gallehaut. Dante's comparison is that just as Manoalt's wife showed Lancelot what he was to do about the Queen, so Beatrice showed Dante what to do about the blessed Cacciaguida.

If Beatrice's laugh is to ridicule Dante for too much respect for ancestry, the purpose of the passage is edification, even though the story referred to can hardly be one easily adapted to strict morality. If Beatrice is compared with Manoalt's encouraging wife, as Lana and the others wish, the incongruity is striking. That these commentators were right—in spite of their advantages for knowing what romantic stories were in circulation—we can hardly assume. Yet whatever explanation we prefer, we still do well to remember that the pious early commentators were willing to accept the possibility of bawdy comedy even in Paradise.

With this suggestion of the comic, we cannot but ask whether in other respects Cacciaguida is a figure touched with comedy as well as a serious speaker. He talks at greater length than any other of the blessed encountered in Heaven. To indulge in reminiscence, the traveler Dante, eager to learn about early Florence, encourages him, asking: "Who were your ancestors and of what sort were the years in which you spent your youth" (*Par.* 16. 23)? On his descendant's "blandishments," Cacciaguida's soul increases in brightness and replies in more than a hundred lines. Already he had responded in more than fifty lines to a request for his name. After the old crusader has talked at greater length than any other shade in Paradise, the Florentine traveler observes from the action of the flame surrounding his ancestor that he "wishes to speak to me somewhat further" (18. 26). The spirit then names souls in the Heaven of Mars. Otherwise he is almost confined to Florentine details—naming some thirty city families. Indeed, the whole approaches a satire on the old man full of minutiae from his youth and delighted to find a listener. The traveler need not be penetrating to observe that his great-great-grandfather wants to do more talking. Perhaps the author is amused at his own concern with Florentine details, which he foresaw would less interest the "men who call the present time ancient," as the traveler-poet says to Caccia-guida (17. 120). By assigning his concern to a man who is comic in his desire to indulge himself with talk of Florence, Dante hints that he knew his own Florentinism likely to be thought excessive. Cacciaguida may be looked on as Virgil's Anchises adapted to comedy.

Justifying Benvenuto da Imola's Horatian doctrine that comedy was to deal with citizens rather than nobles, Dante's Florentines usually are not so prominent as to destroy their comic possibilities: Ciacco the glutton, Filippo Argenti in the mud of the Styx. Brunetto Latini, a little comic as an author over-estimating his work, loses his dignity as he makes up time by running at a speed unlikely in an elderly scholar. Such mingling of respect with ridicule suggests a historical basis in Dante's knowledge of Ser Brunetto, though perhaps we have here the poet making his opportunity.

The indignity of various punishments does something to counteract their seriousness. Devils scourge the panders and seducers: "O how they made the sinners lift their heels at the first strokes! Not one of them waited for seconds and thirds" (*Inf.* 18. 37). The dignity-stripping quality of this punishment is accented when Virgil points to Jason as a partial—but only partial—exception: "Look at that tall man who is coming. You cannot see him shed a tear for pain. How much of his kingly appearance he still retains" (18. 83). The solitary regal exception moves with some of Farinata's epic dignity.

Dante's world had reason to dread the followers of Moham-med, yet the poet deprives the prophet of dignity:

When a cask loses from its head the middle piece or one of the cants, it does not gape so wide as one I saw who was split from chin to farting place. Between his legs were hanging his entrails; his heart and the organs about it were visible, and the loathsome sack that makes what is swallowed into turd. While I was all intent on seeing him, he looked at me, and with his hands opened his breast, saying: "Now see how I split myself; see how Mohammed is ravaged" (28. 22).

In Purgatory, Pope Adrian, in spite of his undignified position, with his "hinder" turned to the sky (*Purg.* 19. 97), is still in his humility a great man. Instead of allowing his visitor to kneel in respect to papal dignity, the penitent says: " 'Straighten your legs; rise up brother. Do not mistake. I am with you and all men a fellow servant of one power' " (19. 133). But in the Inferno the popes, plunged headfirst into holes and shaking their upturned legs (*Inf.* 19. 22), lose their dignity.[2] The traveler, ignorant of their identity, is not initially respectful, and Pope Nicholas adds to the indignity of the scene by addressing the timid sightseer as though he were Pope Boniface, and in no respectful tone.

Remembering the falsifiers, the returned tourist gives some thirty lines to the words and blows of a vulgar quarrel such as he might have witnessed among the citizens whom Benvenuto thought the proper actors for comedy (*Inf.* 30. 100). By rebuking the absorbed onlooker for his interest, the Latin poet emphasizes the vulgarity of the scene. Yet one of the participants is from Virgil's "tragedy," the Greek Sinon, through whose courage and composure in deceit Troy fell.

In Purgatory, Dante smiles and invites his readers to smile when Virgil and Statius are caught in mild and pleasant embarrassment. Statius expresses devotion to the *Aeneid* as his poetic mother and nurse, declaring that to have lived in Virgil's time he would gladly add a year to his purgatorial penance.

These words turned Virgil toward me with a face that in silence said: "Keep still." But will power cannot do everything, because laughter and tears follow so fast after the feeling from which either springs that in the most truthful men they least follow the will. I did smile, as does a man who is giving a private signal. So the shade was silent and looked into my eyes, where the expression is especially plain; and he said: "As you hope to succeed in your great effort, tell me why your face just now showed me a flash of laughter." So now I am attacked on both sides: One man tells

2 On this passage see Chapter 6, p. 158, below.

me to keep still; the other begs me to speak. At this I sigh, so that
my teacher hears me (*Purg.* 21. 103).

Then Virgil allows himself to be revealed, and all goes well.

Even the redeemed in Heaven are not always allowed all the
dignity of their rank. Cunizza was a great lady, yet the commentators suggest other than a solemn view of her. Benvenuto
writes on *Paradiso* 9:

> She was truly a daughter of Venus, always amorous and promiscu-
> ous, of whom I speak in explaining the sixth book of the *Purgatorio*,
> on how she carried on with Sordello of Mantua. Yet at the same
> time she was pious, kind, merciful, helpful to the wretches whom
> her brother cruelly tortured. Properly, therefore, the poet feigns
> that he found her in the sphere of Venus. For if the heathen in
> Cyprus made a goddess of their Venus, and the Romans of their
> Flora, a very beautiful and wealthy harlot, how much more worthily
> and decently the Christian poet was able to give salvation to
> Cunizza! . . . The ignorant wonder that a famous harlot should
> be in Heaven, not considering that her vice is natural, usual and
> almost necessary, especially to the young.

About Cunizza's affair with Sordello, Benvenuto in his comment on *Purgatorio* 6 tells "a very amusing story" which he has
heard but will not declare true. Sordello, to reach a back door
where Cunizza would admit him, had a servant carry him
through a hog yard. The lady's brother Ezzelino, disguised as
the servant, once carried Sordello to the door and, when he left,
carried him back through the yard. Then revealing himself,
Ezzelino said: "This is enough. Hereafter you will not go to a
business so filthy through a place so filthy." Sordello, promising
never to return, asked pardon. Yet the wicked Cunizza got him
back into his sin.

Lana asserts that Cunizza

> was so free with her love that she would have thought it very knav-
> ish on her part to deny it to any man who courteously requested
> it of her. Now in allegory Dante mentions her, since, as she was
> generous and courtly with worldly love, so those who are generous
> and courtly and on fire with divine love possess the blessedness
> and glory of the greatest fame.

At least these early commentators remind us of Boccaccio who,
as pious as they, wrote the *Decameron*, with its range from
pathos to bawdy comedy.

COMMON LIFE IN THE ACTION

As a medieval writer of comedy, Dante shows universally pleasing scenes from common life.

Inferno and Purgatorio. In Limbo, Virgil and his pupil see four shades. Virgil tells who they are, just as nowadays one would name to a stranger men of importance seen in any public place:

"See the man with a sword in his hand coming ahead of the three like a lord. He is Homer, the master poet; the next is Horace; the third is Ovid; and the fourth Lucan" (*Inf.* 4. 86).

As the travelers move along the dike of the stream flowing through the burning desert, they meet a group moving in the opposite direction on the sand below:

One of them recognized me, seized the bottom of my coat, and shouted: "How strange!" As he stretched out his arm toward me, I so fixed my eyes on his cooked visage that his burned face did not prohibit my recognizing him. Moving my face toward his face below me, I replied: "Are you here, Dr. Brunetto?" (*Inf.* 15. 23).

Another homely instance of pointing out men in the street, as it were, occurs among the diviners. Virgil says:

"That man whose beard reaches from his cheeks down to his brown shoulders was an augur . . . and with Calchas he set the time at Aulis for cutting the first cable. Eurypylus was his name, and so my high tragedy somewhere has it. . . . That man so thin in the flanks is Michael Scott" (*Inf.* 20. 106).

Virgil and his pupil stand on the brink of the *bolgia* of the thieves, talking and not noticing who passes, when someone interrupts them by calling, "Who are you?": "I did not know him, but it happened, as it often does in such a situation, that one needed to give another's name, saying: 'Where is Cianfa dawdling?'" (*Inf.* 25. 40). By saying it "often happens," the poet indicates one of the situations that men like to relate as interesting. The coincidence reappears in the lowest circle, when Bocca refuses to give his name and one of the other spirits addresses him (32. 106).

In Ante-Purgatory, the travelers encounter a crowd of souls:

I saw one of them come forward to embrace me with such great affection that it forced me to do the same. O bodiless shades, except in appearance! Three times behind him I brought my hands together, and as often I returned them to my own chest. I know I showed my wonder in my face. So the shade smiled and drew back. I, following him, moved ahead. He gently asked me to stand still. Then I knew who he was, and begged that he would stop a little to talk with me. He replied: "As I loved you when in my mortal body, so I love you when I am free from it; hence I shall stop. But you—why are you going?" "My Casella, to come back again to this place I am making this journey," I said, "but how have you lost so much time?" (*Purg.* 2. 76).

However combined with the Virgilian incident of the shade without substance that cannot be embraced, this is also a scene from daily life, a failure to recognize on an improbable meeting. Striking is the courtesy with which the puzzled stranger responds to the shade, though still unable to "place him," as we say. Then he recognizes the old friend when he speaks, and Casella tells the latest news about himself. The living man then politely requests Casella to sing one of those songs of love that "used to calm all my longings," for it will "comfort my soul, which with my body is so wearied with my journey here." For the moment, all miraculous quality in the visit disappears and the speaker is a wearied traveler, not thinking of Heaven even in expectation. Casella, consenting to sing, enraptures his audience with one of Dante's *canzoni.* Like a street crowd witnessing an extraordinary event, the listeners forget everything in their interest. Then the irate Cato breaks the charm by reminding them that they have forgotten the urgent business of preparing to appear before God. Overwhelmed by this violence of authority, they rush off toward the mountain "like a man who starts without knowing where he will come out. And our departure was not less hasty" (*Purg.* 2. 132). On recovering his composure, the visitor, in his ignorance of the path, can only turn to Virgil, who also has been discomposed by Cato, though soon "his feet gave up the hurry that deprives every action of dignity" (*Purg.* 3. 10). Here Virgil is the great man made for the moment as ridiculous as any in the common herd, scuttling off with dignity destroyed.

As the breathless climber complains of the steep ascent, and Virgil promises rest at the top, they hear a voice saying:

"Perhaps you will need to sit down before that." At the sound we both turned, so that we saw at our left a large rock which neither Virgil nor I had noticed earlier. We went to it, and there were persons sitting in the shade behind the rock, as men sit shiftlessly. And one of them, who seemed tired, was sitting and embracing his knees, holding his face low between them. "O my dear master," said I, "look at that man who acts more shiftless than if laziness were his sister." Then the man turned and looked at us, raising his face along his thigh, and said: "Now go on up, if you are so vigorous." Then I knew who he was, and that strain which still made my breath come fast did not keep me from going to him. When I reached him, he just raised his head, saying: "Have you really seen that the sun drives his chariot on your left side?" His actions and his brief words moved my lips a little to laughter; then I said: "Belacqua, I don't feel at all sorry for you now. But tell me why you are sitting here. Are you waiting for a guide, or have you merely resumed your old habits?" He said: "Brother, what is the use of going up? The angel of God who sits at the gate would not let me go to the sufferings. First the sky must circle around me outside the gate as long as it did in my life—because I delayed to the end my holy longings—if before that time prayer rising from a heart that lives in grace does not aid me. Of what use is any other, which is not heard in Heaven?" (4. 98).

Belacqua, unknown except as mentioned by Dante, is the citizen proper for comedy. To various critics, as well as to the smiling wayfarer himself, the comic quality of this lounger's intrusion upon a passerby has been evident. It is the comedy of the public square.

Pia, though among the negligent, is unusual in her thoughtfulness for the traveler, who will be weary on finishing his journey: "When you are back in the world and rested from your long trip, remember [to pray for] me" (5. 130). A thumbnail sketch of one unselfishly understanding daily infirmity!

Again the travelers must ask the way. Instead of telling them, the man addressed, though dignified as a couchant lion, is inquisitive about their country and their rank. Virgil begins his reply with the word "Mantua." Needing no more, the other shouts: "O Mantuan, I am Sordello from your city." And they embraced each other (*Purg.* 6. 74). Here is the comedy of travelers enormously interested in those they meet merely because they come from the same city or the same state. Why should Dante have selected the dignified Sordello for this naive role? Perhaps because he, like Virgil, was from Mantua; hence he can be used in transition to Dante's digressive attack on Italian party strife:

Sordello feels affinity for an unknown man from his own town, yet many Italians are at enmity with those within the same city walls. When the feelings proper to compatriots have been expressed, Sordello again asks: "Who are you?" (*Purg.* 7. 3). On Virgil's answer, Sordello is vividly the man hearing something so extraordinary that he can hardly credit it:

Like a man who suddenly sees something before his face that makes him wonder, so that he believes and does not believe, saying: "It is true; it isn't," so Sordello appeared (*Purg.* 7. 10).

Then he wishes to know whether his countryman is from the Inferno. After some conversation, Virgil returns to his first request: "What is the shortest way to the entrance to Purgatory?"

While Sordello is still guiding them, there is another realistic street scene:

I saw a man who kept looking at me as though he thought he knew me. It was so late that darkness was coming on, but not so much but that between his eyes and mine there was light enough to show what had been hidden. He came toward me and I went toward him. Noble Judge Nino, how pleased I was when I saw that you were not among the damned! No pleasant greeting between us was omitted. Then he asked: "How long since you came to the foot of the mountain over the wide waters?" "Oh," said I, "I came out of the dreary regions this morning, and I am in the first life, though by my journey I am gaining the second one." As soon as they heard my answer, Sordello and Nino started back like men suddenly bewildered. One of them turned to Virgil, and the other to a man who sat there, shouting: "Conrad, come and see what God in his grace permits." Then he turned to me (*Purg.* 8. 47).

Nino asks Dante to take a message to his daughter and speaks conventionally of his wife and of women generally. Thereupon the visitor's attention is attracted elsewhere and Judge Nino drops from the poem, not even bidding Dante farewell. Such departures without formal leavetaking are frequent, indeed almost necessary if the poem is not to be cluttered with a multiplicity of good-bys. Conrad Malaspina, however, after his attention is roused, continues to gaze upon the visitor who has escaped from Hell, while angels put to flight an intruding serpent. At the first opportunity he speaks, eager to get news of his home on earth. The reply is Dante's device for expressing personal thanks to the Malaspina family, since he says nothing about current affairs in the Val di Magra. Up to that point the scene is wholly lifelike.

Having passed the souls repenting of sloth, the visitor dreams. Dreams are frequent in the poetry of adventure, but one detail is hardly heroic. The dreamer, roused by the stench of the foul siren when she is exposed, opens his eyes to hear Virgil say: "At least three times I have called you. Get up and come on" (*Purg.* 19. 34).

From ordinary life comes the unexpected meeting of the wayfarer with his friend Forese Donati. After he has beheld the repentant gluttons famished almost to skeletons, one of these sufferers turns upon him eyes so sunken that they seem in the "depths of his head" and looks steadily at him.

Then that shade gave a loud shout: "What a blessing this is to me!" I never would have known him from his face, but his voice made plain to me what his appearance alone had suppressed. This spark wholly rekindled my recollection of that changed countenance, and I saw again Forese's face. "Pay no attention to the dry scabies that discolors my skin," he begged, "nor to my lack of flesh, but tell me the truth about yourself, and who the two souls escorting you are. Don't be slow about speaking to me." "Though I wept for you when you died," I answered, "your face makes me weep now with no smaller sorrow, since I see it so drawn. Therefore now tell me for God's sake what so withers your leaves. Don't make me talk while I am so astonished, because a man can hardly speak who is full of other thoughts." [Forese explains how souls are purified from gluttony.] Then I said to him: "Forese, five years have not gone by since that day on which you exchanged the world for a better life. If your power for further sinning was ended before you reached that hour of rightful grief which remarries us to God, how have you come so high as this? I expected to find you down below there, where time atones for time" (23. 42, 76).

Forese explains that his wife's prayers have brought him out of Ante-Purgatory early. Then he attacks the women unlike her in Florence, predicting their punishment. Returning to the personal, he continues:

"Now brother, don't conceal your condition from me any longer. You see that not merely I but all this crowd here are looking at the place where you blot out the sun." So I said to him: "If you bring back to your mind what you were to me and what I was to you, your remembering now will yet be an affliction" (23. 112).

These words, when taken as prosaic autobiography, are held to indicate wicked lives led by Dante and Forese. Yet the fictitious situation has claims. The visitor says to his friend that the mountain "straightens you whom the world made crooked" (23. 126). Forese is purging away the sin of gluttony, and his friend expects to return for the punishment of his pride (13. 137). They can hardly assert lives without reproach.

Benvenuto da Imola speaks of their wasting their time in indulgences, loves, and other vanities, and of their pursuit of undignified pleasures. He also says that Forese the glutton was otherwise a good man. Buti comments on the word "life" (23. 118): "that is, vicious." Yet no vice is set down in the text, and it is not a necessary inference, as Scartazzini says (Note on *Purg.* 23. 116). The *Anonimo Fiorentino* quotes from one of Dante's sonnets to Forese; other early commentators do not notice them. That these sonnets are deplorable seems a recent notion. Until they are proved bitter and hostile, they may be supposed jocose and friendly. If so, the scene with Forese befits comedy, as showing the pleasure of long-separated friends on an unexpected meeting. The visitor continues in an intimate tone, with his only utterance of Beatrice's name before her appearance (23. 128). As an old literary friend, Forese is acquainted with the *Vita Nuova.* As the two walk on, the newcomer asks after Forese's sister: "Tell me, if you know, where Piccarda is" (*Purg.* 24. 10), to be answered: "My sister, of whom I cannot say whether she is more beautiful or more good, is already happy in her crown, as she triumphs in high Olympus" (24. 13).

Forese introduces to Dante an older poet, Bonagiunta of Lucca, to whom the younger writer explains his theory of the *dolce stil nuovo.* This is a social occasion, in which one man meets another whom he has long known by reputation. Then there is more talk with Forese, in the tone of pleasant, fortuitous encounter:

"When shall I see you again?" "I do not know," I replied, "how long I shall live, but I assure you that I shall not return so soon that I shall not wish to be even earlier on the shore [of Purgatory], because the place where I have been put to spend my life reduces its goodness further every day and I believe is now in a state for sad overthrow" (*Purg.* 24. 75).

After foretelling the death of his brother Corso, one of the chief disturbers of Florentine peace, the penitent apologizes:

"I cannot explain more clearly. Now I must leave you, because in this kingdom time is so precious that I am losing too much of it by going along with you at your pace." Just as sometimes a horseman comes from a troop of cavalry at the gallop, as he goes to get honor from the first encounter, so Forese left us with long steps, and I walked along with those two who were such famous men in the world (*Purg.* 24. 89).

Thus Dante adapts to Purgatory a scene from the life of Florence. Nothing could be more in the spirit of Horatian comedy as the Middle Ages conceived it.

When the Earthly Paradise is reached, Virgil ends his pupil's tutelage, releasing him to his own free will. In this interlude between liberation by his first guardian and the rebuke with which Beatrice reestablishes her old mastery, the traveler enjoys the garden, with its beautiful trees and singing birds. Soon he comes to a stream of marvelous clarity. In the distance he sees a lady, appearing "like something that, coming suddenly, turns the beholder's thought aside in astonishment." She is singing and gathering flowers. The poet then lowers the dignity of this scene that might come from a romance to the commonplace level of his traveler who, with an eye for a pretty girl, says:

"Lovely lady, who warm yourself in the rays of love (if I may trust your looks, which usually reveal the heart), won't you please come toward this stream, so I can hear what you are singing? You make me remember where and what Proserpina was on the day when her mother lost her, and she lost the spring" (*Purg.* 28. 43).

As an educated man, the traveler knows about Ovid's Proserpina. The lady does move toward him among the flowers, until he can hear the words she sings, but what they are he does not tell. Then (with further reminiscence of Ovid),

as soon as she reached the place where the grass was wet with the waves of the pretty stream, she favored me by raising her eyes. I do not believe that such light shone under Venus' brows when she was wounded by her son (contrary to his wont). Standing erect, she was smiling from the other bank as she arranged with her hands many colors [flowers] which the rich earth yields without seed. Three steps apart the stream kept us; but the Hellespont where Xerxes crossed—still a bridle for all human pride—did not get more hatred from Leander for spreading its waters between Sestos and Abydos than that stream did from me because its waters then did not yield passage (*Purg.* 28. 61).

Later it appears that the waters are not over the traveler's head (*Purg.* 31. 94). Dante's hero, with Virgil and Statius forgotten behind him, standing on the bank of a stream three steps wide and comparing it to the Hellespont—magnified by Dante's Lucan (2. 675)—could hardly have been imagined by the poet without amusement. The lovely lady, however, makes no amorous suggestion, but tells the traveler she will answer his questions. With comically abrupt abandonment of the romantic, he asks explanation of the wind and water of Purgatory, for Statius' account seemed to exclude them (*Purg.* 21. 43).

Paradiso. In the *Paradiso*, scenes showing genial observation of daily life and zest for it occur less often. In the Moon the blessed souls are somewhat distinguishable, though in higher heavens they are wholly concealed in light. In the Moon the traveler, observing a soul ready to speak with him, says to it: "I shall be greatly obliged if you will kindly tell me your name and your position" (*Par.* 3. 40). The soul replies: "If you search your memory, my being more beautiful will not disguise me, but you will recognize me as Piccarda." The traveler apologizes: "In your marvelous appearance gleams something or other divine that transforms you from what I earlier knew. Hence I was not quick in remembering you, but now what you say helps me, so it is easier for me to make you out" (*Par.* 3. 58).

Important in the *Paradiso* (occupying two and a half cantos) is the examination given the visitor by the three disciples, Saints Peter, James, and John, on the fundamentals of Christian faith: faith, hope, and charity. By making the examination as easy as he does, Dante perhaps wishes to indicate how simple Christian doctrine fundamentally is. Otherwise, indeed, the test is strangely elementary for a man of the historical Dante's supposed philosophical attainments, though not unsuitable for the feigned Dante of the poem. It assumes the existence of the Church, but nothing of an ecclesiastical sort is mentioned; it is almost a return to the primitive New Testament, touched with such bits of neo-Platonic symbolism as that the good of the world is a light from the ray of God, the Essence (*Par.* 26. 31).

But however solemn the doctrines presented, Dante gives the scene something of the comedy he had observed in dealing with men in academic life, both pupils and teachers. The examinee appears before Saint Peter as the bachelor of arts undergoing examination for a higher degree. Beatrice, in the role of expert observer, believes him well prepared, so that the test, like many academic examinations, is a matter of form. The nervous candidate prepares himself with every sort of argument as well as he can, hoping to be a credit to the examiner and to himself. Happily, he answers with readiness, so that the questioner expresses satisfaction. Dante catches the spirit of the affair, as suited to an eager and well prepared but not highly gifted candidate, such as the fictitious visitor to Heaven. This amusing scene from academic life is touched with satire as the test goes forward. Saint James, a benevolent questioner, encourages and yet warns the candidate:

"Lift up your head and compose yourself, because what comes up here from the mortal world must adapt itself to our rays" (25. 34).

The returned traveler draws on his memory:

This encouragement came to me from the second fire, so I lifted my eyes to the mountains which earlier bent them down with such great weight (25. 37).

This seems to mean that the candidate has been so deeply impressed by the reputation of his examining professors that he needs more assurance. The kind catechizer puts the candidate at his ease. Beatrice also interposes to insist on the examinee's qualifications. She applies the metaphor of departure from Egypt, somewhat as when the new arrivals from the world in Purgatory give thanks, in asserting that he has been thought worthy to be brought from earth to Heaven to learn by observation (*Par.* 25. 55; *Purg.* 2. 46). The candidate then answers Saint James's question "as does a pupil who reflects his teacher's thought, ready and eager on the subject in which he is well prepared, so that his excellence may be made plain" (*Par.* 25. 64). In this subservience to his teacher, the candidate refers to the master's Epistle; this, though primarily on faith, also treats hope, that is, patience in the expectation of the Lord's coming (James 5. 8, etc.). No displeasure in the pupil's reference to the examiner's composition is expressed by the latter, but, "while I was speaking, within the dazzling breast of that fire was trembling a light quick and frequent, like a lightning flash" (*Par.* 25. 79).

As the saint questions further, the pupil says that the questioner next to come, Saint John, has in the book of Revelation dealt with the garments of the redeemed "much more explicitly" than has Isaiah (*Par.* 25. 94). The effulgence of Saint John is as bright as the sun. Apparently inquisitive about this saint's body as about that of Saint Benedict (22. 58), the visitor looks fixedly at the splendor that hides it, recalling the legend that the disciple was taken up to Heaven in the flesh. On its falsity the saint pleasantly enlightens him. Continuing, the examinee makes another reference to Revelation in the quoted words "Alpha and Omega." [3] He further says that he has learned about love from his questioner's writings, without specifying which (*Par.* 26. 43). Dante represents his traveler's catechism as an academic exercise conducted by professors gratified by references to their own writings. Whether or not the poet had been at the University of Paris, he had looked with amusement at academic foibles.

When in the highest heaven the souls appear in their bodily form, characteristically earthly incident is again possible. Under Beatrice's supervision, the visitor has been looking at the celestial rose. Then with the desire to question that never fails him:

I turned with reawakened desire to ask my patroness about matters that were taxing my mind. I directed myself to one and another answered; I expected to see Beatrice and I saw an old man clad like the people in glory. His eyes and his cheeks expressed gracious happiness, and his attitude was compassionate, as befits a tender father. But "Where is she?" I said at once (*Par.* 31. 55).

So throughout, Dante's traveler—returned to earth—takes pleasure in telling of the amusing incidents of private life.

We have seen that the observer of the three kingdoms, even though by divine appointment (*Inf.* 3. 95; 5. 23, etc.), is yet a timid soul, childish in his thought, as Beatrice says (*Par.* 3. 26).

3 Revelation 1. 8. Some think that Dante knew *omega* only as O. His son Pietro uses the form *omega* in his comment on *Paradiso* 26.

Virgil treats him like a boy to be bribed with an apple (*Purg.* 27. 45). Yet the Trinity is figured with no such crude anthropomorphism as the sort of triple Janus, suitable to the naive mind, which later was condemned by Pope Urban VIII. Is the reader then to think all the splendid lights of Heaven dominated by a spiritual religion rather than by one suited to such countrymen and citizens as comedy after the Horatian theory deals with? Is any part of the heavenly glory designed for a childish observer whose mind and words are inadequate (*Par.* 14. 81; 23. 45; 33. 121, etc.)?

In the Heaven of Jupiter the holy lights enclosing the blessed souls fly through the air like birds and arrange themselves in the shape of letters. Dante as poet at this point calls on the Pegasean Muse to aid him in presenting the figures he has "conceived," and to show her power in his scant verses (*Par.* 18. 87). The word rendered "scant" is *brevi*, taken in its literal meaning of "short" by some of the old commentators, though by some later ones understood as "inadequate." Such an invocation of the Muse is usual when a poet is about to write something difficult, as when Virgil summons the Muses to help him relate the burning of the Trojan ships (*Aeneid* 9. 77). Did Dante think the matter he now was to present especially elevated or very difficult, or did he feel that its strangeness demanded apology? Frequent in modern times is the forming of letters from groups of men or from flowers or from fireworks; especially the latter are suggested in these light-formed letters in Heaven. They are combined in words of solemn warning to princes, taken from the Apocrypha: *Diligite justitiam qui judicatis terram*—"Love righteousness, ye that be judges of the earth" (*Wisdom of Solomon* 1. 1). As the letters disappear, only the final M remains.

Then, as at the stirring of burned logs numberless sparks rise— from which fools tell fortunes—I saw rise up more than a thousand lights, and some of them went high and some not far, as the Sun which set them afire distributed them (*Par.* 18. 100).

The simplicity of the comparison likens it to that of Ulysses and his fellows concealed by flames: "The farmer who is resting on a hill . . . sees down in the valley great numbers of fireflies. So

the eighth *bolgia* was everywhere made brilliant by a like number
of flames" (*Inf.* 26. 25). The sparks rising up, as the marvelous
lights shift, so place themselves about the M as to produce the
head and neck of an eagle, sign of the Roman Empire, and thus
of political justice. In the next two cantos this unnatural bird,
though made up of many souls, each swathed in light, speaks as
a single being, on both divine and human justice. Among the
lights or souls combined in the eagle are two from the pagan
world: Ripheus, a character from the *Aeneid*, and the Emperor
Trajan. The eagle's reasoning on the salvation of these pagans
suggests Dante's tendency to stretch the commonly accepted
boundaries of divine justice (20. 70). Part of the eagle's discourse
is elicited by questions from the visitor. Throughout this interview Beatrice is unmentioned.

Four times the eagle is called an *image* and four times a *segno*.
The latter word once refers to the figure of the eagle which
formed the Roman standard (19. 101).[4] Indeed, it is a synonym
for *image*, as it means a carved figure in the pavement of the
terrace of the proud (*Purg.* 12. 47, 63; cf. lines 18, 38). Thus no
life is given to the eagle; may we call it a robot? Its workmanship
is divine: "That One who there acts as artist has no one who
directs Him, but He directs. From Him derives that power which
provides form for nests" (*Par.* 18. 109). The image of the eagle
bears the "imprint of the everlasting will" (20. 76). The traveler
reiterates that with his own eyes he saw the lights as they formed
the words and the eagle (18. 70, 86, 97, 107; 19. 10, 37; 20. 17,
84, 146), and as returned sightseer affirms: "What now I must
report voice never uttered, nor ink wrote, nor was it ever grasped
by imagination" (*Par.* 19. 7). Certainly the poet here strives to
show the deep impression the eagle made on the traveler.

Yet for what level of taste did Dante plan this extraordinary
experience? Had he been astonished by some marvelous display
of fireworks, making use of the latest development of gunpowder,
or even of the older Greek fire known to Florentine warfare? Did
he regard the mechanical image of the eagle as so impressive that

---

4 The figure of the legionary eagle frequent on Roman coins makes
probable Dante's knowledge that the imperial eagle was not placed on
a cloth banner.

all men must look upon it as dignified, or may he have had some
of that pleasure in the crowd's taste with which we now can look
upon such wonders? Is this a marvel fit for Dante the traveler,
whose "childish" thought is pleasantly accepted by Beatrice
(*Par.* 3. 26)? We must regret that she does not comment on the
vision of the eagle. Each reader is to judge for himself whether
this speaking statue or robot formed of manifold lights is a display for epic or for comedy. Does Dante hint anything when in
illustrating the formation of the solemn words, *Diligite justitiam*,
he mentions the credulous men who use sparks in fortune-telling
(18. 102)? The lesson of just government is for all.

SIMILES FROM DAILY LIFE

Dante nowhere mentions the notion, repeated by Benvenuto
da Imola, that comedy deals with the affairs of simple life.
This concept seems to have been encouraged by Donatus the
grammarian, whom Dante puts in the Heaven of the Sun. Moreover, Dante knew the word *privatis* in Horace's *Ars Poetica* 90,
indicating comedy as concerned with daily life or private affairs. Still more important than any theory known to him is
his practice. From ordinary life come many of his comparisons.

As Virgil and his pupil walked on the dike confining the
waters of Flegeton, they met a group of spirits who on the
level below "were following the embankment's course. Each
of them stared at us as in the evening one man stares at another under the new moon; and they strained their eyes upon
us as an old tailor does upon his needle" (*Inf.* 15. 16). The
panders and seducers are like a city crowd: "Because of the
large crowds in the year of Jubilee, the Romans have taken a
way of making the people move across the bridge so that on
one side they all have their faces toward the Castle and go
toward Saint Peter's, and those on the other side go toward
the mountain" (*Inf.* 18. 28).

In the course of the bizarre and comic episode of the Malebranche, the devils push one of the sinners under the surface
of the boiling pitch, shouting: "Here you have to dance under
cover, so that, if you can, you may play at odd and even in
concealment" (*Inf.* 21. 53). Guido da Pisa's explanation of

this passage has not been taken into modern commentaries; it rests on the word *accaffi*, "play at odd and even":

In Tuscany there is a child's game called *a caffo*. A boy shuts up in his hand coins or beans or something of the sort to an even or odd number, and says to his playmate: "Guess." The latter says either "even" or "odd." This game is called, as I said, *a caffo*. In the same way the grafters in their proceedings keep their hands closed, and what they give the appearance of putting in one box, they put in another.

This suggestion of a scene in the life of the streets is followed by one from the kitchen of a great house; the devils with their hooks push the sinners under the surface "just as cooks make their helpers push the meat into the middle of the kettle with their hooks, so it will not float" (*Inf.* 21. 55). The sundered body of Mohammed is compared with a broken and gaping barrel (*Inf.* 28. 22). From the domestic hearth are two sinners in the *bolgia* of the falsifiers leaning against one another like pans placed to warm (*Inf.* 29. 73).

The *Purgatorio* also has its scenes from common life. Around the living visitor gather inquisitive souls:

As upon a messenger who carries an olive branch the people crowd to hear news, and nobody is squeamish about treading [on toes], so every one of those fortunate souls fixed his eyes on my face, as though oblivious of going to make himself beautiful (*Purg.* 2. 70).

The people, seeing a messenger from an army perhaps, are absorbed in curiosity about his news. They lose every thought of hurting or being hurt and forget for the moment even important business on which they are engaged. This is quite the medieval comedy of citizen life. Similar is a scene that suggests realism among the lower classes:

When the game of *zara* [craps?] is over, the loser is left grieving; he goes over the throws and while downcast learns [how to play with more success]. With the other man all the bystanders go off. One walks ahead, and another takes hold of him from behind, and a third attracts his notice at his side. He doesn't stop, yet notices this man and that. Any to whom he extends his hand press against him no more, and so he protects himself from the mob. Such was I in that thick crowd, turning my face to those on one side and the other, and by making promises I got rid of them (*Purg.* 6. 1).

When Virgil tells Dante that one of the letters impressed on his forehead by the angel at the gate has been removed, Dante so acts as to remind himself of a situation that brings inevitable laughter: "I acted like those who have something on their heads that they know nothing about unless the gestures of other people make them suspect. So the hand tries to learn, and hunts and finds, doing the duty that sight cannot do" (*Purg.* 12. 127). On the ledge of gluttony Dante sees souls eager for food growing on a tree; they remind him of a common sight: "Greedy and silly children who are begging for something, but the one begged does not answer, but, to make their desire greater, holds high what they want and does not hide it" (*Purg.* 24. 108). A perennial source of amusement to city men is the countryman in town: The amazed mountaineer is worried and gazes about in silence when as a rough backwoodsman he comes into the city (*Purg.* 26. 67). Dante had seen children "too awed in speaking before their elders, so that they do not get the sound of their words to their teeth" (*Purg.* 33. 25).

In Paradise also the traveler still has the urge to make homely comparisons with what he sees. In a time when the bow was still a practical weapon, Dante knew its workings. Of swift motion he says that "it was like an arrow which hits the target before the bowstring grows still" (*Par.* 5. 91).

The returned traveler draws on his humble experience to describe the action of souls in the lucent moon: As in a fishpond where the water is still and clear, the fish approach anything in such a way coming from outside that they think it food for them, so I saw more than a thousand shining ones move toward us (*Par.* 5. 100).

In the Crystalline Heaven the aspiring souls are described with what has been called a "tender recollection of family life," an aspect of the private life that Horace assigned to comedy. These souls are "like the baby that stretches its arms toward its mamma after it has taken milk, because of the spirit that warms it even externally" (*Par.* 23. 121).

Even the excellence of the Florentine coinage did not dispense with need for the testing of coins on the touchstone to guard against counterfeits of the florin, and in a city so commercial as Florence in Dante's time a monetary illustration would have come easily to many citizens. So the traveler, after his simple religious faith has been examined, is addressed by Saint Peter in a figure of speech well suited to his background:

"The combination of metals in this coin and its weight have passed their test, but tell me if you have it in your purse." I replied: "Yes, I have it, so shining and so round that I am sure it is genuine" (*Par.* 24. 83).

Naive the trader who supposes that glitter and shape assure the coin's worth.

To markets in the cities he knew, we may suppose that Dante often saw animals brought for sale in bags. Such a homely idea he applies in describing the action of Adam's soul: "Sometimes an animal that is covered wriggles so that its effort appears in the response its wrapping gives to its motions. So the first of the souls made appear through its covering how pleased it was to accommodate me" (*Par.* 26. 97). The notion of "a pig in a poke" is fitted only to comedy.

In the *Vita Nuova*, Dante speaks of pilgrims as normal in the life of the roads. So in the highest heaven the sightseer—with unquenchable thought of his reminiscences when back on earth—compares himself with "the pilgrim who with enjoyment gazes about in the church he has vowed to visit, and even then imagines telling what it is like" (*Par.* 31. 43).

There are also comparisons in which the interest is less in the scene from life than in the object presenting likeness. These may be so matter-of-fact that Dante seems through them to indicate the mind of his fictitious traveler, sometimes moving on no exalted plane. The pit in which Pope Nicholas pays the penalty for simony is prosaically like those connected with the font in the Baptistery of San Giovanni in Florence. Indeed the traveler Dante (dare we say the historical Dante?) once broke one of them. Equally prosaically, the face of the gigantic Nimrod is "as long and as broad as the pine cone at Saint Peter's in Rome" (*Inf.* 31. 58). Such apparently literal comparisons become poetical. The traveler, approaching the giants around the walled pit of Hell, sees what a plain man would: a city with a round wall surmounted by towers. This simple equivalence becomes one of the poem's memorable passages:

In su la cerchia tonda
Montereggion di torri si corona.

Above her rounded wall Montereggione is crowned with towers (*Inf.* 31. 40).

Perhaps the imaginary traveler's amusingly prosaic mind is most evident when he looks at the half moon from Purgatory; she is "shaped like a big copper kettle that shines brightly" (*Purg.* 18. 78). This is the kettle seen from the side; it appears straight across the top, and the remainder is a half circle; it approaches in shape the waning moon and, as brightly polished, resembles her in color and luster. In Paradise the sparks in which souls reside are twice treated literally:

As at the stirring of burned logs countless sparks rise—from which fools tell fortunes—I saw rise up more than a thousand lights (*Par.* 18. 100).

In the same way as iron throws out sparks when it boils, the circles threw out sparks (*Par.* 28. 89).

Even the admired description of the Venetian navyyard, with its details of boat repairing, first says that the pitch seen in Hell was like that used in Venice (*Inf.* 21. 7).

GENERALLY RECOGNIZED COMEDY

A number of passages in the *Commedia* have, by one or more writers, been labeled deliberately comic. Such a choice depends on the reader and even on his mood when he reads. A few passages are here considered.

Minos, the judge of Hell, a dignified figure in the *Aeneid*, by Dante is made grotesque. He circles his tail around himself as many times as are needed to indicate the number of the circle to which a sinner under judgment is assigned (*Inf.* 5. 6, 11; 27. 124). Minos' position, with Dante's repetition of the "belting," suggests that dignity is not the first quality of the *Inferno.*

In the forest of the suicides, the traveler sees two souls running at full speed pursued by savage dogs. One of them, failing to keep the necessary pace, shouts to the other: "Lano, your legs were not so speedy at the jousts of the Toppo" (*Inf.* 13. 120). At the jousts or battle of Pieve al Toppo, Lano was killed as though he could not run fast enough to save himself. It is the jest of the "Battle of the Spurs." Ariosto puts it thus: "He who wanted to escape had no better weapon than the one he carries lowest down [*i.e.*, his shoes]. Lucky is he whose horse is a runner, for the amble and the trot are not worth much here" (*Orlando Furioso* 26. 25). Similar is the joke repeated by the soldiers of modern wars: "I got one of the enemy; he had heart failure trying to catch me."

There are also the mock-heroic passage of *Inferno* 31, the traveler's discovery that one P has gone from his forehead (*Purg.* 12, 127), and the recognition of Virgil by Statius (*Purg.* 21. 103). Even in the *Paradiso*, comedy has been recognized in the use of "you" rather than the less respectful "thou" to Cacciaguida (*Par.* 16. 10), and in Beatrice's "not merely in my eyes is Paradise" (18. 20). Once the returned traveler remembers that he smiled in amusement, as from the Heaven of the Fixed Stars he looked down upon the remainder of the world: "With my gaze I returned through all of the seven spheres, and I saw this globe such that I smiled at its mean appearance" (*Par.* 22. 133). The earth, "that tiny bit of ground that makes us so proud" (22. 151), is comic to the observer because foolish men make it so important.

Of all the comic passages, the most extensive and usually recognized is that dealing with the Malebranche, or Badclaws, occupying *Inferno* 21, 22 and nearly half of 23. Coming to the elevated center of the arched medieval bridge over the fifth *bolgia*, Virgil and his pupil look down into the trench below them. It is full of boiling pitch, like that used in making boats watertight. Nothing is to be seen except the bubbles from the heat. Suddenly Virgil cries: "Watch out, watch out!" and pulls his charge to him. What happened then the returned tourist narrates:

I turned like a man who cannot wait in his impatience to see something he needs to run away from, and yet sudden fear so takes his strength that he does not stop to look. I saw behind me a black devil come running over the bridge. Oh, how savage he

looked! And how dangerous he seemed as he moved, with his wings
spread, and so light of foot as he was! On his shoulder, which was
lean and strong, a sinner rested on both haunches and the devil
held him by gripping the tendons of his feet. From the bridge
we were on, the devil said: "O Badclaws, here is one of the magis-
trates of Lucca, Santa Zita's city. Stick him into the pitch; I am
going back for more to that city which has plenty for me. Every
man there is a grafter, except Bonturo. For money, in that city
they make *no* into *yes*." Into the ditch he chucked him and along
the hard rock he went back; never was a mastiff let loose so swift
in following a thief. The sinner went under and came up twisted.
But the devils, from whom we were hidden by the bridge, yelled:
"The Holy Face of Lucca doesn't matter here. You don't swim
here as you did in the Serchio. If you don't want our hooks, don't
rise out of the pitch." Then they nicked him with more than a
hundred prongs, saying: "You have to dance under cover here, so,
if you can, in secret you may play at Odd and Even." In the same
way cooks make their helpers push meat down into the middle
of a kettle with their hooks, to keep it from floating. My good
teacher said: "So they can't see you are here, squat down behind
a rock that will give you some cover; and whatever harm is threat-
ened me, don't be afraid, for I understand the business and have
been in such a tussle before." Then he went down from the end
of the bridge and when he stepped on the sixth embankment, he
needed to show a bold face. With the speed and the noise of dogs
rushing out against a poor little man, who at once calls for help
where he stands, the devils came out from under the bridge and
raised all their flesh hooks to hit him. But he shouted: "Don't be
ugly. Before any of your hooks hits me, let one of you step forward
to listen to me, and then think about using your hooks on me."
They all yelled: "You go, Badtail." So one of them started and
the others stood still. He came up to Virgil saying [to the other
devils]: "What good will it do him?" My teacher replied: "Do you
suppose, Badtail, that I could have come as far as this, safe from
all the weapons of Hell, without the will of God and favoring fate?
Let me go on, because it is Heaven's will that I show somebody
this wild road." Then his pride so fell that he let his hook drop
to his feet and said to the rest: "Now we can't hurt him." And
my guide said to me: "You who are all hunched up among the
rocks of the bridge, now you can safely come to me again." Then
I started and quickly joined him, but the devils all moved forward
in such a way that I was afraid they wouldn't keep their agreement.
So once I saw the infantry afraid who came out of Caprona on
terms, when they saw themselves among so many enemies. I
crowded as close to my guide as I could and did not take my eyes
from their looks, which were not good. They lowered their flesh

hooks and said to one another: "Shall I touch him on the rump?"
And they replied: "Yes, give him a nick." But the devil who had
talked with my guide at once turned and said: "Steady, steady,
Bigcomber." Then he said to us: "You can't go farther by this
bridge, because the sixth arch lies down in the ditch entirely
smashed. If you really want to go farther, move on along this bank.
Nearby is another bridge that gives passage. Yesterday, five hours
later than this present moment, it was one thousand two hundred
and sixty-six years since passage here was broken off. I am sending
in that direction some of my men to see if anybody is airing himself. Go with them; they won't hurt you." And at once he said:
"Move forward, Wildhunter, and Brinerubber and you, Uglydog;
Curlybeard is to command the ten. Hotblast can go too, and
Uglydragon, Boartusk, Dogscratcher and Devilmaycare and Crazy
Redskin. Inspect all the boiling glue. These men are to be secure
as far as the next bridge, which goes over the dens all complete."
"Oh, teacher, what do I see?" I cried, "Oh, let us go alone, without any escort, if you know where to go, because I'm not asking
for escort. If you are as wide awake as usual, you see how they are
grinding their teeth, and their eyes threaten us with damage."
He answered me: "Don't be afraid; let them grind their teeth as
they like; they do it for the sinners who are boiling." The devils
turned on the left-hand bank. But first each one scraped his tongue
between his teeth as a salute to their leader; and he made a
trumpet of his arse.

CANTO 22

I have seen horsemen changing position and beginning combat
and drawing up for review and sometimes retreating. I have seen
plunderers in your territory, O Aretines, and I have seen foragers
march; I have seen tournaments celebrated and jousts run, sometimes with trumpets and sometimes with bells, with kettledrums
and with signals from a castle, both by Italian methods and for-
eign ones. But never until then did I see cavalry move in response
to such a strange horn, or footmen, or a ship on indications from
land or from star. We went along with the ten devils. Oh, savage
companions! but in church with saints and in a tavern with gluttons. I was intent on the pitch, to see everything the *bolgia* held,
and the people boiling there. Like dolphins when they signal to
sailors with the ridge of the back to make every effort for saving
their ship, so sometimes to lighten their pain, some of the sinners
showed their backs and hid themselves quicker than lightning.
And as at the edge of a ditch, frogs rest with only their noses out
of the water so that they conceal their feet and their bodies, there
were sinners all along. But when Curlybeard came near, like those
frogs they went back under the boiling pitch. I saw—and still my

heart beats faster when I think of it—one of them wait, just as
happens when one frog stays and another disappears. Then Dogscratcher, who was nearest him, caught his hook in the sinner's
pitchy hair and dragged him out, looking like an otter. I now knew
all the devils' names, I had so marked them when they were chosen,
and when they named each other, I took note. "O Redskin, set
your claws to his back until you skin him," yelled all those cursed
fellows together. And I said: "Teacher, learn, if you can, who the
wretch is who has come into his enemies' hands." My guide went
close to him, asking who he was, and he replied: "I was born in
the kingdom of Navarre. My mother, who bore me to a ne'er-do-
well waster of himself and his property, put me in the service of
a baron. Next I was servant to the good king Tebaldo. There I
went to practising graft, for which I pay the penalty in this heat."
Then Boartusk, from whose mouth stuck out on each side a tusk
like a boar's, made him feel how one of them could tear. The mouse
had fallen among bad cats. Curlybeard held him tight with his
arms and said: "Keep off, as long as I have him between my
prongs." And he turned his face to my master, saying: "Keep asking, if you want to know more about him, before the others spoil
him." So my guide said: "Now tell us: Among the criminals, do
you know of any Italian under the pitch?" He replied: "I just now
left a man who was from near Italy. Don't I wish I too were covered
up like him, so that I wouldn't fear either claw or hook!" Then
Hotblast said: "We've waited too long," and snatched the man's
arm with his hook, so that, tearing it, he carried away a muscle.
Uglydragon also wanted to get hold of him down on his legs, so
that their sergeant turned this way and that with an angry look.
When they were restrained a bit, my guide without delay questioned the man, who kept looking at his wound: "Who was the
man from whom you say you parted unluckily to come to the
bank?" He answered: "It was Brother Gomita of Gallura, full of
every sort of fraud, who had his master's enemies in his power and
treated them so that each one was grateful to him; he took from
them money for himself and left them unarraigned, as they say.
In other duties too he was no small grafter, but the very chief of
them. His companion is Master Michael Zanche of Logodoro,
and their tongues are never tired of talking about Sardinia. Alas!
see how the other is grinding his teeth! I should like to say more,
but I'm afraid he's getting ready to scratch my itching hide."
And their big chief, turning to Devilmaycare, who was rolling his
eyes to find a place to strike, said: "Move off, evil bird." Then
the frightened Navarrese went on saying: "If you want to see or
hear Tuscans or Lombards, I will make some of them come. But
let the Badclaws keep a little distant, so the souls will not fear
their attacks, and I, sitting right here, will get seven of them to

come instead of me only, when I whistle according to our habit when one of us gets out." Uglydog raised his snout at such a speech, shaking his head, and said: "Just listen to the trick he has thought up for getting under again." Then the sinner, who was rich in schemes, answered: "I'm a very spiteful trickster when I bring more trouble on my friends." Wildhunter did not hold back, but opposing the others said to him: "If you dive, I shall follow not at just a gallop but I shall flap my wings over the pitch. We'll leave the ridge and the bank will hide us, so we can see if you by yourself are smarter than we are." O you who read, you will hear of new sport. Each devil turned his eyes toward the other slope, he first who was most opposed to doing so. The man from Navarre chose his moment well, braced his feet on the ground and at the same instant leaped and freed himself from the chief devil. They all felt the sting of blame for this, especially the devil who had caused the failure. So he started with a yell: "You are caught." But that did not help him, since his wings could not move faster than fear. The grafter went under the pitch, and the devil threw back his chest, flying up. In the same way the duck makes haste to plunge under when the falcon comes near, and the pursuer rises up wrathful and defeated. Brinerubber, maddened by the trick, flew right behind Wildhunter, hoping the shade would escape, for the sake of having a fight. So when the grafter disappeared, he turned his claws on his companion and grappled with him over the ditch. But Wildhunter was also a good sparrow hawk at clawing, and both fell into the middle of the boiling pond. The hot pitch was a quick ungrappler, but all the same there was no getting out —the pitch had made their wings so sticky. Curlybeard, annoyed like the rest of his troop, had four of them fly to the other bank with all their hooks, and quickly they went to their stations on either side. They stretched out their flesh hooks to the devils stuck in the pitch, who already were cooked inside their crusts. And we left them in such trouble.

CANTO 23

. . . As we moved on, a thought came to me that doubled my earlier fear. What I thought was: "These devils are because of us so tricked to their injury with such a hoax that I believe it will make them very angry. If wrath is mixed with their malice, they will follow us more savagely than a dog does a rabbit that it snaps up." I already felt all my hair standing straight up with fear, and my attention was turned backward, when I said: "Teacher, if you don't hide yourself and me quickly, I am afraid of the Bad-claws. Already they are after us. I imagine them so strongly that now I hear them." Virgil answered: "If I were a lead-backed mirror, I would not catch your likeness quicker than I realize what you are thinking. Moreover, your thoughts have just assumed the same action and the same face as mine, so that I make a single idea of both. If the right slope lies so that we can get down into the next *bolgia,* we shall escape the pursuit we imagine." He had not finished telling me his plan when I saw the devils coming with their wings spread, not far off, expecting to catch us. My guide at once seized me like a mother who, roused by a noise and seeing flames mounting up near her, snatches her child and flees and does not pause, more careful of him than of herself, so that she wears only a shirt. And from the summit of the solid bank he let himself slide on his back down the sloping cliff which formed one wall of the next *bolgia.* Water never ran so fast along a race to turn the wheel of a mill on land when that water comes nearest to the paddles as my teacher did down that cliff, carrying me on his breast as though I were his child, not his companion. No sooner were our feet on the bottom of the gorge than the devils were on the summit above us. But we had no fear, because the high Providence that made them servants of the fifth *bolgia* took from all of them power to leave it (*Inf.* 21. 25–23. 57).

This comic tale of the Malebranche so pleases Dante that moral purpose flags. He forgets narrative consistency, beginning with a devil hastening to Lucca and ending with the restriction of the fiends to their own *bolgia.* Moreover, the grafters, though glad to escape the sticky boiling pitch, find it a desirable refuge (22. 68) from the rending hooks of the guardians and move easily in and out of it. Yet those demons, when they fall into its fiery viscosity, can escape only with assistance, and are quickly cooked inside their crusts, like meat pies. The comic suggestion of the kitchen is carried on from the lines in which the devils pushing the sinners under the surface are likened to kitchen workers pushing meat down in boiling water. Satire of the military epic appears in the pseudowarlike evolutions of the devils, with mock-heroic quality reinforced at the beginning of Canto 22. The last line of the Rabelaisian Canto 21 may be contrasted with *At tuba terribilem sonitum procul aere canoro/ Increpuit; sequitur clamor, caelumque remugit* (*Aeneid* 9. 503). Apologetically, Dante's son Pietro says that his father reports "what those devils did, 'de ano etc.' [*sic*], that he might show the base manners and acts of such as they. He is excused for saying such things because he is a poet, whose business is to bring about something tending to good by an indecent pres-

entation, as Thomas says on the first of the *Posterior Analytics*."
On the beginning of Canto 22, Pietro comments:

The author wishes to excuse himself for the base speech that he
wrote at the end of the preceding canto by taking over the words
of Socrates: "I judge that what is base when done cannot even
be spoken of decently." But since speeches are to be formed according to the matter dealt with, as the Philosopher says in the
first of the *Metaphysics,* so the author writes. What Tully says
bears on this: "In a coarse matter to use refined speech is in-
correct."

This is Chaucer's apology for his "Miller's Tale," concluding
with a caution to be heeded by readers of Dante: "And eek
men shal nat maken ernest of game." Benvenuto da Imola finds
moral reasons for Dante's Milesian tale, but also comments:
"I wonder whether our author . . . was not laughing when he
feigned these events with his mind or when he was writing
them with his pen." If Pietro di Dante had said something of the
sort, we could feel that he had more sympathy with his father
and better comprehension of his work.

Dante's traveler "doth protest too much" for the sake of
calling attention to an experience that would have delighted
Baron Munchausen:

I saw something that I would be afraid, without more proof, only
to relate, if it were not that I gain safety from conscience—that
good companion who sets a man free under the armor of knowing
he is blameless. Absolutely I saw—and I think I see it still—a body
walking along without a head, just as the others of that wretched
flock were walking along. And the body held the head by the
hair, dangling from his hand like a lantern, and the head looked
at us and said: "Oh me!" Of himself he made a lantern, and they
were two in one and one in two. How this can be, He knows who
so ordains. When close to the foundation of the bridge, the shade
raised the arm holding his head to get his words nearer to me
(28. 113).

Here the poet makes his mock apology, dealing at once with the
comic grotesque of the scene and the serious matter of civil
war which it signifies. So far as I have observed, the commentators treat this passage with seriousness, even to the extent of
making Dante's asseveration emphasize his solid poetic belief in

the reality of his inventions. As to them, this passage can be called recognized comedy only by a sort of *lucus a non lucendo*. But we can turn to the testimony of the poets. The comedy of the situation was evident to the author of *Sir Gawain and the Green Knight*, composed in the fourteenth century and resting on earlier tales of magic wonders. As part of the trick he plays on Sir Gawain by enchantment, the knight allows himself to be beheaded, as it appears. He then mounts his horse, holding his head by the hair. Toward the dais on which King Arthur sits, he turns the face, which lifts up its eyelids and addresses Sir Gawain. Ariosto later used the comic possibilities of the situation in the combat of knights with the enchanted giant Orrilo. When he is beheaded and his head thrown into the river, he swims after it, seizes it by the hair or nose, replaces it, and returns to the combat. Finally Astolfo cuts it off and rides away; the giant in pursuit wishes to cry out: "Stop, stop, come back," but the knight has carried away his mouth. I cannot but feel that Ariosto, who knew Dante well, profited from Bertran de Born's example; at any rate he has added to his basis in Boiardo's *Orlando Innamorato* such a detail as holding the head by the hair and the possibility of speech from the severed head. But perhaps he drew on romances now lost which Dante also had read.

4 · Religion

In Dante's *Monarchia* appears his prosaic view of the relations of Church and Roman Empire, if ever he wrote scientifically rather than poetically. The first two books consider the divine origin of the empire. In their slight reference to the Church, they briefly attack those but pretending to be her sons (*Mon.* 2. 11, 12). In the third book, Dante professes such respect for the Church as an affectionate son owes his parents and declares himself loyal to the pope. Yet he attempts to destroy any ecclesiastical claim to temporal power. He condemns Constantine for weakening the empire by unjust grant of some of her wealth and functions to the pope. He cannot find in the Bible any allowance of temporal power to the clergy (3. 14). The Church, especially her chief shepherd, the pope, should feed her sheep and lambs (3. 15). The pontiff is to lead men to eternal life in accord with revelation (3. 16). No details of this function or means for performing it appear, nor is there any notice of the clergy other than the pope or any suggestion of the sacraments or of any ecclesiastical functions. In the last paragraph of the *Monarchia*, Dante concludes that the activity of the monarch is necessary to the world, that the Roman people justly obtained supreme rule, and that the sole ruler is directly dependent on God. Then, as though by an afterthought, he continues:

This truth is, however, not to be so strictly accepted that the Roman Emperor is not to be in anything subordinate to the Roman

Pontiff, since the happiness of mortals on earth is to some extent brought about for the sake of immortal happiness. Caesar therefore should show Peter such respect as a firstborn son should show to his father, so that, made splendid by the light of paternal favor, he may more vigorously enlighten the sphere of the earth, over which he has been set by That One who alone is the director of all spiritual and temporal things (3. 16).

This tardy recognition of the pontiff's office is not intended to diminish the force of anything said earlier, for the *Monarchia* concludes with a stout assertion of the independence of the emperor as God's immediate appointee.

In Dante's other minor writings nothing contradicts the *Monarchia*. In the *Convivio* he accepts the hours as the Church arranges them, mentions the orders of angels, approves the teaching of the Church, "the Bride of Christ," that the angels are innumerable, and allows that "as Holy Church teaches, who cannot speak falsely," the Empyrean is the abode of the blessed (*Conv.* 2. 3, 4; 3. 6; 4. 23).

In the *Comedy*, doctrine appears in the examination of the traveler on faith given by Saint Peter, the first holder of the keys, the first pope. The dramatic quality of the passage does not forbid clarity:

"Faith is the substance of things hoped for; it causes the expectation of things not seen. This seems to me what it is. . . . The free outpouring of the Holy Spirit which covers the Old and the New Parchments has given me so cutting an argument for Faith that, compared with it, I hold every other demonstration dull."

Then I heard Saint Peter say: "The Old and the New Proposition that so convinced you—why do you believe them divine utterances?"

I replied: "The proof revealing the truth to me is in the events that occurred, for which Nature never heated iron or pounded anvil."

The answer was: "Tell me, who makes you certain there were such events? The very book you are trying to establish, and nothing else, swears it to you."

"If the world turned to Christianity," I said, "without miracles, that alone is so great a miracle that the others are not a hundredth part of it, because you went into the field poor and hungry to sow the good seed, which then became a vine and now is turned to a thorn. . . .

"But now," I said to Saint Peter, "you wish me to show the

form of my active belief, and you ask also its cause. So I reply:
"I believe in one God single and eternal, who moves all the Heaven,
though himself unmoved, with love and longing. And for such a
belief I have not merely physical and metaphysical proofs, but I
also get it from the truth that rains down on me from above by
means of Moses, the Prophets, the Psalms, the Gospel, and by
means of you who wrote when the fiery spirit inspired you. And I
believe in three Eternal Persons, and believe them a being so single
and so triple that it allows *are* and *is* to be united. The profound
divine relationship that I have just mentioned, the Gospel teaching
many times impresses on my mind. This is the beginning; this
is the spark that grows to so bright a flame and shines in me like
a star in Heaven" (*Par.* 24. 64–147).

Simple is the creed here expressed. It is so brief as to exclude
matters that Dante held important. For example, in the *Convivio* he asserts that "of all bestial opinions, that is most foolish,
most disgusting, and most harmful which declares that after
this life there is no other." After some discussion he says that
"the completely true teaching of Christ, the way, the truth, and
the light, assures us of it" (2. 8). Dante the traveler speaks of
the Virgin as "the fair flower whom I always call upon both
morning and evening" (*Par.* 23. 88). Her great importance
throughout the *Commedia* is axiomatic. Yet two such weighty
matters do not appear in a statement so pleasing to Saint Peter
that

as a master who gets a message that pleases him, for which he
embraces his servant in thanks for the news as soon as he has
finished his tale, thus, blessing me with a song, as soon as I was
silent, three times the apostolic light at whose command I had
spoken encircled me. So much what I said pleased him (*Par.* 24.
148).

If such a confession so gratifies the first holder of the keys, can
the poet think it less than enough for the popes of the fourteenth century, for such a pope as Dante's *Monarchia* implies?
The "good Christian's" examination by Saint James and Saint
John harmonizes with that by Saint Peter.

Dante's Saint Peter holds early popes worthy to succeed
him:

The bride of Christ was not nourished on my blood and that of
Linus and of Cletus to be used for the gaining of gold, but to gain

happiness in Heaven. Sixtus and Pius and Calixtus and Urban shed their blood after much weeping. It was not our intention that on the right hand of our successors part of the Christian people should sit, part on the left hand, nor that the keys granted me should become an emblem on a standard for fighting against the baptized, nor that I should be a figure on a seal for exemptions sold and deceptive, for which often I blush and throw out sparks. We here in Heaven see in all the pastures ravening wolves in shepherds' clothing. O vengeance of God, why do you still delay? The men of Cahors and the Gascons [on the papal throne] prepare to drink our blood. O good beginning, to what a wretched end have you been forced to fall! But the High Providence which through Scipio defended for Rome the empire of the world, will quickly rescue [the Church], as I believe (*Par.* 27. 40).

When speaking in the Church's behalf, Saint Peter makes Providence the protector of the Roman Empire, which Dante in his *Monarchia* declares, like the Church, divine in origin. This touch is especially appropriate when the Church's spiritual quality—the only quality allowed her in Dante's treatise—is in question. So Linus and the early papal martyrs contrast with popes of Dante's time, John XXII from Cahors and Clement V from Gascony. In Heaven there shines the light of one pope only, John XXI, mentioned as Peter of Spain without reference to his high office. In Purgatory, Martin IV pays the penalty for gluttony; no further indication of his character is given. Adrian V, undergoing purification from avarice (*Purg.* 19. 99), is treated with sympathy by Dante. The other popes of Dante's lifetime are marked out for punishment in Hell and otherwise attacked for their wickedness. Nicholas III is among the simoniacs (*Inf.* 19. 70). Boniface VIII is by anticipation similarly condemned and is elsewhere censured (*Inf.* 19. 53; 27. 70, 85; *Purg.* 20. 86; *Par.* 12. 90; 27. 22; 30. 148). Clement V is also among the simonists and is condemned in other passages (*Inf.* 19. 82; *Purg.* 20. 91; *Par.* 17. 82; 27. 58; 30. 142). The avaricious in Hell are "clerics, popes, and cardinals" (*Inf.* 7. 47). Dante's characters inveigh against not only papal wickedness but against all corruption in the Church. With an echo of the *Monarchia*, Marco Lombardo says that

the Church of Rome, by mixing within herself the two kinds of authority [religious and political] falls in the mud and defiles herself and her burden (*Purg.* 16. 127).

Folco of Toulouse bewails the avarice of the ecclesiastical organ-
ization:

Because of this [love of money] the Gospel and the great Doctors
are abandoned, and only the Decretals are so studied that their
margins show it. That is what interests the Pope and the cardinals.
Their thoughts do not go to Nazareth, where Gabriel spread his
wings. Yet the Vatican and the other chosen parts of Rome, which
entomb the soldiers who followed Peter, speedily shall be free
from adultery (*Par.* 9. 133).

Thomas Aquinas and Saint Bonaventura deplore the degeneracy
of the Dominicans and the Franciscans (*Par.* 11. 124; 12. 115).
Saint Benedict thinks his order corrupt: "The buildings that
once were abbeys are now dens, and the cowls are sacks full of
bad flour" (*Par.* 22. 76). Religious teaching has failed, declares
Beatrice:

Every writer strives for appearance and produces his own inventions, and the preachers discuss these things and do not mention
the Gospel. One says that the Moon reversed herself at Christ's
Passion and came between [Sun and Earth], so that sunlight did
not pour down. Yet he lies, for of itself the light hid itself, so that
such an eclipse affected the Spanish and the Indians as well as the
Jews. In a year more such fables are shouted out in the pulpits
everywhere than there are Lapi and Bindi in Florence. Hence the
sheep, which do not understand, come back from feeding fed with
wind, and not to see their injury does not protect them. Christ did
not say to his first apostles: "Go and preach nonsense to the
world," but gave them a true foundation, and that only was heard
from their mouths, so that for fighting to kindle the faith they
made shield and lance of the Gospel. Now men go to preach with
jokes and clownishness, and if they raise a laugh their hoods swell,
and they ask nothing else. But such a bird is nesting in the cowl
that if the people saw it, they would understand the pardoning
they rely on. For this reason folly so increases on earth that without support by any testimony the people rush to believe every
promise. This fattens the Saint Anthony pig and many others who
are still bigger hogs, as they pay counterfeit money (*Par.* 29. 94).

Various other references to the clergy are not complimentary.
Among the joys of Paradise the traveler exclaims:

O senseless trouble of mortal men, how defective the arguments
that make you beat your wings on earth! One man takes to law,
one to [medical] aphorisms, one employs himself with priest craft,

another in ruling through force or deceit, another in stealing, and another with citizen's business; one gives effort to fleshly delights and another surrenders to laziness (*Par.* 11. 1–9).

The tone of this is like that of Dante's assertion:

He cannot be called a true philosopher who is a friend of knowledge for profit, as are the lawyers, the physicians, and almost all the clergy, who carry on study not in order to learn but in order to get money or high position (*Convivio* 3. 11).

The word "priest" is applied by Guido da Montefeltro in Hell to Pope Boniface VIII, the "grand priest" responsible for his damnation (*Inf.* 27. 70). It occurs also in the passage on the "courteous priest," the "impious pastor" who, for the sake of party, delivered to death at their enemies' hands four men who came to him for refuge (*Par.* 9. 53, 58). "Cleric" is four times used of sinners punished in Hell (*Inf.* 7. 38, 46; 15. 106; 18. 117). "Shepherd" (*pastor*) several times appears in invectives against the papacy (*Inf.* 19. 83, 106; *Purg.* 16. 98; *Par.* 9. 132; 15. 144; 27. 55). It also signifies "modern pastors who order some of their servants to steady them on both sides, and others to lead them (they are so heavy!), and others to prop them from behind. Their mantles so spread over their mules that there are two animals under one hide" (*Par.* 21. 130). To sarcastic Manfred, the archbishop who disinterred his body and gave it insulting burial is "the shepherd of Cosenza" (*Purg.* 3. 124). "Shepherd" also appears with no suggestion of sarcasm; Aquinas applies it to Saint Dominic (*Par.* 5. 77; 6. 17; 11. 131).

The word "sacraments" is not found in the *Comedy*. Baptism, as Virgil said to his pupil, was "the gate of the faith that you hold" (*Inf.* 4. 36); without it, the "innocence" of infants was confined to Limbo (*Par.* 32. 83). In his unquenchable desire to return to Florence, Dante says that he hopes "at the font of his baptism to receive the poet's wreath" (*Par.* 25. 8). Yet here, as in another reference to baptism, the tone is rather patriotic than religious (*Par.* 15. 134; cf. 16. 25). Priestly confession serves the poet only for an image of himself as he stands by the hole in which Pope Nicholas was placed as an assassin might be (*Inf.* 19. 49). The traveler confesses his shortcomings only to Beatrice (*Purg.* 31. 6, 38). Guido da Montefeltro uses the word "confession" in a religious sense as he speaks of his faith in an ineffective absolution (*Inf.* 27. 83, 118).

Excommunication is a serious matter. For all his attack on the clergy, Manfred tells the travelers that a man who dies in contumacy of the Church must spend in Purgatory thirty times the period of his defiance, even if he repents (*Purg.* 3. 136). Yet he furnishes no details.

In explaining vows, Beatrice says that "Holy Church absolves them" (*Par.* 5. 35), though she does not tell how, vaguely declaring that Christians "have the teaching of the New and the Old Testaments, and the Pastor of the Church [the Pope] as guide" (*Par.* 5. 76). Such possibility of guidance in interpreting the Bible appears in Dante's writings here only. Is Beatrice to be understood as speaking the author's mind? Dante gives little impression of hesitating to interpret for himself "the Scripture which is above" Christians as their proper guide for conduct (*Par.* 19. 83). His Biblical quotations and references number above two hundred.

The *Comedy* offers nothing connected with the functioning of church services, though it tells how Dante broke part of the font at San Giovanni (*Inf.* 19. 20), and the thief Vanni Fucci admits stealing from the sacristy "some splendid furnishings" (*Inf.* 24. 138). Seemingly Dante makes him imply that he was therefore worse than a merely secular thief. The word "altar" is not used in the *Commedia*.

Thus in the poem the Church seems treated as in the *Monarchia*. Dante expresses great respect for her, but that respect—however sincere—is not particularized. What in detail any Church officer is to do—except that the wicked among them should reform—we do not hear. Preachers are to refrain from improper sermons, but receive no positive directions (*Par.* 29. 109). A highly religious poet could hardly say less about the ceremonies and practices of the Church. His sole reference to organ music (*Par.* 17. 44), for example, is less descriptive than Milton's lines

> Let the pealing organ blow,
> To the full-voiced choir below,
> In service high and anthems clear,
> As may with sweetness, through mine ear,

Dissolve me into ecstasies,
And bring all Heaven before mine eyes (*Il Pens.*).

Dante the traveler asserts that he prays morning and evening
to the Virgin (*Par.* 23. 89), yet nowhere indicates that any of
his devotions require ecclesiastical assistance. His is a personal
religion. Can we infer the same thing for the historical Dante?

THE EMPTY CHARIOT

The most elaborate of Dante's allegories, apart from that
pervasive one showing through the state of the dead the truth
about living men, is that of the Earthly Paradise. It has two
parts: the first is a procession in which the books of the Bible
and the virtues, pagan and Christian, accompany a chariot
drawn by a griffin; the second shows in allegory the Church in
the Divine Plan, with her relation to the politics of Dante's
time and to political power in general. The whole is entwined
with the appearance of Beatrice and her reception of her lover.

To consider details, as the visitor walks along the River
Lethe, his attention is seized by sweet music. Soon, as he mistakenly thinks, he sees in the distance seven trees of gold; in
reality they are seven candles, with flames so large that as they
move they leave in the air stripes colored like the rainbow. Then
come in procession twenty-four old men, representing the books
of the Old Testament, followed by four beasts, the familiar
symbols of the writers of the four Gospels. In the midst of the
four is a two-wheeled chariot, such as the Romans used for
triumphal processions. This is drawn by a griffin, an animal
half lion, half eagle. How is it harnessed? The griffin is said to
draw by its neck (*Purg.* 29. 108), as though with a band of
leather, yet the chariot has extending from its front a single
pole such as is used for two animals, instead of the parallel
shafts provided for a single beast of draft. The griffin's eagle
wings extend between the inner ribbon left by the candles and
the outer three, rising so high in the air as to be out of sight.
Three ladies, one red, one emerald, one snowy white, dance
by the right wheel. By the left wheel dance four clothed in
purple. Her three eyes identify one of these as Prudence; hence
the other three are Justice, Temperance, and Fortitude. If so,

the three dancers, as their colors indicate, are Love, Hope, and Faith. No rider in the chariot is hinted at. Here is a situation strange to the triumphs of Rome and of the Renaissance: a triumphal procession with no triumphing hero. Some of Dante's other uses of the word "triumph" imply a procession, and commonly an individual triumphs, such as Caesar (*Purg.* 26. 77; *Par.* 1. 29), the poet (*Par.* 1. 29), Christ (9. 120; 23. 20), and Saint Peter (23. 136). In describing the car drawn by the griffin, he mentions the triumphs of Scipio and Augustus (*Purg.* 29. 116). It is strange, then, that he gives no rider to the chariot in this procession. Following the chariot are two old men, one looking like a physician and the other carrying a sword: Saint Luke's book of Acts and Saint Paul's Epistles. Then come four of humble appearance: the minor Epistles. Last is an old man sleeping: the Revelation of Saint John. The procession then pauses.

The animals and men symbolize the books of the Bible, not their writers. If authors were indicated, Saint Jerome's number of twenty-four for the Old Testament would not fit. For the New Testament, Saint John would appear three times, for his Gospel, the Epistles bearing his name, and Revelation. These books are symbolized by the eagle, one humble man, and the old man asleep. Failing to distinguish the books of the Bible represented in allegory from their writers, the early commentators had difficulties in explaining the procession. Dante's son Pietro makes the twenty-four elders the books of the Old Testament. The four beasts he expounds as the Evangelists themselves, not as their four Gospels. The two old men who follow, the sword-bearer and the physician, are Saint Paul and Saint Luke. The four who come next are to Pietro doctors: Augustine, Ambrose, Gregory, and Jerome. The old man asleep who concludes the procession is Saint Bernard. With minor variations, Jacopo della Lana, Benvenuto da Imola, and the *Anonimo Fiorentino* make the same type of comment. To Buti, however, the animals signify the four Gospels rather than their writers, and the seven men are the remaining books of the New Testament.

Buti's exegesis, making the procession a consistent representation of the whole Bible, has generally been accepted since the sixteenth century. To Dante the passage probably seemed so clear that his intention could not be mistaken, yet his own son misinterpreted it. Can a better illustration be found of Dante's remark that allegory requires the author's explanation (*Convivio* 1. 2)? In the same passage he hints that readers can be trained to understand allegories. The training of some of the interpreters of the procession in Eden was not adequate; otherwise they would have been in agreement. Or are we to suppose that mutually exclusive allegories can be hidden under one literal covering? Even the now prevailing interpretation of the groups accompanying the chariot assumes a systematic allegory of the whole Bible. Can we be sure that it was intended? Such an allegory is a simple one. Animals and men represent, we suppose, historical characters or books. Identification seems easy. Luke, supposed the author of Acts, is in Colossians 4. 14 called a physician. How could the fourteenth-century Benvenuto da Imola have avoided identifying a physician connected with Saint Paul or with the New Testament as Luke? Yet Benvenuto thinks the allegorical physician not Luke, because that evangelist has already appeared as the ox among the four beasts. If practiced allegorists fail (that is, if modern interpreters are right) in so simple an identification, can they be trusted when one of the truths hidden by the allegory is announced as an abstraction, such as one of the sacraments or reason or theology? At least an allegorist can avoid the assertion that his interpretation is necessary or certainly true.

After the procession has been viewed, around the chariot rise up—like souls newly embodied at the Resurrection—a hundred angels who throw a cloud of flowers in which Beatrice appears (30. 28).[1] Does she at that moment descend from Heaven

---

[1] How illustrative is the comparison of the hundred angels with souls rising from their tombs at the Resurrection? For one commentator the word "speedy" (30. 14) is the sole explanatory part of the simile: the angels are as rapid as the resurrected dead. But where, in this scene for the eye, do we see the angels standing or flying? Some think them crowded on the chariot. Yet will the chariot accommodate a hundred, however much we reduce the literalness of the round number? These are hardly angels standing on the point of a needle. Is the commentator right who supposes the angels crowding the chariot invisible until now? Do they

(31. 107)? Is it possible that she has been riding in the chariot? In spite of the long time since he has been in his lady's presence, the narrator recognizes her, perceiving the power of the love he felt in boyhood. Weeping because he finds that Virgil has left him, he is arraigned by Beatrice, who tells him he shall have other cause to weep. She is compared with an admiral who walks the length of his ship to direct his entire fleet, though in the chariot she has no space for so much movement. We are then told that she stands in the car, at the left side to be nearer her lover as she rebukes him. Like a proud queen she continues to speak, bringing her hearer to penitent confession. To this rebuke is given much of the thirtieth canto and all of the thirty-first.

Early in the thirty-second, the observer again turns to view the procession, which moves on, bending to the right. Beatrice descends from the chariot near a lofty tree, to which the griffin fastens the car. At this point the reader is again reminded that the griffin, being "double born" (32. 47), is a "beast that is one being only, with two natures" (31. 80, 122; 32. 96). Soon the observer inexplicably falls asleep. Waking, he asks in fear: "Where is Beatrice" (32. 85)? to be told that she sits at the root of the Tree of Knowledge, with the seven nymphs or Virtues around her. "The others, following the griffin, are going away,[2]

vacate the chariot for Beatrice as admiral? Can we imagine the throwing of lilies in such a way that the cloud of flowers rises and falls both inside and outside the chariot (30. 30)? If the simile illustrates more than speed, are we to suppose the angels, like the later dragon (32. 130), rising from the ground like the dead from their graves (30. 13)? Or are we not to ask whence they come? If the angels surround the chariot instead of crowding in it, the flowers when thrown can rise and fall. The crux is in the words *in su* (30. 16); for Dante do they mean not "on" but "near"?

2 This is usually taken to mean: "The others, following the griffin, are going up to Heaven." The last five words represent the *sen vanno suso* of the original. *Suso* usually does mean "up," as in *men vo suso* (*Purg.* 16. 38). However, in *Purg.* 22. 138 *suso* is by some commentators thought not to mean "upward," and in *Inf.* 18. 29 (cf. *Purg.* 11. 29; *Par.* 24. 39) *su per lo ponte* evidently is "across the bridge," with no "up." More generally, the participants in the procession are allegorical; they are not shades. The human and animal figures are Biblical books. The griffin is allegorical, though thrice called a *fiera* ("wild beast") and once an *animale* (*Purg.* 31. 80, 122; 32. 47, 96). In Dante's Heaven there are no allegorical characters, and he puts no mythical animals there, though the latter appear in Hell. Divinity is represented by a point or circles of light.

with a sweeter and nobler song" (32. 89). The less sweet song of
this comparison is the melody Dante heard before the procession
came in sight and as it reached him (29. 22, 36, 51, 85) and as
it moved and paused (32. 33, 62). Thus the procession vanishes
with sweet music as it appeared with such music. We are not
told whence it came or whither it goes. As a spectacular interlude, but only an interlude, it requires no earlier or later
mention.

With the disappearance of the allegorical procession, except
the chariot and the Seven Virtues or nymphs, the atmosphere
becomes more political. Beatrice sits at the root of the Tree of
Knowledge (32. 87). The chariot is bound to the tree, which
has put forth leaves and blossoms on its naked boughs. An eagle
descends from the sky, tearing the bark, flowers, and leaves of
the tree, and so striking the chariot that it reels like a ship in a
tempest yet is unharmed. Then a famished fox appears in
the chariot. Beatrice drives the animal away—how we are not
told. Thereupon the eagle descends upon the chariot, leaving it
"feathered" with eagle plumage. Then a voice from Heaven
says: "Oh my little ship, how badly you are burdened" (Purg.
32. 119). Thereupon from the earth between the chariot wheels
rises a dragon which pierces the car with its tail, then withdraws
its sting and moves away. In an instant the chariot is covered
with feathers, as rich earth is covered with grain; even the
wheels and the pole are feathered. Next, the chariot puts forth
seven heads, three above the pole and one at each corner of the
body; the three heads have each two horns and the four
have one each, ten in all. On the chariot, the observer sees a
harlot seated, with a giant beside her. Even as the two are
kissing, the harlot turns her shifting eyes on the viewer. In
jealousy the giant beats her from head to foot. Then in rage he
looses the transformed chariot—twice called a monster (32. 147,
158)—and drags it through the forest until in the distance the
trees conceal the harlot and the "strange animal" (32. 160),
that is, the transmuted chariot.

When the griffin and the figures symbolizing Scripture de-
part, Beatrice remains as "guardian" of the chariot (32. 95).
Of its various assailants, she opposes only the fox (32. 121),

though she speaks at length on the others (33. 34). Her imperfect guardianship suggests that Dante did not thoroughly work out her function in the Earthly Paradise.

Of the general meaning of this story of the chariot bound to the tree, no readers of the Biblical Revelation 12, 13, 17, and 18 can feel much doubt. Here, however adapted, is the beast with seven heads and ten horns, and here is the harlot on whose forehead was written "Mystery, Babylon the Great, the Mother of Harlots and Abominations of the Earth." This harlot has for so many centuries been interpreted as Rome that we may suppose her to signify papal corruption, so often attacked by Dante. Nevertheless, the diverse expositions of the mysterious Book of Revelation are to be remembered. In an earlier attack on papal avarice, Dante also employs the harlot-beast of Revelation (*Inf.* 19. 106). Dante's son Pietro understands both passages as censures of the dissolute conduct of the popes, although he sees the seven heads as the seven virtues and the ten horns as the Ten Commandments. Yet having no assurance that he heard his father so explain the passage, we must be satisfied with the indications that the poet intends the harlot and the beast as symbols of ecclesiastical corruption. Un-Biblical details also must remain uncertain. Why, for example, is the innocent onlooker a subject of the giant's jealousy (32. 135)? The poet's warning in the *Convivio* must come before us once more: "The true meaning [of one of my poems] cannot be seen by anybody unless I explain it, because that meaning is hidden under the figure of allegory" (1. 2. 17). To the same effect Beatrice speaks to her pupil after the chariot vanishes in the forest: "Perhaps my narrative, dark as Themis and the Sphinx, less convinces you because like them it confuses the intellect, but actions will quickly be Naiades to solve this difficult enigma. . . . I see your intellect made of stone and, as turned stony, so colored that the light of my saying dazzles you" (*Purg.* 33. 46).

Dante's narrative has been as dark to his readers as the allegorical actions were to him when—in his fiction—he observed them. Certainty of more than the Church's corruption by political power and luxury, and inevitable punishment we can hardly attain. Need we ask for more, or does enjoyment of the poem require more? There is no received explanation of the "five hundred ten and five" who is to kill the thief.[3] Dante's great expectations from Henry VII make that monarch an inevitable candidate. But if he be chosen, Dante must be held to have retained in his poem after Henry's death in 1313 a prophecy written before it. Most attempts to make damnatory passages definite break down. On the side of generality may be urged that the feathering of the chariot often is interpreted as the Donation of Constantine in the fourth century, deplored by Dante in *Monarchia* 3. 10, etc., and in *Inferno* 19. 115; *Paradiso* 20. 55. For all the succeeding ages, the Church for Dante showed the ill effects of receiving political power. Would he then have the giant who beats the harlot symbolize one ruler and only him? On the death of Henry VII did Dante give up all expectation of delivery for the Church even in a distant future?

Various other puzzles appear throughout the scenes in the Earthly Paradise. What is the symbolism of the griffin? A chariot must be drawn by some draft animal. The Romans used horses. Petrarch in his *Trionfi* assigned beasts especially fitting. For example, the triumphal car of Chastity is drawn by unicorns, symbol of virginity. Dante suggests no special suitability for his draft animal. It combines the natures of lion and eagle. This double nature has led to a suggestion that it symbolizes Christ. But Christ's two natures are God's and man's (*Par.* 2. 42; 7. 35; 13. 26) though he may be called the Lamb of God (*Purg.* 16. 18; *Par.* 17. 33), the Pelican (*Par.* 25. 113), or the Lion of the Tribe of Judah (Revelation 5. 5). The Pelican is an obvious metaphor for helpfulness, and the animals are Biblical. That the griffin is a "two-formed wild animal" (*Purg.* 32. 96), without other Christly characteristics, is hardly enough to make it a type of the God-man. The "double beast" (*Purg.* 31. 122) is addressed by the characters of the procession: "Happy are you, griffin, that you do not with your beak pluck from this tree fruit sweet to the taste, since it afterward is griping in the bowels" (*Purg.* 32. 43). The "twin born animal" (32. 47)

---

3 Some exegesis as late as 1961 emphasizes Scartazzini's comment on the passage: "Dante wrote *a five hundred ten and five* and not at all *DXV*" (the Roman numerals).

answers in the only speech he utters: "So is preserved the seed
of all justice" (*Purg.* 32. 48). The tree in question is that
despoiled by Adam when he fell (*Purg.* 32. 37; 33. 55; *Par.* 26.
115), and in the beholder's presence rent and stripped by the
eagle (*Purg.* 32. 113). In its interdict appears God's justice (33.
71). Can there be any reason for attack on the tree by Christ,
for his taking its fruit with the beak of a symbolical griffin? Is
his representative to be commended for eschewing such violence? On the contrary, "Whoever plunders or rends that tree,
with the blasphemy of his deed displeases God, who for his use
only created it holy" (*Purg.* 33. 58). Would a creature typifying
Christ so displease the Father? Adam only sins by tasting the
fruit of the tree.[4] So the griffin cannot be said to have obviously
Christlike qualities. "As in Adam all died, even so in Christ all
became alive." Christ's work is atonement for Adam's sin. The
griffin's one cryptic line most naturally refers to the effect of the
tree: it seemed sweet to Adam but was bitter in its results, as
justice required (*Purg.* 32. 44), for Adam's "going beyond
limits" (*Par.* 26. 117) kept him in Hell more than 4,000 years.

To make the griffin a "wild beast" (*Purg.* 31. 80, 122; 32. 96)
is not in accord with Dante's habit in representing divinity. In
his awe of the Trinity, he does not dream of that monstrous
representation that displeased Wycliffe, in which the Trinity is
a deformed human being with three mouths. Such a representation will do for Satan in Hell. Indeed, is Satan a satire on those
who would so materialize theology, even if his threefold power
to torture comes from the mosaic in Dante's fair San Giovanni?
Dante will give no material form to the Godhead, or show the
Son in human form in Heaven. His representation of the
Trinity—with apology for falling short—is this:

In the deep and shining being of the exalted light I saw three
circles of three colors and one extent. One by the second—as rainbow by rainbow—seemed reflected, and the third seemed fire breath-
ing equally on every side . . . O Eternal Light, which only in yourself abide, you only understand yourself, and known by yourself and
understanding yourself, you love and smile. That revolving circle

---

4 In *Purg.* 32. 39, 114, Dante mentions leaves and flowers but not
fruit. In *Purg.* 32. 44; *Par.* 26. 115, fruit is not mentioned, though implied.

which, so conceived, appeared in you like light reflected, so far as my eyes could gaze on it, within itself seemed painted in its own color with our image, so that my eyes were altogether intent upon it (*Par.* 33. 115).

Or in the Heaven of the Fixed Stars, Christ appears as the Sun, as the Shining Substance. Having the Virgin in human form, the poet less needs to present the Son as he appeared in Judea. He knows that Scripture condescends to human powers by attributing feet and hands to God (*Par.* 4. 43), yet he himself presents no anthropomorphic God. Even the Holy Spirit as a dove, however Biblical, has no place in his poem. In representing divinity, he concedes to human weakness as little as he can. Is it likely that he abandons such a practice to typify the Second Person of the Trinity as a mythological draft animal? But the poet is in the reader's hands; each man may interpret the allegory as he will.

THE TRAVELER'S SINS

The inscription over Hell Gate (Canto 3) declares that the Inferno exemplifies divine justice, power, wisdom, and love. But what effect on Dante's own life was wrought by observing the loving and just punishment of wickedness? One hint at such impact applies to mankind generally; looking at the sinners in the river of blood, he exclaims: "O blind greed, O insane anger which so incite us during our short lives and then in eternity so wretchedly steep us!" (*Inf.* 12. 49)! On leaving the *bolgia* of the thieves and approaching that of the men whose "deeds were not lion-like but those of the fox" (27. 74), the observer makes further application to himself: "I sorrowed then and now I again am sorrowful when I remember what I saw; and I check my disposition more than usually, so that it will not run where goodness does not guide it. If my happy star or something better has given me what is good, I hope I shall not repine at my state" (26. 19). The reference of this speech is not clear. The traveler-poet hardly needed a warning against theft, not being inclined toward it. Perhaps he is moralizing on the whole Inferno. Or is he anticipating the fox-like men he is to see? Ulysses devised the stratagem of the wooden horse, through which Troy fell, and the trick that gained Achilles' aid—also necessary to the destruction of that city. These clever actions so little deserve Hell that perhaps they are punished because directed against Troy, ancestor of Rome, divinely selected —says Dante's *Monarchia*—for imperial rule. Thus we have shrewdness misdirected rather than flagrant evil. Did Dante think that he might so act? Guido da Montefeltro, the other vulpine character who speaks in this *bolgia,* turned his shrewdness to devising treachery.

In Purgatory, Oderisi the illuminator says on the poet's fame: "One Guido has taken from another renown in the [Italian] tongue, and perhaps one has been born who will chase both of them from the nest" (*Purg.* 11. 97). If, as commonly is inferred, the newcomer is the poet Dante, Oderisi's words still do not reveal the emotions of the listener. The illuminator continues on the vanity of worldly reputation, perhaps still representing the views of Dante the poet. The visitor replies: "Your true words fill my heart with good humility and reduce my swollen pride" (*Purg.* 11. 118). So the speaker is affected by the illuminator's words, but is not moved by observing his punishment. His two lines of answer are not more than courtesy demands; he passes on to display his "inquisitive nature" (*Par.* 5. 89): "But who is the man you were just speaking of" (*Purg.* 11. 120)?

Ere long he admits that pride has been one of his chief vices, saying on the terrace of envy: "Much greater is the fear that racks my spirit of the punishment on the terrace [of pride] below, for already the burden to be borne there weighs heavy on me" (13. 136). Yet very soon when two of the blinded souls ask who he is, he answers not: "I am a sinner who does not deserve to be named," but "To tell you who I am would be useless talk, because as yet my name does not make much noise" (14. 20). Having just admitted that he is prone to pride, the worst of the seven capital vices, he has so little inclination to avoid egotism that his thoughts are concerned with the fame he hopes to attain. Does Dante the poet here join hands with his own fictitious sightseer? Yet something might be done to counteract the egotism for which the traveler expects to suffer the penalty, if we believe Omberto Aldobrandesco when he says: "Here I must bear this weight of my pride until I make satisfaction to God. Since I did not do it among the living, here I must do it among the dead" (*Purg.* 11. 70). Statius, however, seems to imply that Hell, but not Purgatory, can be avoided through repentance (*Purg.* 22. 45). Virgil calls the letters his pupil bears on his forehead wounds closed "through being sorry" (15. 81). Nevertheless, the marked man expresses no pain or sorrow on the wounds' infliction or healing. Indeed, he does not know when they vanish (12. 127). As a matter of course, the angels remove them as the climber leaves each terrace. Perhaps Virgil's words apply vaguely to life on earth. Guido Guinicelli, on the seventh terrace, congratulates the traveler on "taking on experience of our lands in order to die better" (26. 73), that is, on learning to avoid purgatorial penance by counter-acting vices while still alive, as did Guido himself and Provenzan Salvani (26. 93; 11. 142). Yet to this part of Guido's speech the traveler, as though more interested in poetry than in purifica-tion, in no way replies.

On the terrace of wrath, an ecstatic vision brings the way-farer instances of meekness, on which he meditates. Virgil enhances their effect by saying: "What you saw was to keep you from refusing to open your heart to the waters of peace which are poured out by the everlasting spring" (*Purg.* 15. 130). If here we identify this visionary with the poet, Dante shows him-self as in danger from excessive wrath, such as he exhibits in his political letters, or as the traveler-poet turns against Pisa (*Inf.* 33. 79). At least Saint Thomas warns against too great fierce-ness even in righteous anger (*Summa Theol.* 2. 2. 158).

In the Earthly Paradise, Beatrice recalls her adorer to per-sonal feeling: "What claim have you to approach the mount? Do you not know that here man is ready for Heaven (*felice*)" (*Purg.* 30. 74)? Part of the pilgrim's shame is that he realizes himself unworthy, though part is the embarrassment of the lover of the *Vita Nuova* before his idol. Beatrice proceeds with her arraignment, including her assertion: "Such was his fall that all persuasions for his well-being (*salute*) were too weak except to show him the people who are lost" (*Purg.* 30. 136). Apart from Beatrice's omission of Purgatory, the word *salute* with all its possible meanings is to be examined. Usually it is rendered "salvation," in a theological sense. Certainly that is one of its meanings. Yet Dante says that he gave himself to Virgil for his *salute* (*Purg.* 30. 51). Is this spiritual salvation? Beatrice, when she visited Virgil in Limbo, spoke to him of Dante's *campare* ("rescue," "escape"); Virgil uses the same word in telling Cato of his assistance to the man lost in the dark forest. Yet commentators make *campare* mean "*salvation.*" In a poem on love and his lady (*Donna mi priega*), Guido Cavalcanti wrote that, wishing to speak to her,

> I find myself with such slight *salute*
> that I do not dare to hold the thought.

Before crossing Lethe, Dante must repent, says Beatrice, and he must confess. This he does, like a schoolboy mute and ashamed, and at last he is so pricked by conscience that he falls "overcome" (*Purg.* 31. 89). Matilda had told him that Lethe takes away the memory of sin (*Purg.* 28. 128). Does this mean a wicked life in the usual sense? Beatrice had rebuked him for infidelity to herself. Can Dante's sin stop there?

Can there be an allegory of his failure to keep his promise, at the end of the *Vita Nuova*, to write of Beatrice? In order to do so, after years of neglecting her as a theme, he writes of Hell (and Purgatory), for by passing through them he makes his visit to Heaven more probable. Is *salute*, then, the poetical health required to compose the *Commedia*? But this, like most allegories, is the work of the reader, not the poet. The medieval commentators and many moderns have preferred religious allegory. One at least has even insisted on "moral aberration" which made Dante's sonnets to Forese Donati "a furnace where behind heavy, creaking bars a hellish fire rages." To obtain this view, it is necessary to read "between the lines" of Beatrice's reproaches, and to blacken Dante's relations with Forese.[5] We may again remember the suggestion in *Convivio* 1. 2 that readers cannot see the truth hidden under allegory unless Dante explains it.

The *Paradiso* opens with the glory of God, director of the universe, to be celebrated by the poet returned to earth. He is able to write because of the sights he saw. Though they were too great for mortal vision, he will tell what he can, hoping that so he may deserve the poet's crown. Thus as a writer to address

5 For Forese, see Chapter 3, p. 88, above.

other men rather than a seeker for personal salvation, he enters
that part of the universe where God's light especially shines.

Almost to the end, his visit depends on Beatrice, "beloved of
the First Lover, goddess, whose speech so rises in waves above
me and warms me that more and more it gives me life" (*Par.*
4. 118). Yet even Beatrice's close association with divinity does
not make her its equivalent. In the Heaven of the Sun, "all my
love was so fixed on God that it eclipsed Beatrice and made me
forget her. She was not displeased but so smiled on me that the
glory of her smiling eyes divided my united mind among various
objects" (10. 59). Hearing a celestial melody, the listener is enchanted:

I so loved it that up to then nothing had bound me with chains
so sweet. Perhaps what I say seems too bold, since it sets below
this heavenly melody the pleasure of those beautiful eyes in which,
as it looks into them, my desire is satisfied. But anyone who understands that those vivid seals of every beauty grow more vivid the
higher the heaven, and that not yet had I turned to them, can
excuse me for that of which I accuse myself in order to offer excuse,
and can see that I speak truly, since my holy pleasure in her eyes
is not here rejected; indeed it becomes purer as I go upward (14.
127).

Toward the end of Beatrice's guardianship, her beauty can be
described by saying that God seemed to take pleasure in her
face, that only her maker could fully enjoy her beauty (*Par.* 27.
105; 30. 21). So always the poet is seeing that he may write, the
poet-lover is deifying his lady even above her of the *Vita Nuova,*
and the religious man is believing in the Trinity and God's
power as when he wrote the *Vita Nuova.*

With these interests are seldom connected effects on his own
soul. From the Seventh to the Eighth Heaven the explorer
mounts with such enormous speed that he especially notes it:

Never down here, where we rise and sink naturally, was there
movement rapid enough to equal my flight. As I hope to return,
reader, to that holy procession—and in my longing to return I often
weep for my sins and beat my breast—I swear that you could not
have pulled your finger from the fire—after putting it in—faster
than I came in sight of the sign that follows Taurus and got
within it (*Par.* 22. 107).

This is the visitor's sole expression of fear that his sins after his return to earth may keep him out of Heaven; it is his only sign of contrition for sin. Curiously thrown in incidentally as an oath, the statement is less impressive than if independently spoken, yet hints that the observer, lover, and writer was determined at least once to mention his own sins and need for forgiveness. Did he find that his traveler's preoccupation with the gathering of matter for his poem—to be written from his notes on his return—and with his devotion to his adored lady, gave him little opportunity for thinking about his personal ethics, so that they can appear only so inconspicuously as here?

If when he witnessed the coronation of the Virgin in the Eighth Heaven, the tourist had any thought of his own sins, he does not say so, though in the presence of "the fair flower whom I always invoke both morning and evening" (*Par.* 23. 88). On meeting Saint Peter and his companions, Beatrice petitions for her charge with the words: "Think on his measureless love and sprinkle dew upon him. You drink always from the fountain whence comes what he meditates" (*Par.* 24. 7). What Peter does is satisfy Beatrice's request that her ward be examined in the fundamentals of Christian doctrine. The saint indeed not only rejoices that the candidate can describe the coins of Christian faith but wishes to be assured that he has them in his purse to be spent in holy works (24. 84). Yet when the catechism by the saints is compared to an examination for a higher academic degree, it is stamped as intellectual rather than moral or religious. The candidate has learned the answers; he does not express simply the fullness of his heart.

The Empyrean is the "Heaven which is pure light, intellectual light full of love, love of true good full of gladness. . . . I felt myself rise above my strength and was roused to such new sight that against any light however shining my eyes would have kept their power" (30. 39). This light—so important that we cannot but remember that the traveler was devoted to Saint Lucia, whose name means *"light"*—is full of love, as a warm personal experience, yet it is also intellectual. The seeker has before him a river of light. Beatrice congratulates him on his desire to "take note" (*aver notizia*) of what he sees, in her desire to encourage the reporter; on the other hand, she com-

mands him to drink of the river, as for his personl edification.
Yet immediately after drinking he is again the poet gathering
material and invoking the *"isplendor di Dio,"* the heavenly
muse of light, for strength to make verses on what he saw (30.
97).

His attention is soon taken by Beatrice's demonstration of
the heavenly rose. After gazing, he says: "I turned with my
wish on fire to ask my mistress about things on which my mind
was intent" (31. 55). On fire indeed, but with intellectual
rather than moral or mystical fire. The guide's successor, Saint
Bernard, points to her as she sits in the celestial rose. To her the
pilgrim addresses his thanks:

O Mistress, in whom my hope is strong and who for my rescue
endured to leave your footprints in Hell, for all the many things
I have seen I am indebted to the kindness and the power of your
ability and your goodness. You have brought me from slavery to
liberty by means of all the ways and all the methods by which
you had power to act. Preserve me in your generosity so that my
soul, which you have made healthy, may leave my body in a state
that you approve (31. 79).

Is this the liberty that Virgil told Cato the visitor was searching
for in his expedition to the kingdoms of the dead (*Purg.* 1. 71)?
In expressing thanks to Beatrice, the traveler might easily sup-
press his guidance through Hell and Purgatory. Yet how much
of his soul's health did he owe to Virgil? The Latin poet told
his charge on leaving him: "Free, direct, and healthy is your
will" (*Purg.* 27. 140). For "healthy" he uses the same word as
does the pilgrim when addressing Beatrice in Heaven. That
rendered "will" is *arbitrio*, here apparently a synonym of
volontade, the Latin *voluntas* (*Par.* 5. 22), though the latter is
more likely to indicate the will of God than *arbitrio*, which may
be only a whim (*Par.* 5. 56; 3. 85). In the final lines of the
Paradiso, the word for "will" is the Latin *velle*, there asserted
to be freely in harmony with the Divine Love. Are we to find
significance in Virgil's use of *arbitrio*, and does he give "healthy"
(*sano*) a lower significance than does Beatrice? A fraction of
the philosophical studies mentioned in the *Convivio* 2. 12
would have impressed on Dante the importance Aquinas gave
the human will. The poet has Beatrice declare: "The most

important gift which God in his generosity devised when he created, and the one most in harmony with his goodness and which he values highest, was liberty of the will. With this freedom intelligent beings—each and every one—were and are gifted" (*Par.* 5. 19). This Dante argues in his *Monarchia* 1. 12. At least we may understand Virgil as making an important assertion about Dante's ethical condition.

From his thanks to Beatrice after she leaves him, the observer turns to behold a "peaceful oriflamme," the beauty of the Virgin. As returned traveler he regrets that he cannot express in writing her power to delight (31. 136). As teacher, Saint Bernard then demonstrates the celestial rose, which the pilgrim on his return is to present to readers. After responding to an interrupting query about the angel of the Annunciation prompted by the asker's "inquisitive nature" (5. 89), the saint further expounds the celestial rose. Apparently to check any improper confidence by the visitor, he warns: "But so that when you move your wings you will not, though believing that you advance, go backward, we must ask grace through prayer—grace from her who can aid you. And you are to follow me with such eagerness that from my words your heart will not wander" (32. 145). The pupil makes no answer to this caution and exhortation. The saint then prays for him, begging the Virgin to "keep healthy (*sani*), after all he has seen, his affections. Let your watchfulness subdue his human tendencies" (33. 35). As a result, the pilgrim ends his "burning desire" (33. 48). Returned to earth, he is obliged to report that he retains only a vague idea of "the lofty Light, true of itself," which he beheld. Hence he humbly prays that the Highest Light will "make my tongue so mighty that I can leave to future men just one spark of your glory" (33. 70). He believes that he has made some approach to the "Eternal Power," the love which unifies all things, because as he writes he rejoices. What he recalls he will write briefly—above all the vision of the Trinity: three circles of Eternal Light, the second marked with a human figure. Yet weak and hoarse is his speech before such a concept. Forgetting—with some suggestion of comedy, it seems—Saint Bernard's warning against trying to use his wings unwisely, the privileged visitor "wanted to see how the image [of Christ] fits

the circle [of light] and how it is placed there" (33. 137). With
further reference to Saint Bernard's warning and to men's attempts "to fly without wings" (33. 15) instead of relying on
the Virgin, the reporter admits that his "own wings" (*Par.* 33.
139) were not strong enough to secure him his wish. Nevertheless he is able to say: "My mind was smitten with a lightning
flash in which its wish was fulfilled. To the lofty imagination
power now failed, but of a surety my desire and my will were
turning like a wheel moved steadily by the Love which controls
the sun and all the stars" (33. 140).

Throughout his journey, then, the traveler says little of his
own soul and his own sins. We may remember that in the
Convivio 1. 2 Dante remarks that "in the secret chamber of
his own thoughts a man ought to censure himself and weep for
his faults, but not openly." So, instead of proclaiming himself
the chief of sinners, the seeker for liberty devotes himself to
his earthly career, attempts to see and hear that he may have
something to write. In the course of this activity, he also gains
for himself harmony with the Love that directs the universe.

RENOWN OR REPENTANCE?

To the traveler who will return to write his reminiscences,
Cacciaguida says that in the three realms of the dead, souls
recorded by fame are shown. Whatever exceptions there may be,
the number of popes, kings, and noblemen whom the visitor
sees and converses with is not small. Fame is important throughout the poem: the fame before death of the shades encountered,
the renown they hope for beyond the grave, the fame which the
imaginary visitor himself, become poet, hopes to achieve with
verses on the marvels of the other world.

When the lost and frightened traveler learns that Virgil is
before him, he exclaims: "O you who are honor and light to all
poets" (*Inf.* 1. 82). This signifies, You who give reputation and
example to all the others. The traveler implies that he trusts
this sage or poet to rescue him because Virgil is "famous" (1.
89). Beatrice is then quoted by the Latin poet himself as though
in confirmation: "O courteous Mantuan soul, whose fame yet
persists in the world and will persist in the future as long as the
world does" (2. 58). Is this repetition by Virgil of his own

praises intended to show him as pleased with it, or is the poet introducing awkwardly something he cannot omit? In some earlier version of the *Commedia*, was the scene between Virgil and Beatrice acted rather than reported? According to the continuing report, Beatrice then, as it were, bribed Virgil by saying: "When I shall be before my Lord, I will often praise you to him" (2. 73). Any gain for Virgil from this praise except fame in Heaven is not evident; the "fresh grass" of Limbo will hardly be made more pleasant by Beatrice's intercession. Beatrice's implied concept of her "Lord" is not found in the *Paradiso*. The traveler, enthusiastic over her beauty, believes that only "her Maker fully enjoys it" (*Par.* 30. 21), yet the anthropomorphic God of the interceding Beatrice nowhere appears. She hardly can speak to the "point radiating such sharp light that the eye it sets on fire needs to close against such acuteness" (*Par.* 28. 16).

When the visitor approaches Limbo he sees at a distance that "people worthy of praise occupy that place" (*Inf.* 4. 72), so that to his guide he says: "O you who make famous knowledge and skill, who are these receiving such honor that it separates them from the state of the rest [in Hell]?" Virgil replies: "The deserved praises proclaimed for them in your world [of the living] gain for them such grace in Heaven that so it distinguishes them" (4. 73). Well-earned fame in Heaven has brought them a mild lot in Hell.

Yet desire for fame exists among the damned whose lot is not ameliorated. Pier delle Vigne, who died with his reputation clouded by slander, wishes vindication: "If any of you get back into the world, be kind to the remembrance of me, which still is prostrate before the blow that envy gave it" (*Inf.* 13. 76). The three men met on the burning sands of the sodomites, Guido Guerra, Tegghiaio, and Jacopo, for whom the narrator expresses great respect, ask that in the world he speak courteously of them (16. 85). For Ciacco no virtue is affirmed, though his sufferings invite the visitor to tears, as though in deserved pity. At least he wishes to be recalled to men's thoughts. Brunetto Latini, believing that he lives in his *Tesoro*, does not seek consideration (15. 120). In the lower circles the sinners do not ask that their reputation be preserved. Yet to Ugolino is offered the bribe of an attempt to clear his reputation, with the condition that he has a grievance (32. 136). As a character sympathetically treated, he at once attempts to explain. When the bribe of fame on earth is offered to Guido da Montefeltro, if he will tell his name, he replies:

"If I believed I were answering a person who would ever return to the world, this flame would stand still without more shaking [that is, he would keep silent]. But since never from this depth has a man returned alive, if what I hear is true, I answer you without fear of infamy" (27. 61).

Bocca degli Abati, when his questioner offers fame, declares that he wishes the opposite, with contempt for the ignorance of one offering such inducement in the ninth circle of Hell. The falsifiers, perhaps in harmony with their sin, are not unwilling that their names "live under many suns" (29. 105).

Virgil is conscious of the poet's power over immortality, telling Pier delle Vigne that his companion can refresh the suicide's fame in the world (13. 53). Confident in the great name he has given Ulysses and Diomede, he addresses them: "If I deserved anything from you while I was alive, if I deserved from you much or little when in the world I wrote the noble verses, do not move, but one of you tell where he was lost and died" (26. 80).

These incidents show fame as a Dantesque preoccupation, with smiling satire on those who offer it and those whom it bribes. Brunetto Latini, with a teacher's confidence, says: "Following your star, you will reach the haven of glory, if I judged rightly while alive" (15. 55). The pupil acknowledges that Brunetto taught him "how man becomes eternal" (15. 85). To interpret these words "how man becomes famous" seems more likely than "how man gets to Heaven," for the discourse of the two men is not on pious subjects, and Brunetto is hardly a pious writer. Giovanni Villani calls him a "worldly man" (8. 10). In the same circle some of the other souls say to the traveler what may be rendered: "As you hope your fame will shine after you, tell us about affairs in Florence" (16. 66). Soon after, the traveler becomes also the author of the *Comedy*, swearing "by the notes of this Comedy, reader, and I hope they will not fail of favor far into the future" (16. 127), that he saw

Geryon rising through the air. However genuine the aspiration, its setting deprives Dante's ambition of offense.

In Purgatory, the souls generally seem to ask the prayers of the visitor on his return to earth rather than verses that will make them famous. Buonconte and Sapia do desire to have their reputations cleared (*Purg.* 5. 103; 13. 148), but no more.

The traveler speaks with the illuminator Oderisi, who inveighs against fame:

I said to him: "Are you not Oderisi, who give fame to Agubbio and fame to that art that in Paris is called illuminating?" "Brother, he said, "the pages penciled by Franco of Bologna are more lively. The fame is now all his, and I am put aside.[6] I would by no means have been so courteous when alive, through the great desire for excellence on which my heart was intent. For such pride here the price is paid. And I would not even be here if it were not that while I was able to sin, I turned to God. O vain pride in human powers! For how short a time is the tree green at the top, unless stupid ages come upon it. So one Guido has taken from the other fame in poetry; and perhaps a man has been born who will drive both of them from the nest. Worldly reputation is nothing but a breath of wind, which blows now here, now there, and changes names as it changes direction. What more repute do you have if you lay off a body that has grown old than if you die before you give up baby talk—ere a thousand years have passed? That is a shorter time, in the face of eternity, than a movement of the eyelid is to the circle that moves slowest in the heavens. All Tuscany rang with the man who is walking so slowly ahead of me, and now Siena hardly whispers about him. . . . Your renown is like the color of grass which comes and goes, and He changes its color through whose power it comes fresh from the ground" (11. 79).

Oderisi's speech on the vanity of reputation is suitable to this terrace of pride, on which the visitor on his return after death expected to do penance (13. 136). Even in such a setting, autobiographical interpretation of the *Commedia* has frequently explained the "poet perhaps already born" as Dante himself. If so we take Oderisi's words, he is a little behind the times, for by 1300 Dante not merely was born but had written the lyric poems in which he most evidently competes with Guido Cavalcanti. After the affectionate passage on his "first friend" (*Inf.* 10. 52), does Dante here assert superiority? Or is this

6 Sometimes interpreted to mean that part of his fame remains. Cf. *in parte* at *Inf.* 4. 129.

passage rather poetically dramatic than merely personal? The traveler is aware that his name as yet does not make much noise (14. 21).

The traveler's meeting with Guido Guinicelli again brings up the theme of poetic reputation. Guido d' Arezzo was for a short time extolled by the unthinking who take their views from rumor, but "for the majority truth has now conquered" ignorance (26. 126). With thought of contemporary verse, Dante even qualifies the renown of Guido himself, which is to endure "as long as the modern style lasts" (26. 113). Dante knew that poetic immortality required more than the enthusiasm of his own era.

Hoping to receive the poet's laurel crown at San Giovanni in Florence, Dante for years persisted in the labors that made him thin.[7] The *Paradiso* opens with unabashed eagerness for poetic eminence—called by Statius that which lasts longest and gives highest honor (*Purg.* 21. 85):

O good Apollo, for the completion of my labor make me such a vessel of your worth as you ask [before conferring] the gift of your beloved laurel! . . . O Divine Power, if you so fully lend yourself to me that I show the picture of the blessed realm which is inscribed within my brain, you will see me come to the tree you love and there crown myself with those leaves that the matter and you make me deserve. If seldom, Father, for the triumph of Caesar or poet (the fault and the disgrace of human wills) the Peneian bough is plucked, what gladness should it give the glad Delphic deity when any man thirsts for it (*Par.* 1. 13).

Later he again calls on the Muse, who makes geniuses famous and long-lasting (18. 83). As both traveler and poet, he confesses to Cacciaguida that through timidly befriending the truth, he fears to lose his life in the ages to come. The old man exhorts him to poetical courage as a proof that he deserves renown (17. 118, 135). Almost at the end of his visit to Heaven,

7 *Par.* 25. 1. In his note on this passage, Momigliano, after speaking of the *Paradiso* as anchored to Dante's earthly interests and as affirming his worldly purposes, says that in this canto "in the very center of the last consecration of Dante as worthy of the city of God, from the height of the heavens he lifts the sigh of the exile for his earthly city. The crown to be received from his native city on earth is still dearer than that received from his celestial city."

he expresses the hope that his poetry may be excellent enough to show some spark of heavenly glory to future ages (33. 70).

Among the Aristotelian virtues, Dante listed one concerned with love of honor, as a mean between too great eagerness for fame and contempt for it (*Convivio* 4. 17). Poetic immortality he mentions more often and with more feeling than he does any of the virtues usually conceived to be the goals of the devout. Of such fame Milton, perhaps thinking of Dante's assertion that for years his poem made him thin as he suffered hunger, cold, and sleeplessness (*Par.* 25. 3; *Purg.* 29. 37), wrote:

> Fame is the spur that the clear spirit doth raise
> (That last infirmity of noble mind)
> To scorn delights and live laborious days.

5 · Beatrice

THE EARLY BEATRICE

In the books written about them, few heroines appear so little as does Beatrice. In a much discussed passage in the *Vita Nuova,* Dante says "she was called by the name of Beatrice by many who did not know her name" (2). Beatrice means a woman who confers blessedness. In the *Vita Nuova* she is called "blessed" (*benedetta, beata*—23, 29, etc.), and so in *Convivio* 2. 2, 8, though the meaning of the name is not insisted on. In the *Commedia* she is *blessed* only to Virgil (*Inf.* 2. 53). The reader does well to remember the old debate on her historical existence and the search for a Florentine Beatrice. Whether the early identification with Beatrice Portinari is correct or not, the important matter is how Dante handled her poetically. Possibly, when writing that people called her Beatrice, Dante implies that her real name was not Beatrice. Would he, after making the efforts to conceal his love detailed in the *Vita Nuova,* have furnished so evident a clue as the real name of "the lady of my mind" (2)? How prosaic an autobiography is Dante's early work? Would good manners have allowed him to make a beloved Beatrice conspicuous by naming her? We may recall that Boccaccio's love was not named Fiametta, and Petrarch's not Laura. In later days, problems in English literary history have been: Who or how real were Daniel's Delia and Herrick's Julia? It would seem that whether or not Dante's Beatrice was an actual Florentine woman, her baptismal name was not Beatrice. How strange that Boccaccio (perhaps most responsible for Beatrice Portinari) assumed that Dante would be literal as he himself was not!

According to the *Vita Nuova*, Dante first saw Beatrice when she was in her ninth year; no act or speech of hers is recorded. At Love's command, Dante in his boyhood often managed to behold this "youthful angel," and "saw that her conduct was so noble and worthy of praise that to her could be applied the poet Homer's words: She seemed the daughter not of a mortal man but of a god" (2). Do the words imply acquaintance or only remote observation? At any rate, at the age of seventeen she saluted Dante on meeting him in the street (3). Somewhat later, hearing his conduct with respect to another lady censured, she denied her salute (10). At the lover's display of emotion over this slight, Beatrice joked with other ladies, presumably in Dante's presence (14, 15); no details are given. Dante heard other ladies talking of her tears on her father's death (22). A few words are given to the effect the sight of her produced on those meeting her in the street: So moved were they that they could not return her salute, speaking of her as one of the loveliest of the angels and a marvel. Dante does not say that he saw any of this; a reference to witnesses may imply that he did not (26). Brief is his account of her death: "The Lord of Justice called this most gentle lady to appear in glory under the ensign of that holy queen the Virgin Mary, for whose name great reverence was shown in the speech of this blessed Beatrice" (29). About Beatrice acting and living this is all. The details given are four or five lines on her clothing at his first sight of her and nine years later. We may infer that before he was eighteen Dante sometimes conversed with her; he does not affirm it.

Otherwise, she appears in the author's thoughts about her, in her effect on him, and in his assertion of her place in Heaven. The *Vita Nuova* is much concerned with Dante the poet, who tells—often fictitiously, it seems—how he came to write the various poems in the volume and explains them; he also gives some of his theories of writing. If Beatrice is the ostensible subject, Dante the poet goes far toward being the chief interest. The two unite in the last chapter:

After this sonnet a wonderful vision appeared to me, in which I saw things that made me decide not to say more of this blessed lady until I could deal more worthily with her. To attain that, I

labor as hard as I can, as she truly knows. Hence, if He by whom
all things live determines that my life continue for enough years, I
hope to say of her what never has been said of any woman. And
then may it be granted by Him who is above all courteous that
my soul shall see the glory of my mistress, that is, of the blessed
Beatrice, who gloriously beholds the face of Him who is holy,
world-without-end (42).

Beatrice is often mentioned in the *Convivio*, a more mature
work than the *Vita Nuova*, as their author says (*Conv.* 1. 1).
More than three years after the death of "that blessed Beatrice
who lives in Heaven with the angels and on earth with my
spirit," Dante gave himself to another lady, that is, in allegory,
to Philosophy. To this affection he yielded gradually, for "that
heavenly Beatrice was still holding the castle of my mind"
(*Conv.* 2. 2, 6). After referring to her as *beata* (2. 8) he says
that he is about to end his discourses on that "blessed Beatrice
who lives [in Heaven]." His last reference to her is: "I affirm
that the lady with whom I fell in love after my first love was
that beautiful and honorable daughter of the Emperor of the
Universe, to whom Pythagoras gave the name of Philosophy"
(2. 15).

In the Earthly Paradise that first love again appears. As Dante
the traveler looks at the allegorical chariot, he sees

a lady wearing over a white veil a garland of olive and clad under
a green mantle in the color of vivid flame. Then my spirit, which
had for so long a time not been awe-struck and trembling in her
presence, without getting more knowledge through the eyes, but
through the occult power that came from her, perceived the great
strength of my old love. As soon as in my face struck that great
force which had pierced me through long ago before I was out of
boyhood, I turned . . . to say to Virgil: "Less than a dram of
blood that does not tremble I have left; I know the signs of my
old flame" (*Purg.* 30. 32).

And later, as he looks at Beatrice: "So fixed and eager were my
eyes to rid myself wholly of my ten years of thirst that my
other senses were all inactive, and on either side of them was a
wall of not heeding (so her sacred smile drew them to her with
her old net!)" (*Purg.* 32. 1). This carries him back to his
ninth year, when first he saw Beatrice: "At that moment, I
say truthfully, the spirit of life, which resides in the innermost

chamber of the heart, went to trembling so violently that this trembling showed terrifyingly in my least pulse beats, and, as the spirit trembled, it said these words: 'Here is a god stronger than I am, who when he comes will master me' " (*Vita Nuova* 2). Just as in the Earthly Paradise the traveler is affected by Beatrice's presence before knowing she is there, so more than a decade earlier the youthful lover had such an experience:

Certain ladies of good family had met in honor of a lady who was married that day. . . . So, thinking it would please a friend of mine, I proposed that we wait upon the ladies in this company. And as we were doing so, I felt an extraordinary trembling begin in the left side of my breast and at once spread to all parts of my body. Then I say that I pretended to turn to examine a painting that ran around that room.[1] But, fearing that somebody would notice my trembling, I lifted my eyes and, looking at the ladies, saw among them the noble Beatrice. Then my spirits, when they found themselves so close to that noble lady, were so distressed by the violence Love offered that only the vital powers of sight remained alive, and even these were separated from their means of action, since Love wished to stand in their high place to look on the marvelous lady (14).

BEATRICE AS TEACHER AND GUIDE

To the Earthly Paradise, Dante and Beatrice are transplanted from the unnamed city of the *Vita Nuova*, yet with change. If the slightly delineated woman of the early work is "crowned and clothed with humility" (26), she of the Earthly Paradise might come from one of Dante's *ballate*, "full of disdain," saying: "I shall not be humble toward any man who looks into my eyes" (*Rime* 80). As she stands in the chariot drawn by the griffin, Beatrice appears thus:

Like an admiral who goes to the poop and to the prow to see the men who are serving in the other ships and gives them heart to do their duty, at the left side of the chariot I saw the lady, who earlier appeared to me veiled, accompanied by angels, setting her eyes upon me from across the stream. Like a queen, retaining her haughty attitude, she addressed me, like one who speaks and keeps until the last his hottest words: "Attend to us. We are, we are Beatrice.[2] How are you worthy to approach the mountain? Do you

1 My translation is a guess at the sense of the passage.
2 The text now generally accepted puts this in the singular.

not know that here man is ready for Heaven?" My eyes fell until
they looked into the clear stream, but seeing myself in it, I turned
them to the grass, such shame weighted my brow! A mother to
her son seems haughty as she seemed to me, because acid is the
flavor of her bitter compassion (*Purg.* 30. 58).

A word I have rendered "haughty" is *proterva*. This word
Ariosto applies to Angelica when she decides to make game of
her brave and noble lovers, Orlando and Sacripante (*Orlando
Furioso* 12. 36). It does not fit the lady of the *Vita Nuova*.

Dante's youthful love for Beatrice was known to various
ladies, one of whom asked him:

"What purpose have you in loving this lady, when you cannot
bear her presence? Tell us about it, because surely the purpose of
such love must be very strange." And when she had said this, not
merely she but all the ladies showed by their expressions that they
were awaiting my answer. Then I said to them: "The ultimate
desire of my love was only the salutation of this lady whom I suppose you refer to, and in it dwelt all my happiness, because it was
the consummation of all my hopes" (*Vita Nuova* 18).

This passage probably implies that Beatrice knew of this "very
strange" devotion of his, but she shows no desire for it, though
she does object to his conduct with another woman. Yet in the
Earthly Paradise she attacks him for forgetting her:

"For a time I sustained him with my face. While I showed him
my youthful eyes, I led him along in the right direction. As soon as
I was on the threshold of my twenty-fifth year and exchanged
earthly life for heavenly, this man turned from me and gave himself to others. When I had risen from flesh to spirit and my beauty
and goodness were enhanced, I was less dear to him and less esteemed. He turned his steps into the paths of untruth, following
false appearances of good which fulfill none of their promises. I
accomplished nothing by praying for spiritual aid, by means of
which I called him back in dreams and otherwise. So little did he
attend to them! Such was his fall that all persuasions for his well-
being were too weak except to show him the people who are lost.
For this I visited the courtyard of the dead and to the one who
brought this man here my prayers, as I wept, were uttered" (*Purg.*
30. 121).

So affected that he speaks with difficulty, the culprit answers
with tears: "Earthly things with their false pleasure turned
askew my steps as soon as your face was hidden." Beatrice

replies, in part: "Lay aside all cause for tears and listen. Thus you will learn how my buried flesh should have moved you in a contrary direction. Never did nature or art offer you such pleasure as did the beauteous limbs in which I was enclosed, which now are scattered on earth. And if your greatest pleasure so failed on my death, what mortal thing was worthy to excite your longing? You should, on the first gleam of deceptive things, have attempted to follow me who no longer was subject to mortal error. Your wings should not have been weighed down, so you would await further blows, by either little maid or other empty and short-lived vanity" (*Purg.* 31. 46). Though by this rebuke the repentant lover is reduced to the condition of a weeping schoolboy, censure continues: "If you are sad on hearing, raise your beard, and you will be more sorrowful on looking" (31. 67). Notwithstanding this poisonous speech, the hearer, though Beatrice is still veiled and on the other side of the stream, believes as he looks at her that in beauty she more surpasses her old self than she did other women when she lived. This censorious Beatrice is unexpected to the reader of the *Convivio*. In that book, love for Beatrice seems superseded by devotion to Lady Philosophy, to the writer's satisfaction.

The old commentators allegorized the scene. Dante's son Pietro writes:

In the cloud of flowers [on the chariot] descended Beatrice, that is, Theology. . . . Our author wishes to say in allegory that earlier he delighted in the study of theology, but that later he gave it up. . . . The author devoted himself to worldly and poetical studies that yield no fruit. [Pietro then quotes from Boethius and Jerome on the meretricious and devilish character of poetry.] Further, if he lost such great pleasure when Beatrice died, that is, when interest in theology died in his heart, as a mortal, what mortal things [could seem valuable]? So it was when, abandoning theology, Dante abandoned himself to a little maid, that is, to poetry and other worldly knowledge. Against these Isidore . . . says: Christians are forbidden to read the fictions of the poets, since their pleasure in the stories too much impels their minds to things that stir up their lusts (On Cantos 30, 31).

In general agreement with this, though somewhat less outright in their statement, are other medieval commentaries. It should be observed that Pietro does not accuse his father of any common sort of wickedness, but merely of abandoning theology for more worldly studies. We may suppose that for Pietro his father's poem was so theological that he did not class it with vain poetry, though Pietro's commentary shows that he himself was familiar with Ovid and other poets.

The medieval commentators, we may remember, appear not to have read the *Vita Nuova*. In Pietro di Dante's commentary as printed, the work is unmentioned, and Beatrice is Theology and only that. When in inedited manuscripts of that commentary the early Beatrice appears, an editor must ask: Has there been interpolation? Benvenuto knows of the *Vita Nuova*, but has not read it carefully. He says that Dante's father took him to a party at Folco Portinari's house where the boy saw the eight-year-old Beatrice (On *Purg.* 30). In his *Life of Dante*, Boccaccio says the same. He and Benvenuto evidently are not writing from the early work itself, in which neither Dante's father nor Folco Portinari are named, and where, as Dante reiterates the number nine, Beatrice is put in her ninth year. Buti shows no consciousness of the *Vita Nuova*, identifying Beatrice with a countess who died at Pisa in 1116 (On *Purg.* 27. 34). So, unless we resign ourselves to allegory, forgetting the *Vita Nuova*, the early commentators do not aid with Beatrice, though when they limit Dante's sins to abandoning theology for poetry, they are biographically valuable. (The poet appears as a sensual sinner in the sixteenth-century commentaries of Landino and Daniello on Canto 31.) So on the Beatrice of the *Vita Nuova* and Dante's infidelity to her as a person, these commentators give no aid. They leave every man to interpret for himself.

When Dante the fictitious traveler has been drawn through the River Lethe, the virtues of Faith, Hope, and Charity, attendants of Beatrice, intercede with her for him: "Turn, Beatrice, turn your holy eyes to your faithful [servant], who to see you has taken so many steps. In your grace do us the grace of unveiling your mouth to him, that he may discern the second beauty which you conceal" (*Purg.* 31. 133). When Beatrice next addresses her lover, her tone has changed: "Here for a short time you will be a forester, and you will without end be with me a citizen of that Rome where Christ is a Roman.

Therefore, for the sake of the world which lives wickedly, now keep your eyes on the chariot, and what you see, be sure to write, when you return to earth" (*Purg.* 32. 100). Obediently the traveler follows her directions. This interest in worldly evil is suggested neither by what has immediately preceded nor by anything in the *Vita Nuova*, and equally unexpected is Beatrice's interest in the writer and traveler expecting to return to the world. She next shows herself eager to fit into the spirit of the journey as Virgil's successor. Looking at her charge, she calmly says: " 'Walk faster, so that as I speak to you, you will be in a position for listening.' When I was, as I should be, with her, she said to me: 'Brother, why do you not go to questioning me as you walk along' " (*Purg.* 33. 19)? On the visitor's polite answer, she continues: "From fear and bashfulness I want you now to free yourself" (33. 31). She continues expounding the pageant, with another exhortation to her companion to tell truly, when back in the land of the living, what he has seen, and to that admonition she recurs (*Purg.* 33. 55, 76). Since her hearer's intellect seems to her stony, she tells him his way is far from the divine. When he answers that he does not remember straying from her, she answers with a smile—and seemingly real amusement—that her words will now be so plain as to be evident to his dull sight. Apparently encouraged, partly perhaps by Beatrice's references to his writing, Dante, with great respect, moves to satisfy his temporarily suspended hunger for knowing the names of things: "O light, O splendor of the human race, what water is this which here gushes from one beginning and severs itself from itself" (*Purg.* 33. 115)? Beatrice refers him to Matilda, who explains that she has already informed the visitor on the matter. Beatrice with good humor excuses the questioner and asks Matilda to lead him to the fountain of Eunoë

The Beatrice of the *Paradiso* is to a great extent the Beatrice of the later Earthly Paradise, when censure is done with. She shows nothing of what may be called the jealousy of her early rebukes. Like Virgil, she is assiduous in her care for the traveler, attentive as a mother (*Purg.* 30. 79; *Par.* 1. 102; 22. 4), though not directly so called, while Virgil is repeatedly "Father" (*Inf.* 8. 110; *Purg.* 18. 7, 13; 25. 17; 27. 52, etc.). She is also guide and escort (e.g., *Par.* 23. 34; 21. 23), titles she shares not only with Virgil but with Sordello, and even with Nessus (*Purg.* 7. 42; *Inf.* 12. 100). There can be no parallel to the frequent reference to Virgil as "teacher" (*maestro, dottore, pedagogue*), "leader" (*duca*), "sage," "our greatest Muse" (*Par.* 15. 26)—expressions of Dante's debt to the poet from whom he learned "the beautiful style that has honored me" (*Inf.* 1. 87). Yet Beatrice is a blessed lady (*Inf.* 2. 53), the love of the First Loving (*Par.* 4. 118), goddess (*ibid.*), miracle (18. 63), celestial escort (21. 23) and Saint Peter's "holy sister" (24. 28). The word "holy" here receives dignity from the circumstances. More-over, Virgil includes Beatrice with Saint Lucia and actually with the Virgin when telling the wanderer of the dark forest that "three blessed ladies in the court of Heaven are concerned about you" (*Inf.* 2. 124). If Virgil was on earth a great marshal (*Purg.* 24. 99), Beatrice has a seat high in the heavenly rose.

The wisdom of Virgil, "that noble sage who knew all" (*Inf.* 7. 3), tends in the poem to be limited to his function as guide and director of the journey, though he can also speak on ethical topics (*Inf.* 11), on the efficacy of prayer (*Purg.* 6. 34), on love as the root of both sin and virtue (*Purg.* 17. 85; 18. 16), and on free will (18. 49). Beatrice, "whose beautiful eye sees everything" (*Inf.* 10. 131), and who is a light "be-tween the truth and the mind" (*Purg.* 6. 44), is as much the teacher as Virgil, instructing her pupil on the universe (*Par.* 1. 88), on moon spots (2. 61), vows and their relation to free will (4. 16; 5. 19), the Redemption and immortality (7. 19), the world's reversals (27. 106), and the orders of angels (28. 98; 29. 10). Beatrice as described in the *Vita Nuova* gives no suggestion of such knowledge and expository power.

In the *Comedy* some of her figures of speech are hardly feminine. Three times she mentions the bow (*Par.* 1. 119; 4. 69; 29. 24), once the smith and his hammer (2. 128), the poop and the bow of a ship (27. 146), the shield and the lance (29. 114). No comparisons come from feminine occupations. Her historical allusions are to men, as Saint Lawrence and Mucius the Roman (4. 84); Iphigenia is mentioned in con-nection with her father (5. 70). Beatrice names no female saints. She refers learnedly to Plato and to writers on angels

(4. 24, 49; 28. 130). She uses Latin words (29. 12, 15). In this matter her speeches are not planned for a woman.

She is even more in command of Dante than is Virgil. The word *donna* applied to her often indicates "mistress" rather than simply "lady." Virgil, however, is sometimes *signore* or "lord" (*Inf.* 2. 140; *Purg.* 4. 109). Even more than to Virgil, the traveler looks to Beatrice for detailed instructions and permission. Especially, he seldom addresses the souls he encounters without her approval. Yet in the Heaven of Jupiter she does not appear (*Par.* 18. 64–20 end). Virgil does not so leave his pupil without direction.

Something of masterful quality appears in Beatrice the beautiful lady who guides her charge through the heavens, though this lady in Heaven is derived from the Beatrice of the *Vita Nuova* who has gone to dwell with the angels (31) and looks on the face of Christ (42), and who as a miracle is rooted in the Trinity (29). As Beatrice and her lover ascend the heavenly stairway, the transition from one heaven to that above it is marked by a heightening of her beauty. For example, in passing from the Heaven of Mars to that of Jupiter: "I turned to my right to see in Beatrice my duty indicated either by speech or by sign, and I saw her eyes so pure, so sprightly that her appearance surpassed that at any earlier time" (*Par.* 18. 52). Or from the Fixed Stars to the Primum Mobile:

My enamored spirit, which was ever full of love for my noble mistress, more than ever burned again to turn eyes upon her. And if nature or art ever in human flesh or in pictures of it put attraction to arrest the eyes in order to gain the mind, all of it united would seem nothing if compared with the divine pleasure that shone upon me when I turned to her smiling face. . . . Then she spoke with a smile so glad that I thought God was rejoicing in her face (27. 88).

I turned my face to my mistress . . . and was struck with astonishment, for in her eyes burned such a smile that I believed I was reaching with my eyes the utmost limit of favor and of Paradise (15. 32).

In the *Vita Nuova,* on being saluted by her, he "thought he saw the utmost limits of beatitude" (39). For a man in the Heavenly Paradise, such interest in the beauty of even a

"blessed" lady is bold or somewhat comic. Beatrice herself may
be amused by adoration:

I turned at the loving word of my Encouragement, and the love I
then saw in her holy eyes I now despair of telling, not merely because I do not trust my speech but because my mind cannot rise
so far above itself if another does not guide it. Thus much I can say
of that time: looking upon her, my affection was free from all
other desire as long as the eternal pleasure, sending its rays directly
upon Beatrice, contented me with a reflection from her beautiful
face. Overcoming me with the light of a smile, she said: "Turn
and listen [to Cacciaguida], for not merely in my eyes is Paradise"
(18. 7).

The traveler is warned not to let his individual paradise super-
sede the larger one.

Yet his love may include something rational: "That sun
which first heated my breast with love has, by proving and
disproving, revealed to me the sweet appearance of truth" (*Par.*
3. 1). Here Beatrice is both the lover's sun and the learned
expositor, and we are reminded that Dante found poetical
beauty in truth (*Convivio* 2. 11). "Beatrice looked at me with
eyes full of sparks of love, so divine that, conquered, my strength
turned its back [submitted]" (*Par.* 4. 139). When celestial light
has overcome the visitor's eyesight, and he is told that Beatrice
can cure him as Ananias did the Apostle Paul, he answers:
"At her pleasure either early or late let healing come to the
eyes which were doors when she entered [my body] with the
fire with which I am always burning" (*Par.* 26. 13). In the
Heaven of the Fixed Stars and after his successful examination
on Christian belief, the traveler burns with fire kindled by Beatrice. Beatrice's eyes also provide Love with a rope to catch
him (28. 12). Such figures, later to be developed by Petrarch
and his followers, are already suggested by Dante's predecessors
and contemporaries. For example, in a *canzone* by Dante's
friend Guido Cavalcanti, Love says: "I took from the lady's
sweet smile a sharp arrow which has pierced your heart"
(*Donna mi priega*). As long as Beatrice is with her pupil, her
beauty increases until he is no more able to express it than he
is the wonders of Paradise: "If all I have written about her up

to now were fused into one speech of praise, it would be too little to supply this need. The beauty I saw is not merely far beyond our poetical strength, but I hold for certain that its Maker alone enjoys it in full. By this passage on her beauty I am beaten more completely, I admit, than ever by a part of his theme comic or tragic poet has been defeated, because, like the sun in an eye that greatly trembles, the recollection of her sweet smile deprives me of my mind. From the first day when I saw her face in this life up to the time of this sight in Heaven, to follow where my poetry led has not been denied me, but now I must cease to follow her beauty as I write" (30. 16). So the returned traveler looks back to the *Vita Nuova* as well as upon his experience in Heaven. After displaying this beauty beyond poetic power, Beatrice becomes a "prompt leader," explaining the arrangement of the souls in Heaven and their condition at the Last Judgment. Elsewhere she shifts her role from lover's ideal to lecturer. After a "smile that was enough to make a man happy in the fire" (7. 18), Beatrice resumes a discussion of vows, which one devotee of Dante has called "rather arid." Having so smiled that the adorer believed "God was rejoicing in her face" (27. 105), she explains the order of the world, seasoning her words with an attack on cupidity and the wickedness of man.

How complex Beatrice is! She is the lovely child of Dante's boyhood; she is the rigorous thinker who declares that her charge needs "to go to the root" of a truth (14. 12); her thoughts sound "the abyss of the eternal plan" (7. 94); to Aquinas she is a "beautiful lady" (10. 93), as was Helen to the old men who looked at her from the walls of Troy; to Saint Peter she is his "holy sister" (24. 28) and to Virgil at least she is one of three with the Virgin (*Inf.* 2. 124); yet she can even show what approaches jealousy of the "little maid," or take the part of the lady who laughed when Guenivere began to slip, or be amused when her lover finds in her eyes paradise enough for him. A reader puzzled by this condition, or feeling driven to make it consistent at all costs, may be helped by recalling that though this is the "lofty *cantica*" of the *Commedia*, it still is a *cantica* in a comedy. Moreover, though by enduring hunger, cold, and lack of sleep for many years the

poet made himself thin in laboring on his *Comedy*, yet he
still did not have years enough to let him make everything
precise and consistent.

The early power of the leader of the *dolce stil nuovo*, even
that of some of its lesser lights, is apparent. What even a youthful Dante does passes into the universal. Yet a school is a school,
and to such extent as its poems are manifestos they risk their
poetical value. The poetry conventionally thought of as coming
from the troubadours and their followers lacks what is required
to give it weight with men generally. The skill of Petrarch as a
versifier and the recognition by craftsmen-poets that he had
something to teach them has given him, as sonneteer, a historical reputation hardly justified by the substance of his love
poetry. Or if he does make Laura something more than an
artistic device, the skillful but light-weight versifiers called
Petrarchists proclaim his weakness. It is not strange that for
such sonneteers—even the best of them—all over Europe the
question has been asked: Was there a real Laura or Julia or
Delia? To ask the question—however mistakenly—is still to
approach an answer not wholly satisfactory to a seeker for
poetical qualities beyond verbal skill. Preoccupation—in itself
deserving praise—with the composition of poetry, such as marks
the *Vita Nuova*, rather than with the world's serious activity,
limits even a Dante. For the young poet, it is a proper stage.
He must learn to write. Milton tells us that critics said of his
early verse: "The style, by certain vital signs it had, was likely
to live." Without such style, verse fails of immortality. Yet
however a vigorous young poet may burst the fetters of ap-
prenticeship, he still is immature until he applies his craftsman-
ship to more than mere literary matters. Are we to wonder
whether Dante, so far as he deals with the Beatrice derived
from the *Vita Nuova*, still shows vestiges of such an immature
stage? Is it more probable that any such vestiges come from
early composition of the *cantica* rather than from continued
inability altogether to throw off earlier habits? The *Inferno*,
where the *dolce stil nuovo* is absorbed and transcended, may
be taken as an answer.

As Foscolo has suggested (*Discorso sul . . . Dante* 159),
parts of the *Paradiso* may have been written earlier than the

rest of the *Comedy*. If so, they would have undergone most changes in the long years of revision. When first placed in the *Paradiso*, the Beatrice of the *Vita Nuova* may not have been a scholastic lecturer. We read that she continued her exposition of vows and free will "like a man who does not interrupt his discourse" (*Par.* 5. 17). Did the word "man" (*uom*) once apply to some learned doctor, a theologian from the Heaven of the Sun? Only in the learned speeches of the *Paradiso* does she address her pupil as "brother" (*frate—Par.* 4. 100; 7. 58, 130; cf. *Purg.* 33. 23). But how the poem came to be what it is, though enlightening, is not of highest import. Dante relinquished it as it stands, and we do not know that he felt dissatisfied. Perhaps the standards of artists, who know what it is to construct, are not always those of scholars. Did Dante wish a neat and clarified Beatrice? At least he has without apology put her before us as she is. Let us read of her and be thankful.

BEATRICE IN THE STRUCTURE OF THE PARADISO

In the first seven cantos of the *Paradiso*, Beatrice speaks at such length that her set speeches, to be distinguished from conversation, run to some 440 lines. These speeches come before she takes her pupil into the First Heaven, after they have there completed their interview with Piccarda and are ready to leave, and in an interval between the Second and the Third Heavens. Thus her expositions are in some sense interludes, directed to her pupil when none of the blessed are present. After devoting most of the seventh canto to a discourse on Christ's death, redemption, and immortality, she abruptly ceases to speak at length. The longer expositions are then assigned to the blessed encountered in the various heavens, such as Aquinas and Cacciaguida. Beatrice makes the brief remarks necessary to the managing of the journey. For twenty cantos she refrains from what may be called lectures. Then, after the disappearance of Saint Peter in the Eighth Heaven, she again resumes her function as teacher, giving some forty lines to cupidity (*Par.* 27. 106). In the next canto she delivers two set speeches, amounting together to about seventy lines. In Canto 29 she resumes her early habit, requiring 135 lines for exposition of the angels, with a digression on preaching.

That Dante deliberately planned such inconsistency in Beatrice's role is difficult to imagine. Would not his original plan be such as is revealed by Cantos 8–26, in which Beatrice in her growing beauty acts as guide and "mother" (*Par.* 22. 4) but not as a lecturer? Her extension of Piccarda's explanation of vows is of disproportionate length, even though including the subject—important to Dante—of free will. Among her discourses late in the poem, that on cupidity (27. 121) is not demanded by the situation, though the author has made such connections as he can for a topic of which he did not tire. In Canto 28 her remarks are suited to a guide explaining the Ninth Heaven; at least they are not primarily theological. The exposition of the angels occupying most of Canto 29 may also be held an overextension of the preceding discourse, and the bonds between it and the section on preaching (29. 91) are not tight, however heartily Dante wrote invective against unspiritual sermonizers. In Canto 30 Beatrice again is more guide than teacher, though in the last words given her in the poem— a Dantesque digression—she attacks Boniface VIII.

Were most of these longer speeches written for Beatrice's tongue? Instruction by her is promised in the *Purgatorio*. Virgil is unwilling to speak positively on prayer: His pupil should not believe without confirmation by Beatrice, who will be a "light between the truth and the intellect" (*Purg.* 6. 45). Yet she does not discourse on that subject. She is recommended by Virgil to remove doubts on worldly possessions and love (*Purg.* 15. 77), but this also she fails to do. Similarly, Virgil refers to her as one who, presiding over faith (*Purg.* 18. 48), can do what reason cannot in giving knowledge of love; nevertheless she does not deal with the subject. On free will Virgil also promises her assistance (*Purg.* 18. 73); of that theme she does speak, though briefly and incidentally (*Par.* 5. 19–24). Beatrice is also to enlighten the traveler on his future as an exile (*Inf.* 10. 132); this function is taken over by Cacciaguida (*Par.* 17. 94). Dante gives no sign, then, that he was planning Beatrice's present speeches when he wrote the *Purgatorio*; but was he contemplating others as extensive as her existing expositions?

In Heavens Three to Eight Beatrice displays little learning. Yet, for example, when speaking after the philosopher Aquinas, she says that the traveler "needs to go to the root of another truth" (*Par.* 14. 12). Thus the erudite Beatrice of the first seven cantos and of Cantos 27, 28, and 29 may be distinguished from Beatrice the guide and director who conducts the visitor through Paradise. Her learned and denunciatory speeches are less suited for the pilgrim's "sweet guide and dear" (23. 34) than for some learned man. In his years of writing, the author must have produced much manuscript in *terza rima* and other meters. Shall we suppose that, as the inventor of *terza rima*, he wrote in it little save his *Comedy* as it now stands? Such manuscripts as he esteemed would have been an important part of the baggage carried on his wanderings. In his many years of writing he would modify his plans. So elementary a notion as that he began with *Inferno* 1 and went straight through the poem to *Paradise* 33 without enormous rewriting, excising, adding, shifting, and reconsidering of material needs only to be stated to be rejected. On paper or in his memory, he had stores of material not certainly placed in the *Comedy*.

Having written part of the *Paradiso* about as it stands, and having decided on its total length and its thirty-three cantos, he found, it seems to me, that he lacked some hundreds of lines of the destined number. Various possibilities were before him. He could replan and rewrite on a larger scale. But already he was approaching or perhaps had already passed the span of life—fifty-one years—attained by his great teacher, the author of the *Aeneid*. Moreover, perhaps he had further work to do in bringing the *Inferno* and the *Purgatorio* to the state he desired. Virgil, as Dante knew, had on his deathbed desired that his poem be burned, because not revised to his mind —however admirable it appeared to his readers in Roman times or in the fourteenth century. Did Dante so feel the pressure of years as to resort to the most rapid method, that of inserting in the most suitable places verses that he already had by him, for whatever purpose composed? Thus, by assigning to Beatrice speeches written, it appears, without thought of her, he gave the effect described by Momigliano as that of two

Beatrices (comment on *Par.* 18. 19–21) and of "artistic uncertainty" (on 7. 19). Momigliano writes further:

> Beatrice is after Dante the most complex figure in the *Commedia*,
> but the most incoherent. . . . When upon her lyric personality
> are superimposed the pedagogical and edifying duties derived from
> her introduction into the architecture of the *Commedia* as one of
> the strongest columns supporting it, her poetic figure dies. Her only
> personality having a true poetic life is that of the admonisher and
> rescuer of Dante, when she is a creature which strains toward God's
> light and is glorified in it. That of the professor is darkened by the
> enigmatic struggle. That of the revealer of theological truths
> and of the exhorter to Christianity is overweighted by scho-
> lastic and sermonizing attitudes which Dante presents with frag-
> mentary attention and pleasure, influenced by his own passion for
> theology and for religious rectitude and forgetful of the poetic
> force generating Beatrice. In these isolated personalities Beatrice
> loses her sublimity, that is, her reason for being. Scholastic method,
> syllogistic skeleton, pauses of pulpit eloquence, perorations make
> us forget the divine beauty of Beatrice. The theologian kills the
> woman. Evidently, since the *Commedia* is constituted as it is, such
> a defect was inevitable. Without the exhorter to Christianity, and
> especially without the revealer of the truth, the *Paradiso* would
> have been shorter by a number of cantos; the whole poem, if the
> *Paradiso* was not symmetrical with the other parts, would seem
> maimed (On *Par.* 5. 61).

This passage raises various questions. Perhaps the most important is that of poet and critic: Which determines a poem?
More specifically, were *Inferno* and *Purgatorio* of their present
length before the last *cantica* was composed, so that a shorter
Paradiso would have destroyed symmetry? But dismissing these
for the present, we see that the critic almost implies that the
scholastic matter of the first seven cantos and of the three
later ones came tardily into Dante's poem, perhaps as a result of
his desire to round out his hundred cantos.

6 · Punishments and Rewards

PUNISHMENTS IN HELL

Poets who have written on visits to the world of the dead have had their eyes on its relation to the world of the living. Virgil's Aeneas hears the screams of the wicked punished in Tartarus, and in the Elysian Fields sees those who by conferring benefits have deserved grateful recollection of their deeds (*Aeneid* 6. 664). Dante's greater length permits him to be more detailed than Virgil. From the inscription at the portal of Hell we learn his purpose of exhibiting by example divine power, wisdom, love, and justice. Commentators in the fourteenth century, including Dante himself (if he be the author of what is called his *Tenth Epistle*, directed to Can Grande della Scala), being interested in the allegory of divine justice, saw the *Commedia* as presenting, by means of the shades, man as, in this world, in the exercise of his free will he deserves punishments and rewards from divine justice. In his philosoph-·ical studies, Dante had learned the importance of the human will and of the formation of habit through its exercise. The truly wicked, wrote Aquinas in his Commentary on Aristotle's *Ethics* (Chap. 13, lect. 15), habitually engage in evil actions, in which they find pleasure. If we are to discover a rational system in Dante's Hell, the spirits there justly punished represent living men who have formed the habit of conducting themselves wickedly. They have rejected repentance; otherwise they would have been assigned not to Hell but to Purgatory. They remain in the evil to which they have accustomed themselves as their desired environment. In life they dwell in a hell of sin: "Which way I fly is Hell; myself am Hell" (*Paradise Lost* 4. 75). Thus the shades in allegory representing the unrighteous are in the part of the Inferno that they have chosen and from which they do not attempt escape. That is, they are beyond repenting.

About 1390 the commentator Buti expressed what he thought the principle of the *Inferno*; for example, he wrote: "The punishments which literally the author adapts to the sinners in Hell, according to their fitness to the sin, are allegorically to be understood of sinners in this world. Hence when I have shown the punishments in the text, their allegorical significance will be clear" (On *Inf.* 5. 25). On this principle Buti explains the sinners of the various levels of Hell as they appear to him. The shedders of blood in a river of blood express thereby how they lived (*Inf.* 12. 48). Deniers of the soul's immortality are enclosed in tombs to fit their belief that man does not exist beyond the grave (10. 15). More would be required to symbolize the active daily life of these sinners, for their rejection of immortality, to Dante the height of wickedness (*Convivio* 2. 8), shows only passively a mind in darkness like that of the sepulchre.

Those who have caused discord and strife within social groups suffer such division of their own bodies as they brought upon kingdoms and families. The poet's Mahomet thus explains their punishment: "All those you see here were sowers of division and faction when alive; therefore they are so severed" (28. 34). Another sinner in the same *bolgia*, Bertran de Born, is still plainer: "Because I parted persons so united [as father and son], I am, alas! carrying my brain parted from its source in this body. So in me is carried out the *contrapassum* [counterpassion, *lex talionis*, law of retribution]" (28. 139). Seeing that these men did not suffer in life the division which a devil inflicts on them in Hell, but rather caused division in others, Buti yet tries to explain the slashed bodies of these sinners as an allegory of their earthly activity. Ali, "split from the chin to the forehead," he says was not a disciple of Mahomet's but a Christian cleric who misled him: "This punishment is suitably feigned by the author. Since Ali was one of those clerics who are head of the Church after Christ, he can properly be said to be divided in the head, because he divided himself from the other clerics who are the head. So allegorically we can say that when he was in the world he was divided in the head, for to Mahomet he opened his fraud and the false opinion he had in his head and sowed it in him" (On *Inf.* 28. 28).

Thus Buti fits this punishment into the system of allegorizing wicked life through condition in Hell. His argument omits the devil with the sword who slashes the sinners of this *bolgia*. Who divided the mind of Ali; was he the author of his own dividing? These sinners do not—as they did in life—mangle social bodies; their own bodies are mangled. In Hell the obvious agent for torture is a devil. The bodies of these sufferers are at intervals miraculously healed and then again sundered by their tormenter. To Buti, this means that their punishment is without end and that they never know quiet, since in life they unceasingly destroyed the quiet and peace of faithful Christians and of citizens and relatives and friends and married couples. Thus he gives meaning to what some may think another wonder seen by the visitor to Hell, varied by the rhythm of the renewed punishment. Moreover, endlessness is not peculiar to this *bolgia* but common to all the penalties of Hell. So this punishment illustrates the law of retribution or *lex talionis*, "an eye for an eye and a tooth for a tooth"; that which the sinners did is done to them. Their severed bodies can typify a divided city, but they are not shown causing such division as they brought about when alive.

Unless we adopt some such ingenuity as that of Buti, we allow Dante to be satisfied with such vague similarity as resides in the idea of division, however differently applied. Instead of fitting the punishment into a tight allegorical system, the poet rather asks, what he can make pictorially or dramatically effective in his narrative course. Yet Buti and the writer to Can Grande are not to be wholly rejected when they make the punishments allegories of evil lives. Their analysis is correct in that the poem not only does represent a fitting of the punishment to the crime but also often suggests the state on earth of the sinners dealt with. Yet most of the shades passively accept punishment, though once at least they actively imitate

their earthly employment, for the misers when alive labored
uselessly in heaping up wealth, as in Hell they fruitlessly roll
heavy weights (7. 27, 63). Thus the allegory of earthly habit
is seldom made perfect by Dante. His readers, according as
they wish to exercise ingenuity, can regard him as more or
less attaining it.

Once having read that the carnal sinners in the second
circle of Hell are buffeted by winds (5. 30), we easily believe
that they symbolize men swayed irrationally to and fro by
their passions. We take the flatterers immersed in the filth of
privies as materializing men who practised a filthy sin (18. 125).
Yet if given only the punishment, would we at once decide
upon the sin typified? When Buti says that Dante wishes to
show how foul flattery is, he does not say that since these sinners are foul, we know them as flatterers.

The brevity of Dante's scenes and his habit of showing the
sinners as though they were exhibits in a museum prepared for
the scrutiny of observers, require the souls to be passive under
punishment. To wallow in filth shows the nature of the flat-
terer's soul, but his act of currying favor is not suggested. The
angry in the Stygian swamp attack Filippo Argenti, and he
turns upon himself his own teeth (8. 63), according to the
medieval ethical notion that the angry man injures himself. As
late as Milton, Moloch will rush on to attack at the expense
of forcing the Almighty to "consume" Moloch and his companion devils and reduce them to nothing (*Paradise Lost* 2.
96). But for the most part Hell shows sinners inactively enduring punishments suggesting—not always clearly—their earthly
lives.

Pictorially developed is the state of the simonists. In the
rock of the third *bolgia* are holes like those in which the priest
stood when performing baptism in Dante's San Giovanni:
"From the mouth of each one stuck out a sinner's feet and
his legs up to the thick part, and the rest was inside" (19. 22).
The "thick part" (*grosso*) has usually been interpreted as the
calf, but one annotator at least, noting a reference to violent
movement of joints (19. 26), speaks for the thigh. Elsewhere
Dante uses the same word. The grafters are like frogs that stick
their muzzles above the water but keep under it their "feet

and thick part" (22. 27). Here the whole body is indicated. Virgil, with his pupil suspended around his neck, climbs down Satan's body. Then, "when we were exactly at the point where the thigh merges into the thick part (*grosso*) of the haunches," etc. (34. 76). Does this tell that the simoniac popes are with ridiculous obscenity revealed from toe to buttock, and thus have the fullest opportunity for brandishing their legs so violently that ropes would not hold them? [1] Would most of us, reading of these sinners, at once suppose them punished for simony? Yet Dante, though interested in making them absurd, still points to correspondence between sin and penalty when he has Pope Nicholas jocosely say: "On earth money and here myself I put in a purse" (19. 72). The joke covers the failure in parallel. The simoniacs should be shown in some such relation to money as the manslayers of the Seventh Circle bear to blood. Benvenuto da Imola endeavors to find the correspondence required by his theory, so like that of the letter to Can Grande:

> Their punishment is that they are strictly shut up and buried in holes in the earth with their heads down and their feet up, and the soles of their feet are burned with steady flame. Hence, mad with this torturing heat, they wave their legs and feet, which are above the earth. This is an entirely just punishment for them, since they who ought to contemplate heavenly things and meditate on divine matters, keeping the law of Christ, of whom they pretend to be lieutenants and imitators, on the contrary, by following after vain worldly things, do the opposite, being wretchedly immersed in worldly affairs only. Therefore they are well represented as planted in the earth, since they have their hearts intent on worldly concerns only and their feet turned toward Heaven, as though they would say: "I wholly spurn heavenly matters and my mind is fixed on worldly things," so that they dig in the earth and seek in it for gold and silver, and do not attempt to lay up treasure in Heaven.

How much of this is proper poetic interpretation and how much is commentator's ingenuity, unwarranted by Pope Nicho-

---

1 I have rendered *giunte* (here only in this sense in the *Commedia*) as "legs." *Giunture* (*Purg.* 26. 57) is explained by commentators as "bones" and as "sinews." Of *gambe* (19. 23) Siebzehner-Vivanti's *Dizionario della Divina Commedia* remarks that it is often used "per tutto l'arto inferiore INF. XIII. 121 ecc." Readers can choose how much leg-brandishing they will allow the simoniacs.

las' pun, readers can decide for themselves. Benvenuto has no Dantesque support for making the simonists gold miners. But at least the annotator is right in holding that the states of the damned typify, more or less according to the poet's convenience, wicked earthly lives.

The grafters of the fifth *bolgia* are immersed in pitch, to which Dante gives realism through likening it to that boiling in the Venetian navy yard. The first sinner mentioned is brought by a demon who shouts: "Put him under [the surface]" (21. 39). The other devils warn their prey: "Don't come above the surface." When he does not heed, they thrust him down as a scullion would a piece of meat in a kettle, saying in their enjoyment of their joke: "Here you have to dance under cover, so that, if you can, you may play at odd and even in concealment" (21. 53). Why pitch to conceal them? The notion of mere concealment, such as these sinners are generally explained as seeking for their rascality, seems forced aside by interest in pitch as hot and sticky. Especially does this appear when two of the Malebranche are ridiculously caught in the glue (22. 144).

All sinners destined for circles of Hell below Limbo appear before Minos as judge. To him they confess, and Minos decides how many circles "down they should be put" (5. 12). After Minos' decision, the suicides "fall into the forest" (13. 97), and the sinners in the Tolomea also fall (33. 125, 133). Yet in that part of Hell one of the shades supposes Virgil and his companion passing through on their way to the Giudecca, the lowest division of the last circle, as their allotted place of torture (33. 111). To the fifth *bolgia*, that of the grafters, a devil brings souls directly from Lucca (21. 35). At least Minos is not mentioned. This *bolgia*, however, is so exceptionally developed that it can be put outside the norm. By a devil who appeared as Buonconte died, his soul was carried before Minos with no mention of crossing Acheron (27. 114). In such matters a poet may be allowed variation according to his artistic purpose, even to inconsistency, rather than held to specifications, whether those of critics or his own. The confessions to Minos and the conduct of most of the sinners—unprotesting at their state—indicate that they accept the part of Hell assigned to them. So they must insofar as Hell is an allegory of men on earth deliberately or maliciously living in wickedness and with deadly sin rejecting repentance. Yet in two instances, condemned souls endeavor to alleviate their punishment. The centaurs patrol Flegeton, shooting their arrows at any of the damned who get farther out of the blood than the measure allotted to their sin (12. 72). For the allegory, the grafters of the fifth *bolgia* should keep always under cover, yet they are continually attempting to elude the vigilance of the Malebranche assigned to keep them under the concealing pitch. Here Dante abandons allegory for story. Tortured persons naturally try to escape. Guardian devils are interesting to readers, but what can they do except use their fleshhooks or other weapons on the sinners? Medieval pictures of Hell get much of their vigor from the activity of the devils. Indeed, part of Dante's individuality of treatment is that he so little employs torturers. If in allegory the *Comedy* shows the lives men live on earth, in the freedom of the will, the author has no need of hellish jailers, unless he considers Saint Anthony's tempters factual.

To Dante's contemporaries, especially those who had read the books he knew, some suggestions came easily which now are difficult. For example, the sullen angry of the Stygian swamp are not strange to readers of Aquinas' *Summa* (e.g., 2. 2. 158. 5), on the relationship between sullenness and anger (*Inf.* 7. 121). Yet the medieval commentators sometimes show little advantage over moderns who catch Dante's metaphors. The sinners in the lowest hell, says Benvenuto da Imola, "are tortured in the coldest and stiffest ice, and properly, for the heat of love and the love of charity are always symbolized by fire. . . . Contrarily, cruel hatred causing betrayal is signified by ice. . . . This indicates that all the heat of love and humanity is extinct in the hard and frozen heart of the betrayer" (On *Inf.* 32). The early expositors, making their own guesses, do not find in Satan's chewing and tearing any suggestion of the activity on earth of Brutus, Cassius, and Judas, though the careers of the three may, in Dante's opinion, have been so satanic that Lucifer in person properly attends to their punishment.

For all his underlying principle of representing the life of wicked men by their situations in Hell, Dante may now and then be satisfied with a mere hint at his formula. If at times his presentations be overingenious, as for the sodomites on the burning sands, nevertheless he is always interested in lively description and storytelling, that is, in poetry. When does allegory take the primary rather than the subordinate place? The modern allegorical interpreter is often left to his own devices, as were those of Dante's century. Any punishments which to the poetically minded reader are immediate metaphors for bad earthly life—as the useless and heavy labors of the greedy as they roll their stones—he can accept as symbolical. If he wishes further to accompany commentators old or new in their conclusion or in their methods, so he may. Yet if he holds aloft an invention of his own as the only key to a supposed symbolical passage, he is in danger.

PURIFICATION IN PURGATORY

As the name declares and as Dante repeats, Purgatory is the realm "where the human spirit is cleansed [purged] and becomes fit to ascend to Heaven" (*Purg.* 1. 5). This mountain "takes away men's evil" (13. 3); it "cures the souls" (*Par.* 17. 20). In Purgatory, sinners untie the knot that sin has tied (*Purg.* 16. 24). Most strikingly, Purgatory is "the mountain that straightens you whom the world made crooked" (*Purg.* 23. 125). This straightening is voluntarily undergone by the penitents; as Statius explains, they desire to be tormented on any terrace until purified from the sin purged there (*Purg.* 21. 64). The penalties are opposed or counteractive to the sins. Chaucer, in his "Parson's Tale," after discussing any one of the seven capital vices or deadly sins, gives the remedy against it. To this pattern of opposition the Florentine has adapted his purgatorial penalties, in order to represent man on earth struggling against, and with divine aid ridding himself of, the various vices. To make such an ethical plan poetic is not always easy.

On the terrace of pride the metaphor expressing humility is evident. Benvenuto puts it thus: "What a just and proper punishment the poet gives these proud men! For he feigns that each man carries on his proud shoulders a weighty rock that bends him to the ground, and so burdened he goes slowly on his way. By this the author indicates that he who strives to purge this burdensome vice of pride must bow to the ground his head, which he earlier carried erect toward the sky. In short, he must be as much bent down and humiliated as he tried to be raised up and exalted. This is a great affliction to the proud man who, having striven to appear magnanimous, looks upon it as a sign of extreme wretchedness." Here the voluntarily assumed burden forces the sinner into an attitude contradicting pride (*Purg.* 11. 53).

On the terrace of sloth, counteraction to the sin is literal rather than allegorical. The slothful are getting rid of their vice by running at full speed. Similarly the gluttonous of the Sixth Terrace are so abstinent as to be reduced almost to skeletons.

On the Second Terrace, where envy is purged, the eyes of the penitents are fastened shut with wires. Benvenuto explains: "This was a very just penalty for the envious, since envy is caused especially by the sight. Therefore Socrates well said that the envious man in a city might be punished by having eyes and ears, so that his afflictions should equal in number the instances of good fortune that he saw and heard. . . . Hence the man wishing to be purged of this vice should wholly close his eyes so that he will not become envious on seeing the good fortune of other men." In the commentary by Dante's son Pietro, we read: "The closing of their eyes signifies that any one desiring to purge himself must have his eyes closed to worldly things so that he will not see vanity" (On *Purg.* 13). Thus on four terraces the purging penalties of Purgatory oppose the vices they are to eliminate.

On coming to wrath, Benvenuto explains differently:

The poet offers a fitting method of purging anger. For he feigns that those prone to anger are purged in smoke, very thick, very black, and very bitter, so that no one can see or make out anything in it. The reason is that smoke is caused by fire, and anger is a sort of fire, since it is a flaming of blood around the heart. Therefore, as there cannot be fire without smoke, there cannot be anger without darkness of mind. So he who is to be purified properly from this very injurious vice of anger must be punished in smoke; that is, he must carefully imagine the nature and quality of this vice which so extinguishes the light of reason and covers it with smoke (On *Purg.* 16).

Thus the penalty has the qualities of the vice. Buti uses much the same method, as does Lana. If these commentators had consulted Aquinas' *Summa* 2. 2. 158, they would have read that impetuosity is one of the qualities of anger. Perhaps then they would have noted that the movements of the penitents on this terrace are slow and careful, like those of a blind man. Thus the man prone to the haste of anger can be counteracting his un-Christian habit. Perhaps Dante—the more because this vice is briefly dealt with—intended to suggest opposition in saying that these penitents are "untying the knot of anger" (*Purg.* 16. 24); that is, they are undoing what has been done. At least the poet does not here offer an obvious metaphor. Yet if we do not insist on an inflexible allegory for the *Purgatorio*, we can say: "So these sinners are purified," without asking that the penalty be more than part of Dante's story.

On the Fifth Ledge of Purgatory, the penitents lie on the ground with their faces down. This so piques the traveler's curiosity that to his usual: "Who are you?" he adds: "Tell me why you keep your backs turned up" (*Purg.* 19. 94). Pope Adrian, the sufferer addressed, tells the questioner that he will let him know why "Heaven turns their backsides toward itself," but first must tell his own story. He lived a life of avaricious longing until he came to the papacy. Of his position then he says: "I saw that my heart would never be quiet in that position and yet could not rise any higher in the world" (*Purg.* 19. 109). On such failure of worldly goods to quiet the heart, Dante wrote in his *Convivio*: "These false traitors promise to remove all thirst and all need, and to bring all plenty and sufficiency. And so in the beginning they promise such sufficiency on the attainment of a certain amount. But when that is attained, instead of satisfaction and refreshment, they produce intolerable thirst in the feverish heart, and in place of satisfaction they set a new goal, that is, a greater quantity to desire. . . . Hence the thirst of cupidity is never quenched or satisfied" (4. 12). The Pope explains: "What avarice does is revealed in the purging of the souls that are turned upside down, and the mountain has no more stinging penalty. As our eye was not lifted up, being fixed on earthly matters, so justice here sinks it to earth. As avarice destroyed our love for every good thing, so that our labor was vain, so justice holds us tight here, bound and fastened hand and foot; and as long as the just Lord pleases, we shall be motionless and stretched out" (*Purg.* 19. 115). This passage has caused so much discussion that the reader may properly take what is easily apparent, leaving that for which no immediate solution has been offered. Dante's son Pietro attempts to aid:

This is the figure: Just as the covetous man, or the man living in some such vice, does not cease in laboring and vexing himself, as you have seen in *Inferno* 7, where he feigns that such persons roll rocks, so the man who is pulling himself back from the vice of avarice binds himself hand and foot with the rope of good resolutions so that no longer he runs about and piles up [money] but weeps, keeping his eyes on worldly things in all their vileness, though on account of them he earlier abandoned looking at heavenly things (On *Purg.* 19).

To the avaricious in Hell may be applied Pope Adrian's words on the avaricious in Purgatory: their "labor is vain." The avaricious and wasteful in the Inferno are popes and cardinals, just as Pope Adrian and Hugh Capet, founder of a royal dynasty, represent these vices in Purgatory. The "worldly matters" on which that pope and the Capetians set their minds were the Papacy and kingly power, the splendors of the world. So perhaps Dante's son was right in holding that the avaricious in Purgatory, with their faces on the ground and their limbs bound, are suffering a punishment directed against their sin of gazing on the world's rich prizes and spending all their efforts in attaining them. It may nevertheless be observed that other medieval commentators found the penalty representative of the lives of the expiators, as interested in "vile" earthly things. A sufficiently ascetic view can equate kingdoms with what Bunyan called "muck."

From Benvenuto da Imola in Dante's century down to the present, some commentators have thought the flames on the seventh and last terrace imitative of lust, the vice there purged. Yet Dante's son Pietro writes: "The penalty should fit the sin, and the will should be distressed by the penalty in opposition to the sin. Those who are purifying themselves from the sin of the flesh are as it were in the fire of conscience just as they

sinned in the fire of lust" (On *Purg.* 25). This position seems
supported by Guido Guinicelli's assertion that the sinners "by
their shame aid the burning" of the flames (*Purg.* 26. 81).
Buti says that these sinners

are in the fire to purify themselves from the sin of lust. This fire
is a penalty suited to such a sin, since as in this world they have
been burned in the evil desires of the flesh, so for reformation they
should burn in the flame and desire for continence and chastity.
This method is essential to those in this world who hope to reform
themselves from such a sin. Therefore, the poet feigns it about
those in Purgatory (On *Purg.* 25. 133).

Men in this world should enter the flames of contrition if they hope
to liberate themselves from such a sin. . . . In such burning they
feel pain because of the affliction they bring on themselves, which
comes from the burning love of goodness (On *Purg.* 27. 19).

In the *Convivio*, Dante speaks with more general application
on the flame of love: "The beauty of that Lady [Philosophy]
rains little flames of fire, that is, fire of love and of charity,
given life by a noble spirit, that is, heat directed by a noble
spirit, that is, a just longing, through which and by which is
caused the origin of good thinking. And not only does this fire
of love and charity do this, but it undoes and destroys what is
opposite to it and to good thoughts, that is, the innate vices,
which especially are the enemies of good thoughts" (3. 8).
In a different connection, Benvenuto da Imola writes that
the "fervor of love and the love of charity are always symbolized
by fire" (On *Inf.* 32). In the *Fioretti* of Saint Francis we read
of a brother for whom the fire of his temptation was turned into
the fire of the Holy Spirit (41). Or, as suggesting the spread of
the idea, an English homily from a manuscript of Dante's
century reads:

> This fir calle I charite,
> That brinnand in us au to be.
> It clenses man of sinful lust.[2]

If Dante with considerable ingenuity so devised the penalties
of Purgatory that they all represent opposition to one of the
seven capital vices, or deadly sins, the results of his planning

2 *English Metrical Homilies*, ed. John Small, Edinburgh 1862, p. 104.

were lost even for some zealous readers in his own century. Did he foresee that what he had done would not be clear to everybody? Was he willing here that readers should enjoy poetical qualities even when failing to master rational details?

PARADISE

When writing to Can Grande, Dante (if the letter be his) deals chiefly with the *Paradiso*. Applying his formula for the whole *Comedy*, he says that allegorically this *cantica* shows man in the world as by exhibiting desert he is eligible for just rewards. An argument against the genuineness of the letter is that the *Paradiso* differs from the other *cantiche* in showing men living in the world. All its saints shine in blessedness, while *Inferno* and *Purgatorio* more particularly symbolize men on earth subject to special sins and vices or striving against them.

In the *Paradiso* the grouping of the redeemed takes little account of individual types of goodness. In the Moon are those forced to break vows, in the Sun are literary men, in Jupiter are rulers. In the eagle of Jove, the greatest lights are placed in the bird's eye, but types of goodness and greatness are not differentiated. In the Eighth Heaven no light is brighter than Saint Peter's (*Par.* 24. 21); is his the brightest? On the mountain and in the pit there is less extrinsic grouping than, for example, in Mars, with its religious warriors. In Hell the avaricious are all churchmen (*Inf.* 7. 38), but they are classified for their vice, not their profession. In Purgatory the terrace of avarice and its opposite includes a temporal ruler as well as a pope. The usurers and the diviners in Hell belong to professions esteemed wicked, and in their punishment all of either group are equal. Yet for the diviners Dante makes an effort to show their great variety, which extends from city founder to shoemaker, from Homeric days and lands to Dante's own. An occupational group in the *Purgatorio* is the assembly of rulers in the happy valley outside the gate. The universal ethical formula of the seven vices forbids extrinsic limitation. In Paradise much scope for character, within salvation, is given only in the Heaven of Venus, where the three lovers mentioned are Folco, Cunizza, and Rahab.

Along with grouping by something extrinsic, as occupation, in the *Paradiso* goes limitation in the number of speaking characters. Omitting the eagle, I count fourteen in addition to Beatrice and Saint Bernard. The *Purgatorio* yields twenty-three, besides Cato and Matilda. In the *Inferno*, however, the travelers converse not only with Charon, Flegias, Minos, Plutus, the devils at the city of Dis, the Centaurs, and the Malebranche, but with some forty shades. So in Heaven the number of scenes giving opportunity for allegories of earthly life is not large.

Especially in Heavens Two to Eight, from Mercury to the Fixed Stars, the forms and features of the redeemed are concealed within lights. (Can Dante expect his readers to contrast the concealment within flames in Hell of Ulysses and Guido da Montefeltro?) However important speech is, disguise tends toward impersonality. As the blessed appear in higher heavens, they seem to show increasing tendency to harmonious movement, yet dances of the blessed lights occur early and late (7. 7; 12. 22; 24. 17). Their circular speed in the Sun and in Saturn is compared with that of a revolving millstone (12. 3; 21. 81). A pearl is used in comparison in the Heaven of the Moon and in Saturn (3. 14; 22. 29). Various saints in different heavens are lanterns (8. 19; 21. 73; 23. 28). They are likened to precious stones (9. 37, 69; 15. 22, 85; 19. 4; 20. 16). In all these heavens there are splendors, sparks, and lights. Thus Dante does not differentiate the individual saints as he did the sinners or those under purgation. Though the grades of blessedness emphasized by the different levels of Heaven are distinctive—with the lovers, for example, only in the second heaven— yet as a light a blessed soul cannot be assigned with certainty to one heaven only, as those bearing burdens are assigned only to the terrace of pride in Purgatory. The heavens themselves grow brighter as they are higher, as does Beatrice's smile, but Dante has hardly attempted to transfer such increase to blessed individuals. Are we to assume the greater brightness the higher the heaven, from such passages as this: "As in a flame a spark is seen . . . I saw in this light [of the Heaven of Venus] other lanterns move in circuit with rapidity more or less according to their internal vision" (8. 16)? Though this is a rule for distinguishing individuals, it seldom is applied.

Throughout the heavens the reward of the redeemed is little-differentiated light and motion in harmony with other saints. Indeed, "the glory of Him who moves the whole penetrates through the universe and is here more splendid and there less so" (*Par.* 1. 1), yet, in presenting the shades of the blessed, Dante does not strive to impress upon his readers such difference.

The concept of the blessed as luminous fits Dante's concern with divine light. In recollection of the *Commedia,* Milton might have written:

> God is light,
> And never but in unapproached light
> Dwelt from eternity (P. L. 3. 3).

The last canto of the *Paradiso* is one of divine lucency. Three times the author speaks of Eternal Light, twice of high light, once of the utmost light, twice of living light, as well as using less vigorous terms. From this brilliancy of the Highest Good is derived the light enclosing the blessed (*Par.* 14. 47, 55).

In the Moon, shining investiture adds to beauty without concealing identity. When Piccarda vanishes from Dante she is like something heavy sinking in water (3. 123). In the Heaven of Mercury the splendors, the saints in their robes of light, are no longer to be recognized, yet they retain some appearance if not reality of earthly substance, being like fish in a fishpool. In the splendor of the Sun, where the robes of glory are complete, individual souls circle around the visitors with a sweet song. They often take regular positions, though without distinctive qualities, as in token of happiness they grow brighter. Such are their qualities in the sphere above the Sun, until in the Empyrean they again have recognizable bodily form.

However uniform the appearance of individuals among the redeemed, something of variety comes from the arrangement of the lights veiling the shades in a cross (suited to crusaders) or an eagle (suited to kings) or going up a stairway (suitable to minds intent on heavenly contemplation). Yet similarities, though deliberate, perhaps appeared excessive to the author himself, and even once are amusingly censured. After Saint Benedict has spoken feelingly of his order, the traveler, with

courtesy but yet as though not much interested in what has
been said or in the lights, asks if he can see the saint without his
brilliant disguise (22. 60). The latter politely answers, then
turns back to the topic interrupted by the traveler's irrelevant
inquisitiveness. Are we to suppose the questioner wearied by
the monotonous lack of individuality in the appearance of the
redeemed?

Evidently, no attempt is made to symbolize the specific activity on earth or the state with respect to the cardinal virtues
of any of the redeemed, as in the other *cantiche*, where those
who have divided kingdoms are themselves split asunder, and
the envious do not turn their eyes to the world's pleasant things.
The blessed do exemplify the confidence in the triumph of
good of the saints on earth, even though they behold wickedness or endure personal affliction. The shades who speak,
though obliged to give some explanation of their surroundings,
are largely concerned with the unsatisfactory earth. Piccarda
speaks on her own wrongs and those of Constance. Justinian in
dealing with the Roman Empire comes down to the time when
the Guelfs oppose it and the Ghibellines make the imperial
standard a party symbol. Charles Martel goes from bad government in Sicily to the folly of thwarting the natural dispositions
of men: "If the world down there would give heed to the
foundation Nature lays, conforming with that, its people would
be good; but you twist to religion one who was born to gird on
the sword, and make a king of one fitted for sermons. Hence
your footsteps are not in the high road" (8. 142). Cacciaguida
is concerned with the degeneracy of his beloved Florence. The
voices from the Eagle are directed against corrupt princes (18.
115). Pier Damiano deplores the backsliding of the monastery
of Fonte Avellana and the luxury of modern prelates (21. 119).
Saint Benedict laments the recusancy of his own and other
monastic orders (22. 73). In anger at wickedness at Rome,
Saint Peter, as he declares in an invective against worldly popes,
often turns red and shoots out sparks (27. 54). The blessed
are as much concerned with corruption on earth as when they
were alive. Of goodness on earth they say less, as though not
knowing just kings; against the background of unfaithful clerics
there is no poor parson who "Christes loore and his apostles

twelve/He taughte, but first he folwed it hymselve." The shades in Heaven show the feelings of the militantly righteous on earth. Yet their earthly activity cannot be typified as sometimes in the *Inferno* and the *Purgatorio*. Aquinas is not shown writing his *Summa* with an eye only on the truth or Justinian commanding the codification of Roman law in his love for justice. The seven virtues—faith, hope, charity, prudence, justice, temperance, and fortitude—are not as evidently symbolized in practice as in Purgatory the seven vices are resisted. Yet the harmony of the redeemed has its indication of perfect earthly life. The pilgrim comes among a heavenly people "just and healthy-minded" (*Par.* 31. 39), living in a "safe and joyous realm" (31. 25). The kingdom of Heaven, where men enjoy the reward of well-spent lives and where love rules, allegorizes the perfect empire of the poet's longing.

7 . Outline-Analysis of the Commedia

INFERNO

INFERNO 1. 1 – 2. end. Introduction to the entire *Commedia.*
1. 1–60. Dante in the dark forest.
1. 61–end. Dante's dialogue with Virgil; Dante decides to visit the world of the dead.
2. 1–9. Invocation.
2. 10–end. Dante's courage fails; Virgil encourages him; tells of Beatrice; Dante again decides to follow Virgil.

INFERNO 3. 1–end. Ante-Hell.
3. 1–21. Hell Gate.
3. 22–75. The entrance hall; the neutrals.
3. 76–end. The River Acheron.

INFERNO 4. 1–end. Limbo; First Circle of Hell.
4. 1–22. The brink of the First Circle.
4. 23–45. The unbaptized.
4. 46–63. Christ's harrowing of Hell.
4. 64–151. Homer with other great poets and Aristotle with other non-Christians in a "noble town."

INFERNO 5. 1–end. Second Circle; sexual sinners tossed by violent winds.
5. 1–24. Minos, judge of unrepentant sinners.
5. 25–72. Sexual sinners.
5. 73–end. Francesca.

INFERNO 6. 1–end. Third Circle: gluttons in rain and mud.
6. 1–33. Cerberus.
6. 34–93. Ciacco on Florentine affairs.
6. 94–111. Torments after the Last Judgment.
6. 112–end. Plutus.

INFERNO 7. 1–96. Fourth Circle: avarice and prodigality.
7. 1–15. Plutus, god of riches.
7. 16–66. The miserly and the wasteful rolling stones.
7. 67–96. Virgil explains Fortune, God's servant.

INFERNO 7. 97–8. 64. Fifth Circle: the angry in Styx.
7. 97–end. The swamp of Styx.
8. 1–9. The high tower.
8. 10–30. Flegias the boatman.
8. 31–64. Filippo Argenti among the angry in the swamp.

INFERNO 8. 65 – 9. 105. The Gate of the city of Dis.
8. 65–78. The city at a distance.
8. 79–end. Entrance refused by devils on the walls.
9. 1–33. Virgil's earlier visit to Hell.
9. 34–60. The Furies and the Gorgon.
9. 61–63. An allegory indicated.
9. 64–105. A supernatural being forces the devils to let the travelers enter.

INFERNO 9. 106–11. end. Sixth Circle: heretics.
9. 106–end. The sepulchres of the damned.
10. 1–21. Epicurus and his followers.
10. 22–121. Farinata degli Uberti and Cavalcanti.
10. 122–132. A promise that Beatrice will explain Dante's future.
10. 133 – 11. 5. The brink of Circle Seven.
11. 6–9. Pope Anastasius a heretic.
11. 10–90. Virgil explains the arrangement of Hell.
11. 91–end. Virgil explains usury as a sin.

INFERNO 12. 1–end. Seventh Circle, first ring: violence against neighbors.

12. 1–30. A difficult descent and the Minotaur.

12. 31–45. Virgil tells of Christ's descent to Hell.

12. 46–end. The river of boiling blood, watched by centaurs, where bloodshed is punished.

INFERNO 13. 1–end. Seventh Circle, second ring: the violent against themselves, changed into trees or torn by dogs.

13. 1–54. Trees inhabited by the souls of suicides.

13. 55–110. Pier delle Vigne's narrative of princely ingratitude.

13. 111–129. Wasters of their property torn by dogs.

13. 130–end. The soul of a suicide in a bush.

INFERNO 14. 1 – 17. end. Seventh Circle, third ring: the violent against God, on burning sands in fiery rain. Geryon takes the travelers to the next circle.

14. 1–42. Horrible justice on the burning sands.

14. 43–72. The proud Capaneo.

14. 73–138. Virgil explains the rivers of Hell, flowing from a Cretan statue.

14. 139 – 15. 15. The diked stream.

15. 16–end. Brunetto Latini.

16. 1–89. Three Florentines deserving courtesy; the degenerate city.

16. 90–117. The abyss; the cord thrown into it.

16. 118 – 17. 33. Geryon appears from the abyss.

17. 34–78. Florentine usurers.

17. 79–end. The poets descend, riding on Geryon's back.

INFERNO 18. 1–99. Eighth Circle, first *bolgia:* panders and seducers scourged by devils.

18. 1–18. The plan of Malebolge, the Eighth Circle.

18. 19–99. Venedico Caccianemico; Jason.

INFERNO 18. 100–end. Eighth Circle, second *bolgia:* flatterers in the filth of privies. Alessio Interminei; Thais.

INFERNO 19. 1–end. Eighth Circle, third *bolgia*: simoniacs upside down in narrow pits. Popes Nicholas III, Clement V, Boniface VIII.

INFERNO 20. 1–end. Eighth Circle, fourth *bolgia*: wizards and fortune-tellers, with twisted bodies.

20. 1–30. Dante rebuked for pitying those justly punished by God.

20. 31–57. Virgil names Tiresias, Manto, and others.

20. 58–102. Virgil relates the foundation of Mantua.

20. 103–end. Eurypylus, Michael Scot, and others.

INFERNO 21. 1 – 23. 57. Eighth Circle, fifth *bolgia*: grafters in boiling pitch; comic devils, the Malebranche.

21. 1–21. The *bolgia* compared with the Venetian navy yard.

21. 22–57. A grafter brought directly from Lucca.

21. 58–136. Virgil guards the frightened Dante from the devils.

21. 137 – 22. 15. The comedy of the devilish signals.

22. 16–90. A sinner tells his story.

22. 91–end. That sinner deceives the devils, making them ridiculous.

23. 1–57. Virgil, with Dante, escapes from the angry devils.

INFERNO 23. 58 – 24. 63. Eighth Circle, sixth *bolgia*: hypocrites wearing gilded, leaden garments.

23. 77–109. Dante speaks with Catalano and Loderingo.

23. 110–126. Caiaphas and Annas lie crucified on the ground.

23. 127–end. Virgil learns how to get out of the *bolgia*.

24. 1–21. Virgil disturbed like a shepherd in time of frost.

24. 22–63. The travelers climb out of the *bolgia*.

INFERNO 24. 64 – 26. 15. Eighth Circle, seventh *bolgia*: thieves tormented by serpents.

24. 64–96. The serpents compared with those of Africa.

24. 97 – 25. 16. Vanni Fucci tells of his crime and predicts woe for Florence; he defies God, inveighs against Pistoia.

25. 17–33. The centaur Cacus.

25. 34 – 26. 6. Five Florentine thieves; the serpentine transformations of four of them.
26. 7–15. Dante predicts woes for Florence.

INFERNO 26. 16 – 27. 134. Eighth Circle, eighth *bolgia:* wicked strategists enclosed in flames.
26. 16–54. The flames described.
26. 55–end. Ulysses tells the story of his last voyage.
27. 1–54. Dante tells Guido da Montefeltro about conditions in Romagna.
27. 58–134. Guido tells of his deception by Pope Boniface and his consequent damnation because he did not repent.

INFERNO 27. 134 – 29. 36. Eighth Circle, ninth *bolgia:* causers of division slashed with a demon's sword.
27. 134 – 28. 21. The *bolgia* compared to battlefields.
28. 22–63. Mahomet displays his wounds; speaks of Fra Dolcino.
28. 64–102. Pier da Medicina tells his story and indicates Curio, who advised Caesar to cross the Rubicon.
28. 103–111. Mosca de' Lamberti tells how he caused strife in Florence between Amidei and Buondelmonti.
28. 112–end. Bertran de Born's punishment for setting son against father.
29. 1–36. Dante lingers and Virgil advises haste. Revenge for Geri del Bello.

INFERNO 29. 37 – 31. 6. Eighth Circle, tenth *bolgia:* falsifiers punished by sickness.
29. 37–84. Comparisons to show the horror of the place.
29. 85–end. Dante speaks with Capocchio, an alchemist, who hates the Sienese.
30. 1–21. Theban and Trojan comparisons.
30. 22–45. Capocchio indicates Gianni Schicchi and Myrrha, who played the parts of other persons.
30. 46–90. Dante speaks with Maestro Adamo, a counterfeiter.
30. 91–129. Maestro Adamo indicates Potiphar's wife and Sinon of Troy, liars.
30. 130 – 31. 6. Virgil rebukes Dante for listening to a quarrel.

INFERNO 31. 7–end. Movement from the Eighth to the Ninth Circle.

31. 7–111. The giants like towers surrounding the lowest pit of Hell.

31. 112–end. Antaeus transfers the travelers to the pit.

INFERNO 32. 1–72. Ninth Circle, first ring (Caina): betrayers of relatives, fixed in ice.

32. 1–15. Dante's invocation to the Muses.

32. 16–72. Dante speaks with the Count of Mangona and with Camicion de'Pazzi.

INFERNO 32. 73 – 33. 90. Ninth Circle, second ring (Antenora): betrayers of their country, fixed in ice.

32. 73–123. Dante speaks with Bocca degli Abati.

32. 124 – 33. 78. Ugolino tells his story.

33. 79–90. Invective against Pisa by the poet.

INFERNO 33. 91–end. Ninth Circle, third ring (Tolomea): betrayers of their guests, fixed in ice.

33. 91–150. Dante talks with Frate Alberigo; learns of Branca d'Oria.

33. 151–end. Dante's invective against Genoa.

INFERNO 34. 1–69. Ninth Circle, fourth ring (Giudecca): betrayers of Redeemer and Emperor chewed and clawed by Lucifer.

34. 1–54. Lucifer seen fixed in the ice.

34. 55–69. Judas Iscariot, Brutus, and Cassius seen by Dante.

INFERNO 34. 70–end. Ascent from Hell to Purgatory.

34. 70–99. Virgil assists Dante to climb along Lucifer's sides.

34. 100–126. Virgil explains the center of the world.

34. 127–end. Climbing up, they emerge on the island of Purgatory.

PURGATORIO

Purgatorio 1. 1 – 4. 96. The shores of the island of Purgatory.

1. 1–12. Poet's invocation.
1. 13–108. Cato, the guardian of Purgatory, talks with Virgil.
1. 109–end. Virgil cleanses Dante's face and girds him with a rush.
2. 1–75. An angel brings a shipload of souls to Purgatory.
2. 76–119. Dante greets Casella and listens to his song.
2. 119–end. Cato rebukes the shades for their delay.
3. 1–45. Virgil speaks on human reason and the birth of Christ.
3. 45–102. From a group of shades they learn the path.
3. 103 – 4. 18. Dante talks with Manfred, who died repentant but in contumacy with the Church.
4. 19–96. The travelers ascend the mountain.

Purgatorio 4. 97–end. The first shelf of Ante-Purgatory, where wait those negligent in repenting. Belacqua.

Purgatorio 5. 1 – 7. 63. The second shelf of Ante-Purgatory, where wait those who repented on the point of death.

5. 1–51. Virgil as a spirit and Dante as a solid body.
5. 52–84. Jacopo del Cassero tells of his murder.
5. 85–129. Buonconte da Montefeltro tells how he was killed in battle and his body carried away in the flooded Arno.
5. 130–136. Pia asks him to remember her on his return to earth.
6. 1–27. A simile of a winner at *Zara* annoyed by beggars.
6. 28–48. Virgil instructs Dante on prayer.
6. 49–75. Virgil encounters his countryman Sordello.
6. 76–end. Dante bewails the conduct of Italy and Florence.
7. 1–63. Virgil reveals himself to Sordello, who explains that the travelers must pause for the night.

PURGATORIO 7. 64 – 9. 12. The valley of princes who postponed repentance because of their worldly cares.

7. 64–85. The beauty of the valley, a place of heavenly song.

7. 86–end. Various great rulers.

8. 1–18. An evening prayer.

8. 19–21. The Poet calls attention to his allegory.

8. 22–39. The coming of two guardian angels.

8. 40–84. Sordello leads them into the valley, where Dante speaks with Nino Visconti.

8. 85–93. Dante sees three bright stars in the southern sky.

8. 94–108. A hostile serpent approaches, which the angels put to flight.

8. 109–end. Dante speaks with Corrado Malaspina.

9. 1–12. Dante sleeps.

PURGATORIO 9. 13–end. The gate of Purgatory.

9. 13–72. While Dante sleeps, dreaming of an eagle, Lucia carries him to the gate of Purgatory.

9. 73–end. Steps leading up to the gate. The guardian angel inscribes the letter *P* seven times on Dante's forehead and opens the door.

PURGATORIO 10. 1 – 12. 114. First Terrace: the egotists, bowed down by heavy burdens.

10. 1–21. Ascent through a cleft in the rock.

10. 22–99. The cliff rising above the terrace bears figures in relief showing instances of humility from the lives of the Virgin, King David, and the Emperor Trajan. The figures are so expressive as to seem alive.

10. 100–120. The penalty for pride.

10. 121–end. A meditation on egotism.

11. 1–37. The Lord's Prayer paraphrased by the penitents.

11. 38–78. Omberto Aldobrandesco.

11. 79–end. Oderisi speaks on worldly fame, illustrated by Cimabue, Giotto, Guido Guinicelli, Guido Cavalcanti, and Provenzan Salvani.

12. 1–72. The pavement shows vivid mosaics, giving instances of egotism: Lucifer, Briareus, Nimrod, Niobe, King Saul, Rehoboam, Sennacherib, and others.

12. 73–114. An angel directs them to the stairs to the next terrace and removes one P from Dante's forehead; a Beatitude is sung.

PURGATORIO 12. 115 – 15. 39. Second Terrace: the envious, in haircloth and with their eyes wired shut.

12. 115–end. In a comic scene Dante finds one P erased from his brow.

13. 1–21. Virgil apostrophizes the sun.

13. 22–42. The Virgin and other examples of love.

13. 43–end. Sapia of Siena.

14. 1–87. Guido del Duca and Rinieri da Calboli; Guido on the wickedness of the Valdarno.

14. 88–126. Guido presents the sad condition of Romagna.

14. 127–end. Voices give instances of envy.

15. 1–39. A glorious angel directs them; a Beatitude is sung.

PURGATORIO 15. 40 – 17. 69. Third Terrace: the wrathful concealed in dense smoke.

15. 40–81. Virgil explains the inexhaustible nature of the good.

15. 82–114. Examples of kindness: the Virgin, Pisistratus, Saint Stephen.

15. 115–138. Virgil understands Dante's thoughts though unspoken.

15. 139 – 16. 24. The punishment of anger.

16. 25–63. Marco Lombardo.

16. 64–end. Dante and Marco speak on separation of Church and state.

17. 1–12. The smoke compared with a mountain fog.

17. 13–39. In his fancy Dante sees instances of anger.

17. 40–69. An angel directs the travelers and removes a P from Dante's forehead; a Beatitude is sung.

PURGATORIO 17. 70 – 19. 54. Fourth Terrace: the slothful making great haste.

27. 16–60. Dante fears the flames; Virgil encourages him with Beatrice's name. The three poets pass through unharmed.

PURGATORIO 27. 61 – 29. 12. The Earthly Paradise entered.
27. 61–117. The poets sleep on the stairs.
27. 117–end. Virgil abdicates, giving Dante freedom.
28. 1–36. The beauties of the Earthly Paradise.
28. 37 – 29. 12. The fair Matilda appears singing on the other side of the River Lethe; she explains the Earthly Paradise, the Golden Age of the ancients.

PURGATORIO 29. 13–end. Allegorical Procession of Bible and Church. The books of the Bible and the Seven Virtues escort an empty triumphal chariot drawn by a griffin.

PURGATORIO 30. 1 – 32. 6. Beatrice.
30. 1–33. In a shower of flowers, Beatrice appears in the chariot.
30. 34–54. Dante, recognizing his ancient flame, turns for aid to Virgil, who is gone.
30. 55–99. Beatrice sternly rebukes him for infidelity; he is so cast down that the angels intercede.
30. 100–end. Beatrice shows that he failed of the promise of the *Vita Nuova*; forced her to go to Hell to rescue him; he must repent.
31. 1–36. Dante confesses.
31. 37–90. He is so moved by her further rebuke that he falls senseless.
31. 91–111. Matilda takes him through Lethe, of which he drinks, and to Beatrice.
31. 112 – 32. 6. Beatrice, gazing on the griffin, is implored by Faith, Hope, and Charity to look on Dante; he gazes on Beatrice.

PURGATORIO 32. 7–end. Further allegory of the chariot.
32. 7–60. The procession moves until Beatrice descends near the Tree of the Knowledge of Good and Evil, to which the chariot is fastened.

32. 61–99. Dante slumbers, awakes to find the procession gone
and Beatrice at the foot of the tree.

32. 100–end. He sees the chariot feathered by an eagle, attacked by a fox and a dragon, putting out seven heads
and ten horns like a monster, occupied by a harlot and a
giant; the giant drags it away through the forest.

PURGATORIO 33. 1–end. Preparing to leave the Earthly
Paradise.

33. 1–51. In cryptic language, Beatrice promises the salvation
of the Church and the Empire.

33. 52–78. Beatrice instructs Dante to write what he has seen.

33. 79–99. She recurs to his unfaithfulness.

33. 100–end. On her command, Matilda takes Dante and
Statius to drink of Eunoë. With renewed strength, he is
ready for his further journey.

PARADISO

PARADISO 1. 1–end. Introduction; the Sphere of Fire.

1. 1–36. Invocation to Apollo.

1. 37–81. Ascent to the Sphere of Fire.

1. 82–end. Beatrice explains form and matter in the universe.

PARADISO 2. 1 – 5. 90. First Heaven, the Moon: the blessed
who have broken vows of chastity.

2. 1–18. Warning to readers of difficult poetry to come.

2. 19–30. Ascent to the Moon.

2. 31–105. In answer to Dante's enquiry, Beatrice lectures on
moon spots.

2. 106–3. 6. She explains the influence of the heavenly bodies
on nature.

3. 7–51. Various souls, especially that of Piccarda Donati.

3. 52–90. Questioned by Dante, Piccarda explains that the
blessed are in different grades, but each is satisfied with his
place.

3. 91–123. Piccarda's broken vow and that of the Empress Constance.

3. 124–end. Beatrice too bright for Dante's eyes.

4. 1–63. Answering Dante, Beatrice explains that the blessed all dwell in the Empyrean Heaven but are shown in the various heavenly bodies to signify that "differently they have happy life."

4. 64 – 5. 90. Beatrice informs Dante on vows, their dispensation, and their relation to free will.

PARADISO 5. 91 – 7. end. Second Heaven, Mercury: spirits engaged in practical activity.

5. 91–96. The beauty of Beatrice.

5. 97–end. Beatrice encourages Dante to question the willing spirits.

6. 1–96. Justinian speaks on the Roman Empire.

6. 97–111. Justinian inveighs against Guelfs and Ghibellines.

6. 112–126. Justinian speaks on just rulers.

6. 127–end. The sad fate of Romeo, an honest and just royal minister.

7. 1–end. Dante hesitates to question Beatrice, but she, knowing his wish, kindly explains to him the theory of Redemption and the Resurrection.

PARADISO 8. 1 – 9. end. Third Heaven, Venus: loving spirits.

8. 1–15. Beatrice's beauty increased.

8. 16–39. Loving spirits and Dante's poem on the Third Heaven.

8. 40–84. Charles Martel speaks on bad government in southern Italy and Sicily.

8. 85–end. Charles on the proper use of men's diverse abilities.

9. 1–6. Retribution to come, Charles believes.

9. 7–66. Cunizza tells who she is, speaks of the tyrant Ezzelino da Romano, and predicts woe for Padua and vicinity.

9. 67–125. Folco of Marseilles, on Dante's request, tells who he is and speaks of the Heaven of Venus, in which Rahab the Harlot is prominent.

9. 126–end. Folco attacks avarice, especially that of popes and ecclesiastics.

PARADISO 10. 1 – 14. 78. Fourth Heaven, the Sun: great teachers.

10. 1–27. Address to the reader on the wonders of the universe.

10. 28–63. On ascending to the Sun, Dante for a moment forgets the enhanced beauty of Beatrice.

10. 64–end. Saint Thomas names various teachers who move like a garland in their dance.

11. 1–12. The poet speaks on men's vain occupations.

11. 13–117. Saint Thomas, knowing Dante's desires, speaks on Saint Francis.

11. 118–end. Saint Thomas bewails the degeneracy of the Dominicans.

12. 1–21. The splendor of the heavenly mill as it turns.

12. 22–105. Saint Bonaventura speaks on Saint Dominic.

12. 106–126. He bewails the degeneracy of the Franciscans.

12. 127–145. Saint Bonaventura names his companions in Heaven.

13. 1–30. Dante sees angelic dances.

13. 31–111. Saint Thomas speaks on the wisdom of Solomon, Adam, and Christ.

13. 111–142. Saint Thomas warns against hasty judgment.

14. 1–18. Dante wonders about bodies after the Resurrection.

14. 19–33. Celestial dance and song celebrating the Trinity.

14. 34–66. Glorified bodies after the Resurrection.

14. 67–78. A third circle of souls.

PARADISO 14. 79 – 18. 51. Fifth Heaven, Mars: crusaders and other religious warriors.

14. 79–90. As Beatrice's beauty shines, they rise to the Heaven of Mars.

14. 91–end. Dante beholds the cross, which furnishes him the greatest pleasure he has known in Heaven.

15. 1–31. A light, detaching itself from the cross, greets Dante.

15. 32–36. Beatrice's enhanced beauty.

20. 1–72. After the just princes united in the eagle have sung, they are named: King David, the Emperor Constantine (mistaken in his donation to the Church), Ripheus, and others.

20. 73–129. On Dante's wonder at the presence of Ripheus and Trajan in Heaven, the eagle explains that to accept their love and hope the Kingdom of Heaven adapted its rules.

20. 130–end. By explaining predestination, the eagle makes clear Dante's defective vision.

PARADISO 21. 1 – 22. end. Seventh Heaven, Saturn: contemplative spirits.

21. 1–45. Beatrice's increasing beauty must be tempered to fit Dante's powers. A heavenly stairway reaching upward.

21. 46–72. With Beatrice's permission Dante asks one of the souls (Pier Damiano) why he has descended to speak with the visitor, and why the heavenly song is silent. Immortal grace is great and mortal ears are dull.

21. 73–102. On Dante's enquiry, Pier Damiano explains predestination.

21. 103–end. To Dante's question, Pier Damiano gives his name; he then tells of his life and attacks the luxury of the prelates. Other spirits give a shout which overcomes Dante.

22. 1–21. Beatrice explains that Dante will see the vengeance indicated by the shout.

22. 22–72. Beatrice directs Dante's eyes to Saint Benedict. Dante wishes to behold the saint in his true shape but is told that he must wait until he comes to the highest heaven.

22. 73–99. The saint speaks on the corruption of the monasteries.

22. 100–123. Beatrice directs him upward; he sees and invokes the stars in Gemini.

22. 124–end. Beatrice asks Dante to look downward. He sees the planets and the earth like a tiny field.

PARADISO 23. 1 – 27. 94. Eighth Heaven, the Fixed Stars: Christ, the Virgin, Apostles, Adam.

23. 1–45. Having watched like a bird expecting dawn, Beatrice sees and makes Dante see the glory of Christ surrounded by his followers.

23. 46–87. Dante is now able to look upon Beatrice as she smiles, but she warns him to turn from her face to the throng of "splendors" surrounding Christ.

23. 88–end. Mary follows Christ upward in a procession honoring Saint Peter also.

24. 1–45. Beatrice begs Saint Peter to examine Dante's religious beliefs.

24. 46–end. The Saint questions Dante on faith and approves his answers.

25. 1–11. Dante's reliance on his *Comedy* to secure his return to Florence.

25. 12–99. Saint James examines him on hope.

25. 100–117. Saint John appears, as Beatrice tells Dante.

25. 118–129. He instructs Dante to correct on earth the legend of his transportation to Heaven without death.

25. 130–end. Dante is so blinded by heavenly splendor that he cannot see Beatrice.

26. 1–66. Beatrice will restore sight to Dante's eyes, through which entered the fire of his love for her; meanwhile Saint John examines him on love.

26. 67–79. A heavenly song is sung and Beatrice's gaze restores Dante's sight.

26. 80–142. After Beatrice indicates Adam, Dante speaks with him on the first sin, the first language, and the Garden of Eden.

27. 1–9. All Paradise joins in a hymn to the Trinity.

27. 10–66. Saint Peter inveighs against the wickedness of popes and clergy, charging Dante to report what he hears.

27. 67–94. The blessed mount upward; Beatrice charges Dante to look down upon the tiny earth.

PARADISO 27. 95–30. 12. Ninth (Crystalline) Heaven or Primum Mobile: figurative representation of the Deity and the angels.

27. 95–120. Strengthened by Beatrice's smile, Dante ascends to the Ninth Heaven, which Beatrice explains.

27. 120–end. Beatrice declares that greed has led men astray but that fortune will correct their path.

28. 1–end. First in Beatrice's eyes and then directly Dante sees a point of light surrounded by nine circles. Beatrice explains that all things depend on the point, a symbol of God, and that the circles represent the heavens and the associated hierarchies of angels.

29. 1–81. Beatrice explains the origin and nature of the angels.

29. 82–126. Beatrice digresses to attack preachers who attempt only to amuse their hearers.

29. 127–end. She speaks on the number of the angels, whose splendor reflects that of God.

30. 1–12. Dante gradually loses sight of the point of light and the splendor about it.

PARADISO 30. 13 – 33. end. Tenth Heaven or Empyrean: the true abode of all the blessed, of whatever grade. Dante sees a further symbol of the Trinity.

30. 13–37. Beatrice's beauty is so increased that for the first time since his earliest sight of her his song can no longer deal with it.

30. 38–81. The river of light.

30. 82–132. The celestial rose, where the blessed sit in order.

30. 133–end. Praise of the Emperor Henry VII; censure of Popes Clement V and Boniface VIII by Beatrice.

31. 1–27. Angels flying about the heavenly rose.

31. 28–51. Dante says he has come to the glory of the Trinity on leaving unjust Florence.

31. 52–69. Saint Bernard takes Beatrice's place.

31. 70–93. Dante expresses his gratitude to Beatrice, who sits in her place in the celestial rose.

31. 94–end. Saint Bernard directs his eyes to the Virgin Mary.

32. 1–84. Saint Bernard names various spirits in the celestial rose and indicates the infants there through parental faith.

32. 85–99. Bernard tells Dante to look upon the Virgin, who is celebrated in a hymn.

32. 100–114. Dante is eager to learn the name of the angel who looks upon the Virgin's face; Bernard tells that he is Gabriel.

32. 115–138. The patricians of the heavenly kingdom, Adam, Saint Peter, Saint John, Moses, Saint Anna, and Saint Lucia.

32. 139–end. Saint Bernard prepares Dante to follow his prayer to the Virgin.

33. 1–45. Saint Bernard's prayer to the Virgin.

33. 46–75. Dante's insufficiency for telling what he saw.

33. 76–108. Dante gazes upon the light of Divinity.

33. 109–136. Vision of the Trinity as three circles with the likeness of man on the central one.

33. 137–end. Dante is eager to understand this, but lacks power, knowing only that divine love is controlling him.

A

Adam, Master, 3

Adrian, Pope, 164f.

Aeneas: eager to visit lower world, 75; at Dido's court, 78; in Hell, 4, 155. *See also Aeneid,* Virgil.

Aeneid: Dante's knowledge of, 28; shade embraced, 85; speeches in, 78; imitated, 29; adapted, 44; on Eurpylus, 45; on Ulysses, 46; on heavenly decrees, 49; revision of, 153; as tragedy, 66f., 75; as epic, 67; *Aeneid* 3.56: 24; *Aeneid* 6: 17; *Aeneid* 6.135: 76; *Aeneid* 3.522; 6.640: 43; *Aeneid* 7.641: 29; *Aeneid* 9.77: 94. *See also* Aeneas, Virgil.

Allegory, 29ff., 160, 161, 171; devised by reader, 127; difficulties, 118; four kinds, 29; imperfect, 157ff.; and poetical pleasure, 30, 37ff., 162; of Lady Philosophy, 140; of Beatrice, 143; puzzling, 32, 122; required author's explanation, 33, 121, 127; of *Inferno,* 31, 155ff.; of *Purgatorio,* 162ff.; of *Paradiso,* 32, 167ff.

Antaeus, 69

Apollo, 2, 39f., 61; inspired Dante, 59. *See also* Muses.

Aquinas, 12, 113, 126, 155, 161

Aretino, Leonardo: *Life of Dante,* 2

Ariosto, 19, 27, 72, 101, 108, 142

Aristotle, virtues, 137

Assignment of souls, 24

Audience, limited, 39. *See also* Reader.

Autobiography, *see* Dante

Avarice, of clergy, 112ff., 159, 164f.

B

Badclaws, *see* Malebranche

Baptism, 114

Baptistery, Florentine, 158; Dante's exploit, 1, 8, 99; Satan in mosaic, 123

Bawdry, 78, 83, 106

Beatrice, 13, 16f., 19, 138ff.; in *Vita Nuova,* 138ff.; promise to write of her in *Vita Nuova,* 127; not name of heroine, 138; allegorized as theology, 143; aid to Dante, 130; beauty, 16, 23, 59, 133, 147, 149; jealousy, 145, 149; change in tone, 144f.; and divinity, 128; erudition, 25, 151; in Earthly Paradise, 53, 90, 140; inconsistent, 151, 154; laughter, 79; like a mother, 72; in *Paradiso,* 151ff.; gives permission to speak, 72; teacher and guide, 141, 146; Theology, 143f.; rebukes Dante, 72; com-

KEY TO PASSAGES FROM DANTE
AND HIS COMMENTATORS

8.94: 1, 62
8.104: 68
8.110: 145
9.1: 68
9.13: 68
9.51: 43
9.52: 68
9.55: 34, 68
9.61: 34, 44, 63
9.70: 63
9.85: 35
10.8: 21
10.15: 33, 156
10.52: 135
10.58: 44
10.73: 25, 78
10.85: 21
10.109: 15
10.122: 43
10.131: 146
10.132: 152
11: 22, 146
11.11: 18
12: 26, 71
12.9: 18
12.21: 21
12.30: 18, 71
12.48: 156
12.49: 124
12.52: 7
12.72: 161
12.81: 71
12.100: 146
12.113: 43
13.46: 44
13.53: 134
13.76: 133
13.80: 43, 44
13.84: 15
13.97: 160
13.120: 101
13.121: 159
14.7: 44
14.16: 62
14.19: 7
14.51: 78
14.74: 18
15: 26
15.16: 96
15.23: 84
15.30: 15
15.43: 18

15.45: 15
15.55: 45, 134
15.61: 24
15.85: 134
15.101: 15
15.106: 114
15.120: 45, 133
16.16: 18
16.49: 18
16.66: 134
16.67: 24
16.85: 45, 133
16.94: 23
16.127: 134
16.128: 2, 8, 45, 61, 63, 67
17.85: 69
17.104: 69
18.20: 43
18.28: 96
18.28–33: 26
18.29: 119
18.31–33: 31
18.37: 81
18.40: 9
18.65: 31
18.80: 31
18.83: 81
18.97: 31
18.117: 114
18.125: 158
19.13: 8
19.18: 2
19.20: 115
19.21: 2
19.22: 82, 158
19.26: 158
19.49: 114
19.53: 112
19.70: 112
19.72: 159
19.82: 112
19.83: 114
19.101: 15
19.106: 114, 121
19.115: 122
19.118: 45
20.2: 56
20.3: 45
20.19: 8, 15, 45, 62
20.106: 84
20.112: 45

20.113: 59, 66, 67, 75
20.114: 28
21:26
21.1: 46
21.2: 61, 66, 67
21.7: 100
21.9: 23
21.25–23.57: 101–106
21.35: 160
21.39: 160
21.53: 96, 160
21.55: 97
21.59: 69
21.94: 2
21.127: 69
22: 26, 107
22.17: 21
22.18: 62
22.27: 159
22.31: 2
22.68: 106
22.118: 1, 46
22.144: 160
23: 26
23.19: 69
23.35: 2
23.40: 72
23.110: 9
24: 26
24.1: 23
24.32: 71
24.43: 18
24.70: 9
24.127: 72
24.133: 9
24.138: 115
25.13: 9
25.40: 84
25.46: 63
25.94: 46
25.97: 46
25.143: 46
26.12: 64
26.15: 71
26.19: 64, 124
26.25: 95
26.43: 9
26.79: 46
26.80: 134
26.90: 78
27.3: 43

10.46: 64
10.59: 128
10.70: 57, 64
10.93: 149
10.145: 12
11: 26
11.1–9: 114
11.124: 113
11.131: 114
12.3: 168
12.16: 64
12.22: 168
12.90: 112
12.115: 113
13.1: 12, 57, 62
13.8: 64
13.26: 122
14.12: 149, 153
14.25: 64
14.47: 169
14.55: 169
14.78: 19
14.81: 57, 94
14.103: 57
14.122: 17
14.127: 128
14.130: 57
14.138: 17
15–18: 79
15.22: 168
15.26: 146
15.32: 147
15.85: 168
15.87: 73
15.97: 24
15.134: 114
15.144: 114
16: 26
16.1: 79
16.10: 101
16.13: 23
16.14: 79
16.23: 80
16.25: 114
17.20: 162
17.33: 122
17.44: 115
17.82: 112
17.94: 152
17.109: 57
17.118: 136
17.119: 67

17.120: 81
17.128: 4
17.133: 77
17.135: 136
18.7: 148
18.16: 16
18.19–21: 154
18.20: 101
18.26: 80
18.52: 147
18.57: 23
18.63: 146
18.64–20 end: 147
18.70: 95
18.82: 58
18.83: 136
18.86: 57, 95
18.87: 94
18.97: 95
18.100: 94, 100
18.102: 96
18.107: 95
18.109: 95
18.115: 170
19.1: 12
19.4: 168
19.7: 58, 95
19.10: 95
19.37: 95
19.83: 115
19.101: 95
20.16: 13, 168
20.17: 95
20.55: 122
20.70: 95
20.76: 95
20.84: 95
20.141: 16
20.146: 13, 95
21.1: 20
21.7: 23
21.23: 146
21.29: 13
21.58: 19
21.59: 17
21.61: 13
21.73: 168
21.81: 168
21.119: 170
21.130: 114
21.142: 17
22.4: 72, 145, 152

22.5: 72
22.29: 168
22.49: 74
22.58: 74, 93
22.60: 13, 170
22.69: 13
22.73: 170
22.75: 75
22.76: 113
22.100: 23
22.106: 1, 63
22.107: 128
22.112: 58
22.133: 13, 101
22.151: 101
23: 26
23.20: 117
23.28: 168
23.34: 146, 153
23.45: 94
23.55: 58, 63
23.62: 61
23.87: 19
23.88: 1, 111, 129
23.89: 116
23.93: 64
23.98: 64
23.121: 98
23.129: 17, 64
23.136: 117
24.7: 129
24.14: 64
24.17: 168
24.19: 146
24.21: 167
24.28: 149
24.34: 3
24.39: 119
24.52: 17
24.64–147: 111
24.83: 99
24.84: 129
24.148: 111
25: 26
25.1: 58, 61, 136
25.3: 2, 54, 137
25.8: 114
25.27: 19
25.34: 92
25.37: 92
25.55: 92
25.64: 92

COMMENTATORS ON THE COMMEDIA

THE GOTHAM LIBRARY

Oscar Cargill, General Editor

Robert J. Clements, Associate Editor for Modern Languages

A paperback series devoted to the major figures in world literature and topics of enduring importance

If these titles are not available at your bookstore, you may order them by sending a check or money order direct to: New York University Press, 32 Washington Place, New York 3, New York. *The Press will pay postage.*